From a Roman Window

Five Decades: The World, the Church and the Catholic Laity

To all who have helped or will help us to cross in Hope
the threshold of the third Christian millennium

From a Roman Window

Five Decades: The World, the Church and the Catholic Laity

ROSEMARY GOLDIE

HarperCollins*Religious*
An imprint of HarperCollins*Publishers*

Published by HarperCollins*Religious*
HarperCollins*Publishers* (Australia) Pty Limited Group
17–19 Terracotta Drive
Blackburn, Victoria 3130
http://www.harpercollins.com.au
ACN 005 677 805

Copyright © Rosemary Goldie 1998
All rights reserved. Except as provided by Australian copyright law, no part of this book may be reproduced or transmitted by any form or by any means, electronic or mechanical, including photocopying, recording, or by any information storage or retrieval system, without permission in writing from the publishers.

First published 1998

Typeset in 12/15 Bembo

Printed in Australia by Griffin Press

HarperCollins*Publishers*
25 Ryde Road, Pymble, Sydney, NSW 2073, Australia
31 View Road, Glenfield, Auckland 10, New Zealand
75–85 Fulham Palace Road, London W6 8JB, United Kingdom
Hazelton Lanes, 55 Avenue Road, Suite 2900, Toronto, Ontario, M5R 3L2
and 1995 Markham Road, Scarborough, Ontario M1B 5M8, Canada
10 East 53rd Street, New York NY 10372, USA

The National Library in Australia
Cataloguing-in-Publication data:

Goldie, Rosemary.
   From a Roman Window: five decades: the world, the church and the Catholic Laity.
   ISBN 1 86371 697 1
   1. Goldie, Rosemary. 2 Vatican Council (2nd : 1962-1965) - History.
   3. Laity - Catholic Church - Biography. 4. College teachers - Biography. I. Title
270.092

Our thanks go to those who have given us permission to reproduce copyright material in this book. All rights of copyright holders are reserved. Particular sources of print material are acknowledged in the text. Every effort has been made to trace the original source material contained in this book. Where the attempt has been unsuccessful, the publishers would be pleased to hear from the author/publisher to rectify any omission.

The author and publishers would like to thank and acknowledge the following for the use of copyright material: *Crossing the Threshold of Hope* by His Holiness John Paul II. Translation copyright © 1994 by Alfred A Knopf Inc. Reprinted by permission of the publisher and The Holy See Press Office ; Comitato Permanente Dei Congressi Internazionali Per L'Apostolate Dei Laici, *World Crisis and the Catholic*, Sheed & Ward, London 1958; Albino Luciano, *Un Vescova Al Concilio; Lettere Dal Vaticano II*, Città Nuova Editrice, Roma 1983 ; Susannah Herzel, A Voice for Women, © World Council of Churches, Geneva 1981; John M. Todd, *We are Men*, © Sheed & Ward, London 1955; Extract for *Women and Holy Orders: Being the Report of a Commission by the Archbishops of Canterbury and York* (Church Information Office, 1996) is copyright © The Central Board of Finance of the Church of England and is reproduced by permission; *Commonweal*, 23 August 1997, New York; 'Women Respond to the Pope', *The Tablet* 15 July 1995; John Cogley, *The Layman and the Council* (ed.) Michael Green, © Templegate Publishers , Springfield, Illinois 1964; Philip F. Pocock, *Brief to the Bishops*, © Longmans, Canada 1965; Vincent J. Giese, *The Apostolic Itch*, © Fides Publishers, Chicago, Illinois 1954 ; John Cogley, *The Mind of the Catholic Layman*, © Charles Scribner's Sons, New York 1963 ; Avery Dulles, 'Can the word Laity be defined?', © *Origins* Vol.18.29, 29 December 1988; Avery Dulles, 'Pastoral Response to the Teaching on Women's Ordination',© *Origins*, Vol. 26.11 29 August 1996.

The Scripture quotations contained herein are from the New Revised Standard Version of the Bible, copyrighted, 1989, by the Division of Christian Education of the National Council of Churches in the United States of America, and are used by permission. All rights reserved.

Contents

Acknowledgments vi
List of Acronyms vii
Foreword ix
Introduction 1
Prologue 5

PART I LAITY: POST-WAR – PRE-COUNCIL

1 A world becoming 'one' 15
2 In the crisis of the modern world 31
3 Living internationally as Christians 43
4 The emerging theology 52

PART II AT LAST...VATICAN II

5 An Ecumenical Council 64
6 The post-Conciliar Congress 88

PART III LAITY IN THE POST-CONCILIAR CHURCH

7 Why speak about 'laity'? 114
8 Associations, movements, communities, 'charisms' 120
9 Council 'on', 'of' or 'for' the Laity 136

PART IV THE LAITY, CONTINENT BY CONTINENT

10 A voyage of discovery 156

PART V CONCERNING WOMEN

11 'I'm not a feminist but . . . !' 192
12 The Women's Ecumenical Liaison Group 199
13 Commission on women in Church and society 207
14 *Ordinatio Sacerdotalis*: The ordination debate 218
15 John Paul II and women 232

Epilogue 236
Sources 240
Index 242

Acknowledgments

It would take another book to name all who have helped to guide and sharpen my vision from the Window, and most of them appear already in these pages. But special thanks are due for special help. First of all, to Edmund Campion — priest-historian, writer and friend. When the 'Roman Window' was no more than an idea, he encouraged me to attempt a daunting task that seemed necessary, and that ended with this 'very personal book' of which he has written with such understanding and characteristic acumen.

But the idea could not have grown into a book without the generous help of many other friends. Corinna De Martini, Josette Kersters and Patricia Molloy, who typed, computerised and proof-read at an early stage. The librarian-archivist of the Pontifical Council for the Laity, and his assistant — Gabriele Turella and Angelo Sala — who patiently accompanied my research. Paula Turella, who brought her camera and her expertise to catch me at the Window. Sr. Sophie McGrath, RSM, Sr. Irene Breslin, SU and Donna Orsuto who undertood a careful reading of the manuscript. And, in the decisive stages, the publishing and editorial staff of HarperCollins, who brought both skill and friendliness to their professional involvement: Cathy Jenkins, Adrienne Ralph, and my particular editors: together with Susannah Burgess, Brigid James, whom I came to know as we 'faxed' one another across the world through a long and (for me) hot month of August.

I thank all who have given permission to use quotations from books and articles, beginning with the editor of *The Revue d'Histoire Ecclésiastique* (Louvain) who allowed me to use in translation my article of 1993, 'L'avant-Concile des "Christifideles Laici"', which became the basis for most of Part I.

Finally, if errors or omissions have emerged in the sifting of this mass of heterogeneous material, I crave indulgence.

Rosemary Goldie

List of Acronyms

AFAMP Association of Women Aspiring to the Priestly Ministry
AFL–CIO American Federation of Labor–Congress of Industrial Organizations
CAP Catholic Action of the Philippines
CCR Catholic Charismatic Renewal
CELAM Episcopal Council of Latin America
CEPAC Conferentia Episcopalis Pacifici (Episcopal Conference of the Pacific)
CFM Catholic Family Movement
CIO Catholic International Organizations
COPECIAL *Comitato Permanente dei Congressi Internazionali per l'Apostolato dei Laici*
CW Catholic Worker
CWL Catholic Women's League
FABC Federation of Asian Bishops Conferences
FAO Food and Agriculture Organization
FUCI Italian Federation of Catholic University Students
ICMICA International Catholic Movement for Intellectual and Cultural Affairs
IMCS International Movement of Catholic Students
IWY International Women's Year
JOC Jeunesse Ouvrière Chrétienne (Young Christian Workers)
JWG Joint Working Group
MIAMSI International Movement for Apostolate in Independent Social Milieux
NCCM National Council of Catholic Men
NCCW National Council of Catholic Women
OCIPE Catholic Office on European Problems
PCL Pontifical Council for the Laity
SECAM Symposium of Episcopal Conferences of Africa and Madagascar

SODEPAX Committee on Society, Development and Peace
UCFA University Catholic Federation of Australia
UNESCO United Nations Educational, Scientific and Cultural Organization
UNIAPAC International Christian Union of Business Executives
WCC World Council of Churches
WELG Women's Ecumenical Liaison Group
WUCWO World Union of Catholic Womens' Organization
YCS Young Catholic Students
YCW Young Christian Workers
YMCA Young Men's Christian Association
YWCA Young Women's Christian Association

Foreword

Early in 1954, Eris O'Brien, the scholarly archbishop of Canberra-Goulburn, spoke at a conference of university Catholics. In the front row was Rosemary Goldie and O'Brien said how pleased he was to see her there. He praised her book on French poetry, telling us something of its publication in Paris a few years earlier. In his introduction the critic Albert Béguin had recounted how Rosemary Goldie brought him the manuscript to read but he had put off doing so. Her topic was ambitious, difficult, a booby-trap for foreigners: what could she contribute? Then, after he had read the work Béguin admitted he had been wrong. To his great surprise, he wrote, she proved to be in touch with French 'spiritual geography'; the gaucheries which one almost always detected in outsiders writing about France were quite absent. 'A young Australian woman speaks about our poets as if they were her own' - how Eris O'Brien relished Béguin's phrase, 'une jeune Australienne', rolling it round his mouth like a morsel of fine French cuisine.

Rosemary's opuscule was something of a farewell to the delights of academia, for by the time Eris O'Brien introduced her to us, she had exchanged postgraduate research for full-time work in Catholic international bodies. Under a bewildering variety of names, acronyms, groupings, her life since then has been dedicated to elucidating the possibilities of being a lay Catholic in today's world. Famously, this dedication took her to a post in the papal court. A woman in the curia! How the tabloid press could play with that! Truth to tell, her work in the curia seemed not very different from her previous job experience. In that very clerical world she spoke, as she has always done, with a lay voice; and her line of country, the laity, remained the same.

Her Roman experience affords her the viewing platform, as well as the title, for this book. Here is a Roman view of what has been happening in the Vatican II decades, told by a unique Roman observer whose watchtower allows her to see the big picture across the Catholic (and ecumenical) world. No one else alive today could have written this book. *From a Roman Window* is about ideas rather than organisations, the story over the past century of our changed thinking about church. It will be a necessary book for anyone who wants to know more about the church of our times.

It is also a very personal book, although those who skim it in a bookshop may miss some of this. An early member of The Grail, Rosemary Goldie has learnt to be self-effacing. Her characteristic style is subtle, ironic and understated. Nevertheless, if her wit speaks in a low voice, it is powerfully present. For decades she has been an acute observer of clerical psychologies, not least in the Vatican, and *From a Roman Window* records some of her findings. Historians of the Roman curia will read this book attentively.

Her Grail background accounts for another characteristic of her book. Over the years The Grail has formed self-reliant Catholic women who set their own spiritual agendas. From the first generation of Grail women in Australia, Rosemary Goldie was always aware of the part women could play in the story. When blokey attitudes and neanderthal thinking obstructed their contribution, her disappointment was manifest. Her closing pages have her ruminating on the role of women and the lessons taught by her experience. This is creative writing which will encourage readers to think again about questions they may have considered definitively closed.

Edmund Campion
Catholic Institute of Sydney
November, 1997

Introduction

This book is titled *From a Roman Window*. The 'window' is that of my office, the room cluttered with books, papers and boxes where I still batter away at a manual typewriter dating from well before the dawn of the computer era. The window looks out on the Square of Santa Maria in Trastevere (St Mary's across the Tiber) from the older part of the Palace of St Calixtus, once the property of the Benedictines of St Paul's-without-the-Walls (where they retreated, it is told, when the River Tiber rose too high for them to return to their Abbey). The modern Palace, however, was built in the 1930s by Pius XI, in the monumental style of Fascist Rome.

At the time this story begins, St Calixtus housed six of the Sacred Congregations, Departments of the Roman Curia (the sacrality was dropped in 1983). When these moved closer to the Vatican, the Vicariato — the Chancery offices of the diocese of Rome — moved in. But John XXIII decided, logically, that the diocesan offices should be attached to the Cathedral of Rome, the Basilica of St John Lateran, and promptly evicted a missionary museum from the Lateran Palace. This made the Palace of St Calixtus available as a home for a series of new Curial bodies later created by Paul VI for the implementation of Vatican II: the Pontifical Councils for the Laity, for Justice and Peace, for the Family, for Culture.

'San Calisto', Paul VI once remarked, had the advantage of being 'ecclesiastical, but not clerical' — an appropriate place for 'non-clergy' involved in the work of the universal Church at its centre. This is where I have spent the greater part of my time, in one or another capacity, since 1952.

The Palace is one of a number of extra-territorial properties in Rome that were recognised as belonging to the Vatican under the Lateran Treaty of 1929 between the Holy See and the Fascist regime. It was to have been linked by a thoroughfare to the Vatican, but this plan was never carried out and it has remained enclosed, incongruously, in this popular quarter of old Rome. In the 1950s Trastevere was still something of a village, where families knew one another and shopkeepers catered for children. But today, behind the facades that have been slightly retouched, there are restructured luxury apartments, and across the road from our main gate, where once there was a toy shop, there is now a beauty parlour.

The Square is dominated by the Basilica of Santa Maria in Trastevere, whose 'modern' history goes back to the twelfth century. It has been taken over by the Community of St Egidio. On Christmas Day, the Basilica opens its doors to a festive meal served by the young people for the homeless and the hungry, who at other times are assisted in less spectacular ways.

Theoretically, at least, the Square is a pedestrian island. But this does not exclude the trucks driving in for the works that are always in progress wherever you go in Rome, nor the vans serving cinema or television sets. (Trastevere and its cafes are still photogenic, though the 'dolce vita' is no longer in evidence). Then there are motorcades for weddings or funerals in the Basilica, and other peaceful invasions: children in carnival costumes or staging some folklore pageant; an ecological display; a fair for books and crafts; pilgrims, tourists and beggars. There are also visitors and staff, crossing over to enter our Palace by the 'Piazza San Calisto'. Once they would have been distinguishable by flowing cassock or nun's coif; today, you may need to look closely for a discreet cross or medal distinguishing a 'religious' among the 'Vatican women' arriving on foot, by car or bicycle.

Over the years my window has been looking out on a varying parade of the world. This parade may disturb the pigeons perched on window-sills or round the fountain, but otherwise it makes for reflection, at least when the bells of the Basilica are not pealing out — or breaking into a telephone conversation.

It is the world, as reflected in the life of the Church — and especially of the lay members of the Church alive to a worldwide dimension — that this book is all about. It concerns the Church at a particular period in history: approximately five decades, from the post-Second World War years to the end of a twenty-five-year period following the Second Vatican Council. It traces a journey through nearly half a century of events with which I have been in one way or another associated. My purpose is to give an account (necessarily subjective, but as far as possible factual) of the emergence, growth and occasional momentary decline of a sense and concrete expression among lay men and women of belonging to the Church — to the Roman Catholic Church, but also, more and more, to the wider context of the whole People of God in their striving towards unity and full communion. At the centre is the Second Vatican Council, the point of both arrival and departure for renewal in the life of the Catholic Church, and a significant landmark for the Christian world as a whole.

It may seem that I have given excessive importance to congresses and international meetings. Our Permanent Committee, which figures so prominently in this history, once received a letter addressed to the 'Committee for Permanent Congresses'. That is certainly no ideal for a life commitment of service to Church and society! But, if Vatican II is our central landmark, the international meetings leading up to it and away from it have been milestones marking progress in both the quantity and quality of lay involvement in the mission of the worldwide Church.

In Part I I have tried to show that the decisive contribution of Vatican II in giving a new sense of belonging and responsibility to the laity did not just happen. The impression is often given that, before the Council, lay people were all passive — called only to 'pray, obey and pay' — and that after the Council, by some miracle, they jumped into activity.

This book, however, is not meant only for those who never experienced the pre-Vatican II Church, or whose memories of it have remained vague. It is also for those (and most of us are in this category) who find the post-Vatican II Church at times confusing, and who may take courage from sharing experiences that can be an invitation to 'cross the threshold' of the Third Millennium — with John Paul II — as a 'threshold of hope'. In the past such sharing has been gladly undertaken with Christian men and women of other communions, and I like to think that recalling it now may contribute to further dialogue and deeper commitment to the cause of unity. Others also, interested observers of the Christian world, may glimpse here some ways of working together for the good of the whole human family.

What I share concerning women in Part V can open up horizons for dialogue and collaboration, but it also reveals a complexity of problems that concern both women and men, and that call for much patient effort if we are to discover and show to the world the true face of the Church. Readers sensitive to gender issues will find that I have made use whenever possible of inclusive language. But it would have been an anachronism to change texts quoted from a time — not so distant — when 'layman' could be used indiscriminately for the man or the woman in the pew.

The Prologue explains how I came to be personally involved in this history, starting from a first experience in international life as an Australian student in Paris from 1936 to 1938. But the book is not an autobiography or a collection of memoirs. Although it necessarily relies on many memories, these have been validated by considerable research in the interests of historical truth, and have made use of many articles, interviews and other sources contemporary with the events recorded. These events cannot always be given in chronological order, and each of the book's five Parts could supply material for a volume longer than this one. But there is one thread running throughout, leading towards and from Vatican II — a thread registering growth, often in unpredictable ways. This thread involves a variegated multitude of men and women — lay people, religious, priests, bishops, popes — who have contributed to this growth of the whole People of God.

Prologue

It was July 1936. The Orient liner was ploughing its way over the Indian Ocean, out from Fremantle, on to London. I looked up from the book I was reading in a sunny spot on deck and it hit me all of a sudden: I was on my own, going to France for two years. The hectic ten days before leaving Sydney — a month or so earlier than expected — had left no time for realising what it meant to have won the French Government Travelling Scholarship. Here I was, on my way to 'enjoy the literary and artistic life of Paris' (the bait Professor G. G. Nicholson had dangled before my eyes to encourage me to make the extra effort in my final year at Sydney University). It hit me with an attack of homesickness that would last for three months in Great Britain doing the tourist things (seeing five Shakespearean plays in four days at Stratford-on-Avon, touring in Scotland and Wales), and on through my initial months as a 'Sorbonnarde' in Paris. It left me before my second year, by which time I had become the 'Parisian', happy now to be part of the local colour in the days when foreign students were still a manageable group, and beginning to dread a little the prospect of returning to family and friends. Much-loved as they were, they might never be able to realise how changed I could be after two years and a twenty-first birthday in Paris.

Those were, I think, the most formative two years of my life, even if I had little time to become involved in the literary and artistic life of Paris. I was even less involved in the political upheavals that were taking place. I learned much later what the 'Front Populaire' meant and what to think of the diametrically opposed interpretations of the Spanish

Civil War. I endured unhappily the gleeful reactions of the French press to Britain's discomfiture over the abdication of Edward VIII ('On ne Baldwine pas avec l'amour'!). But my great discovery was what it meant to be a Christian — a Catholic — in the heyday of a French Catholicism that, in later years, was to nourish the streams leading up to Vatican II. What is left of my student library still bears witness to those days: Charles Péguy and Paul Claudel, Ernest Psichari and Stanislas Fumet; and a 1936 edition of *Humanisme intégral*, bought in Paris while I was commuting between the philosophical complexities of the Sorbonne and the serene metaphysical depths of Jacques Maritain's lectures at the Institut Catholique.

This was the heyday also of 'Catholic Action', in France and worldwide. The term had been used generically to mean any action, even in the social, economic and political fields, to defend the interests of the Church and her mission. But now Pius XI had defined it as a call to lay men and women to 'collaborate in the apostolate of the Hierarchy', with a 'mandate' from their bishops. In France, this meant especially an 'apostolate of like to like' in one's own social milieu, along with a method — 'see–judge–act' — to change that milieu where it needed changing. This was devised by a young Belgian priest, Joseph Cardijn (later Cardinal), a miner's son who had mobilised the boys and girls of the working class in what would become Jeunesse Ouvrière Chrétienne (JOC) — the worldwide Young Christian Workers (YCW) movement.

Paris was to be my entry into international living. I was welcomed there in October 1936 by Professor Nicholson himself, who was enjoying a sabbatical year. He advised me about my courses at the Sorbonne, and installed me as a paying guest of a family on the Boulevard Saint-Michel, where I would have no temptation to speak English. He gave me my first introduction to the historical, and Christian, treasures of the Latin Quarter.

I was welcomed, too, by Nancy (Anne) Taggart (later Lady Kerr), who had been the Travelling Scholar from Sydney University the previous year and was now a seasoned Parisian. In her memoirs,[1] Anne devoted a chapter to our shared experiences. It was she who introduced me, among other joys, to the 'Cercle International de Jeunesse'

(International Youth Club) run by a kindly American Quaker couple. She recorded that our membership included students, young and not so young, from about thirty countries, among them 'a Hindu, Krishna Keskar, who was nicknamed Gandhi' and who had served a prison term as a fighter for Indian independence. Later he was to be Indian Minister of Information. There was also a Hungarian who spent some time with the International Brigade photographing the Spanish Civil War and later became a Hollywood film star. I was the only member identified as a Catholic, but the 'Cercle' respected every individuality. When I left Paris in 1938, the members presented me with my treasured copy of Bernanos' *Journal d'un curé de campagne*, bearing all their signatures.

As the first Catholic Australian to reach the Sorbonne on a French Government Scholarship, I enjoyed also extra-curricular activities which provided a different kind of international apprenticeship and that went some way towards preparing me for my Roman career. During my undergraduate years, I had been a member of both the Newman Society of Sydney University and the University Catholic Group. The latter was founded by Agnes McFadden, to bring Catholic culture nearer to the people. I had left Sydney fortified by a recommendation from the Newman Chaplain, Dick Murphy, SJ, to a Jesuit in Paris. The Jesuit promptly dispatched me to a Dominican, Marc Dubois, OP, Chaplain of *Veritas*, a small group of Catholic women students at the Sorbonne. There I made some good friends. And another discovery.

I discovered that, as a member of *Veritas*, I was automatically a member of the French Federation of Catholic Women Students, and thereby a member of Pax Romana — the International Secretariat of Catholic University Students, founded in Fribourg, Switzerland, in 1921 — an organisation of which I had never heard. I was to hear much more of it, for the Sixteenth Pax Romana Congress was to be held in Paris in the summer of 1937, on the occasion of the International Exhibition. As Pax Romana's first Australian contact, I was invited to the Congress and to the Study Days that preceded it. (It was during these days that I had my first taste of liturgical renewal and of the dialogue Mass.) After the Congress, I was so much a part of the Pax Romana family that, in April of the following year, I went to its Interfederal Assembly as an accredited delegate of the French Federation.

Our sessions were held in Vaduz, the village capital of Lichtenstein, a peaceful spot in Central Europe. But war clouds were gathering rapidly. The future Prince Franz-Josef II met the delegates over a friendly meal. Later the Administrative Secretary, Rudi Salat, entrusted me with the task of taking the message of Pax Romana to Australia. None too soon. By the time the University Catholic Federation of Australia (UCFA) was founded, all contact with the Pax Romana Headquarters in Fribourg had been cut off, and would remain so for years. We affiliated instead through the Secretariat set up in Washington headed by the legendary Ed Kirchner. The story has often been told: the Pax Romana Congress, meeting in Washington when war broke out on 1 September 1939; the Polish and German delegations praying together; Rudi Salat, German and anti-Nazi, unable to return to Europe and to his family. When the United States came into the war after Pearl Harbour, Salat left for South America, helping to set up university Catholic Action, wherever a papal nuncio could offer him hospitality.

Back in Sydney in September 1938, I was already booked to teach senior French at the Sacred Heart College, Rose Bay. My teaching career lasted exactly two terms. I inevitably became involved in the Grail Movement, which had arrived in 1936 from the Netherlands, bringing European spirituality, culture and folklore. Most importantly, it brought the possibility of a dedicated life for women 'in the world', a much misunderstood idea at the time, but one which proved to be a gift to the Church through the prophetic (today we would say charismatic) personality and inspiration of the Dutch Jesuit professor, Jacques van Ginneken. The story of my war years in Australia is inseparable from that of the Australian Grail during that time. I owe a great deal to the Grail, to which I am still linked, in an unstructured way. Since the 1950s, when I began to work for the university apostolate, and then for the whole lay apostolate throughout the world, I have found it impossible to identify with one movement.

My activities, like those of the Grail, were varied. Perhaps the most important was my collaboration with Adelaide Crookall to plan a residential course for girls, 'The Quest', started in Melbourne in 1940. But it was my continued association with Sydney University that was instrumental in deciding my future and thus the content of this book.

This included the University Grail Group for which I was responsible, and my role as Assistant Secretary of the newly founded UCFA. There was, above all, normal association with the University through work for a Master of Arts degree, a thesis on 'The Idea of Heroism in French Literature', written as echoes reached us of the struggle for freedom in Europe and the tragedies of occupied France. The degree secured, I had hopes of developing the contemporary part of my thesis into a deeper study for a Doctorate of Literature.

Towards the end of 1944, while visiting Melbourne, I caught sight of a small paragraph in a newspaper announcing five International Fellowships offered by the International Federation of University Women. Encouraged by Professor Nicholson and the Australian Association of University Women, I applied, though I was convinced that so impractical a subject as French literature would hardly be considered in wartime. I returned to Sydney. I was at the Grail house in Springwood when a letter arrived from Washington, shortly before Easter 1945: I had been awarded the Aurelia Henry Reinhardt International Fellowship to study for one year in Paris for my doctorate.

But how to get to Paris? With the help of Dame Enid Lyons (widow of the former Prime Minister, J. A. Lyons) a passage was booked,[2] and I set out on my adventurous journey on 13 May 1945. The war had ended in Europe a few days before, but we were still at war with Japan. Once on the high seas we were allowed to know that our ship was the *Moreton Bay* — the first to take civilians from Australia through Suez since the outbreak of war. But it was only after Gibraltar that captain, crew and passengers knew where we would land in England. It turned out to be Avonmouth, port of Bristol. In the meantime we had taken on a thousand returning servicemen in Colombo and Suez. (The steward delighted in telling us that, if there was not room for all the military, we could be left, baggage and all, in Suez!) There was none of the elegance of my pre-war journeyings, when the Orient and P&O lines offered five first-class passages each year to students travelling to Europe on scholarships. In the Indian Ocean, we experienced anti-aircraft practice, and passengers were in serious trouble if found by the captain without life jackets (even for a party in his stateroom). But it was a journey full of new hope, which not even the ruins left by the London blitz could quench.

During the months spent in England waiting for a student visa for France, I witnessed new — and difficult — beginnings. A conference in Oxford for the Centenary of Newman's Conversion made it possible for a number of people, both from Pax Romana and from the Grail, to reach England. A regional conference of Pax Romana was held in London to pick up the threads after the disruption of the war years. For the Grail there was a crucial meeting of the leaders of the international movement, who brought with them totally different wartime experiences in Europe, America and Australia. It began at the English Grail centre at Eastcote, Middlesex, and — to my joy — continued on the mystic Isle of Caldy, off the coast of Wales. There the group was joined for a few days by van Ginneken, founder of the Grail. Not many weeks later, on 20 October 1945, van Ginneken died in the Netherlands. I have always been grateful for my brief contact with this priest, scholar, poet and lover of Christ, whose vision of women's potential for the 'conversion of the world' has not lost its relevance in a changing world and a post-Vatican II Church.

My year in Paris, starting in October 1945, was lived under wartime conditions of housing and rationing and, apart from the renewal of some pre-war friendships, in a hermit-like devotion to study. This necessary preoccupation was broken twice, once by a trip to the Grail centre in the Netherlands and then by what was to prove another turning point: my participation, as delegate of UCFA, in the Jubilee Congress marking the 25th Anniversary of the foundation of Pax Romana, held in Fribourg in August 1946. At the pre-Congress Assembly a significant decision was taken: to 'refound' Pax Romana as two movements. One was to be for students, the International Movement of Catholic Students (IMCS), and one for 'intellectuals', the International Catholic Movement for Intellectual and Cultural Affairs (ICMICA).

Pax Romana had grown internationally despite the war. A new phase was opening up, but one which would no longer have the inspiring leadership of Abbé Joseph Gremaud, the much-loved Swiss priest who had been General Secretary since 1924. He resigned for reasons of health (although he would remain as IMCS chaplain until his death in March 1953). It was he who, after the Jubilee Congress, accepted my offer to come to Fribourg for four months from December 1946. I knew that Ed and Louisa Kirchner were returning to the United States, after some epic work on Ed's part for the refugees in Europe, and an English-speaking staff member was badly needed.

I cherished the illusion that I could finish a doctoral thesis while working for Pax Romana. The thesis never happened, although a volume of my research was eventually published,[3] and the four months became six years. A new phase was opening up in my own life, deeply linked with the rapidly emerging reality of a Catholic laity — men and women — increasingly aware of their responsibility of 'being' the Church at national and international levels.

It is difficult to recapture the feeling of war-weary Europe. Switzerland was something of an oasis, but the problems of the world pressed in on us from all sides. Communism was considered the big menace. My first Interfederal Assembly as a Pax Romana staff member was held during Easter 1947 at Anzio, south of Rome, still heavily marked by the American 'invasion' of Nazi-occupied Italy. Debate was furious about relations with Marxist-inspired student organisations. Peace was an ambiguous term, appropriated by communist propaganda. The necessary 'democratisation' of the university (making it available to all and not just the wealthy) had ideological overtones; students in France would soon be claiming their rights as 'young intellectual workers'.

But if there were threats there were hopes, too, and new horizons. The United Nations was getting under way and, before leaving Paris in 1946, I was part of Pax Romana's delegation to the first Conference of the United Nations Educational, Scientific and Cultural Organization (UNESCO). There were the first stirrings of decolonisation; India was independent from 1947. The *Pax Romana Journal* carried feature articles on human rights, on UNESCO as seen by Jacques Maritain, on the movement for European unity and on Christian unity.

The Holy Year of 1950 was to be the first great post-war gathering of Catholics from all over the world. During that year, Pax Romana held its Congress in Amsterdam and received this message from Pius XII: 'Be everywhere present in the vanguard of the intellectual combat...' During the Pilgrimage to Rome that followed the

Congress, Mgr Giovanni Battista Montini (who would later become Paul VI) told the pilgrims: 'Faith is a strength — the only language which unites us'. Pax Romana was already collaborating in the preparation of the First World Congress of the Lay Apostolate which would be held in Rome in October 1951.

Officially, I was to take part in this Congress as a delegate of Pax Romana. In fact, I was coopted into the secretariat and spent the week in chaotic activity. Naturally, we had neither computers nor photocopy machines. There was none of the streamlined efficiency of modern congress organisation. There were mountains of papers, a babel of tongues and tremendous enthusiasm.

Operating in the background, however, was no great privation for me. I am not a good congress participant. I have spent many of the years since then preparing for or reporting congresses, and I believe they have their uses; yet I have not been unduly discouraged when told that yes, it was interesting, but mostly because of the people you met in the corridors. Now, looking back from the 1990s, I am convinced that the 1951 congress was providential and even its corridors were worth organising. They were opening into a 'world becoming one', where (as Pius XII had solemnly declared) 'the laity also are the Church'. For me, and for my Roman future, its unexpected follow-up was to be decisive.

Part 1
LAITY: POST-WAR – PRE-COUNCIL

'Who are the laity? ... The Church would look foolish without them.'
J. H. Newman, 22 May 1859

CHAPTER 1

A world becoming 'one': The First World Congress of the Lay Apostolate, 1951

December of the Holy Year 1950. Some eighty people from Europe and the Americas had come together in a retreat house on Rome's Janiculum Hill. They had been invited by Vittorino Veronese, President of Italian Catholic Action, to plan for the First World Congress of the Lay Apostolate. The Congress was to be held in Rome in October 1951, the program of the Holy Year having proved too full to receive it.

On 19 December, Giovanni Battista Montini, Substitute in the Vatican Secretariat of State, brought greetings from Pius XII. We saw a priest in simple black, with no insignia of office, to whom the bishops present deferred and the lay people looked, not so much for authority as for understanding. This Congress, he said, 'will be a terminal point for the efforts of the laity over the past years and, at the same time, a solid foundation for their activity in the future'. He continued:

> All human activity today has an international dimension, and the lay apostolate can be no exception...When the Catholic Church invites us to work at international level, her aim is to open up

wider horizons for our charity ⁴ . . . We may be tempted at times to think that everything has been done. But when we consider needs, we are bound to acknowledge that we are still only at the beginning . . . It is for us to lay the first stone of the whole edifice which will be the Christian reality of tomorrow.⁵

Nearly five years earlier, Pius XII, in an address to the cardinals in February 1946,⁶ had already made his obvious — but epoch-making — statement that 'the laity also *are* Church'. In 1947, in a message to the First International Congress of the YCW in Montreal, he had stressed the worldwide scale of the lay apostolate. Well before that, in Christmas broadcasts during the tragic war years, he had looked towards the future of the world community. It was no longer a time like that between the two world wars, when leaders of Catholic international organisations met almost clandestinely to discuss their collaboration with the League of Nations, knowing that 'internationalism' could be suspected (not altogether without reason) of anticlerical and antireligious tendencies. The 1950s would instead be years of rapid development. 'Catholics', Pius XII would say on 23 July 1952, 'are called to overcome every vestige of nationalistic narrowness, and to seek a genuine fraternal encounter of nation with nation'.⁷

As the new decade dawned, humanity was experiencing what Cardinal Suhard, Archbishop of Paris, had described as a 'world-shaking crisis', a 'crisis of unity'.⁸ 'Ever since it exists', he wrote, 'for the first time the world is "one" '. The challenge for Christians was to achieve 'a humanism that matches the world and the designs of God', a 'cosmic' spirituality, a 'humanism of the person' and a 'humanism of the Cross'. The instrument raised up by the Holy Spirit was Catholic Action: 'a communitarian apostolate of responsible lay people, from all classes of society', gathered at the point of convergence of 'three simultaneous actions: religious, civic and social'.

Pius XI had defined Catholic Action as participation (or collaboration) of the laity in the apostolate of the hierarchy. But the World Congress of 1951 was to have a wider scope than that. Its aim would be to illustrate many forms of lay activity and to explore openings for common action at world level.

When the Congress was first announced, certain modern pioneers of the lay apostolate in Europe feared that the responsibility assumed by Italian Catholic Action, and confirmed by the Pope, would give too Italian a stamp to its proceedings. Joseph Cardijn, founder of the YCW, wrote to Montini suggesting the involvement of priests and lay leaders from other countries. With his Belgian colleagues, Cardijn had been perplexed by the massive involvement of members of Italian Catholic Action in the campaign which successfully barred a communist takeover of the new Republic in the Italian elections of April 1948. However, there was no need to worry about the international credentials of the Congress. From the start, Veronese characteristically exploited his relations with lay leaders, men and women, in many countries. The Preparatory Conference of December 1950 lost no time in appointing a committee to revise the draft program; its chairman was Cardijn.

In the redrafting a problem arose that would constantly resurface throughout the decade leading up to the Second Vatican Council. In promoting lay participation in the Church's mission in the world, should the starting-point be doctrine or the state of the world? It was not a matter of choosing between deductive or inductive thought processes. Everyone accepted the need for doctrinal clarification; and everyone wanted to respond to the needs of the human family. But people tended to feel differently about the relative urgency and effectiveness of doctrine on the one hand and analysis of human need on the other. For this First World Congress Cardijn had his way and the tone of the Congress would be given by his dramatic opening address: 'The World of Today'.

Vittorino Veronese

Who exactly was the initiator of the Congress? Many, in the generations following Vatican II, may not even have heard the name of this layman to whom the Church on all continents — and not the Church alone — owes much.

Vittorino Veronese was born in Vicenza, Italy, on 1 March 1910. He graduated in Law at the University of Padua in 1930. His marriage to Maria Petrarca gave him seven children, three girls and four boys.

His apostolate began when he joined the Italian Federation of Catholic University Students (FUCI), whose national chaplain was Montini, the future Paul VI. The President was Igino Righetti. The impact of the 'FUCI of Montini–Righetti' has lasted, through many vicissitudes, up to the present day.⁹ From 1939 to 1944, Veronese was Secretary of the Graduate Movement ('Movimento Laureati'), founded by Righetti in 1932 as an offshoot of the FUCI. He became General President of Italian Catholic Action in 1946, when the post-Fascism Statutes of this group came into force. (The Fascist regime had been obliged to make certain concessions to the Catholic Church. Catholic Action was able to survive, but only as long as it was entirely under ecclesiastic control. Any exercise of lay independence could be seen as a threat to the State.)

Veronese was an important influence up to and after Vatican II. He died peacefully in Rome on 3 September 1986 — after a period of moral and spiritual isolation.

The 'providential Congress'

The First World Congress for the Lay Apostolate opened on 7 October 1951. After prayer in St Peter's Basilica, national delegations from seventy-four countries, representatives of thirty-eight Catholic international organisations and members of seventeen ethnic groups in exile from communist-ruled states, converged on the newly opened Palazzo Pio, at the Tiber end of the Via della Conciliazione. The Auditorium can hold 2000 people comfortably and is equipped for simultaneous translation (a novelty for which at the time there were few adequate operatives). It would later also house the second and third World Congresses for the Lay Apostolate.

Historians of modern Church history can find the proceedings of this first Congress in two large volumes.¹⁰ The second contains reports (in French) of twenty workshops, with subjects ranging from parish, family and women to work in all its forms and unionism (not yet 'ecumenism'). Major statements in the first volume show 'where we were' in 1951.

Cardijn's address to 'this providential Congress' was a challenge to lay Christians at 'the Church's most missionary hour'. He provided a panorama illustrating demography in relation to religions and ideologies,[11] the progress of science and technology, the economic situation and the 'worker problem', the process of planetary unification.

Not all speeches were wholly devoted to the rhetoric of the occasion. Veronese, quoting an article by Count della Torre, editor of *L'Osservatore Romano*, gave the historical background for the modern lay apostolate:[12] movements for the defence of the rights of the Church and for Christian social action that arose in Belgium, France, Germany, Switzerland, Ireland and England from the middle of the 19th century. These had culminated in the international Congress of Malines in 1864 with 4000 participants, which had opened a new era, marked by the social encyclicals of Leo XIII. Three basic principles had motivated the laity at the time and were no less valid a century later: the *primacy of the spiritual*; an *open and positive* concept of Catholicism (not a besieged fortress); and a readiness to *serve*, not to be served by, the Church.

Two major speeches on 'The Basic Doctrines of the Lay Apostolate' had little in common, except the doctrine itself. Valerian Gracias, Archbishop of Bombay (and later cardinal), quoted not only recent Popes but also Cardinals Newman and Suhard and the laymen G. K. Chesterton and Frank Sheed. He anticipated the Vatican II Decree on Lay Apostolate by referring to the apostolate as 'a necessary and obvious postulate of the Christian vocation'. The Argentinian Cardinal Antonio Caggiano argued that in a society formed of 'unequal parts' (namely, the Church), lay people could only be an 'instrumental cause' of apostolate, subordinate to the 'principal cause' — the 'divinely instituted hierarchy'. However, in addition to Catholic Action, in which lay people collaborate with the apostolate of the Church itself, he also identified the 'action of Catholics' — an 'active and apostolic presence' in civil society of lay members of the Church. Caggiano's doctrine was unimpeachable, but the severe scholastic lesson aroused discreet reactions, if not of dissent, at least of discomfort. The Cardinal himself admitted wryly that some might have seen his speech as an introduction to a *summa contra laicos* — a treatise 'against the laity'!

The Congress moved on from doctrine to life: *What kind* of lay Catholics were needed for what kind of world? The answer to the first part of that question, for every sphere of life, had to be 'formation'[13] (an awkward expression in English, but one for which no adequate substitute has yet been found). This was treated by Giuseppe Siri Archbishop of Genoa and by the President of German Catholic Youth, Joseph Rommerskirchen. In addressing the second part of the question, it was seen that the post-war world called next for a 'Christian Social Order'; this was analysed by the Dutch Secretary General of the International Federation of Christian Trade Unions, Pierre Serrarens, and by the French sociologist, Charles Flory. Finally, an overview of international life, governmental and non-governmental, revealed responsibilities for Catholic lay people:

> The United Nations has now been in existence for six precarious years. It is responsible for the maintenance of peace in the whole world . . . a world made small by the tremendous strides of technical progress, and united in the fear of the great destruction which that progress has made possible.[14]

The speaker was Catherine Schaeffer, Assistant for Relations with the United Nations in the General Secretariat of the National Catholic Welfare Conference of the Bishops of the United States.

The Congress conclusions were drafted by a Commission of some thirty members, mostly lay people, with important input from two future 'periti' (experts) of Vatican II: Gérard Philips of Louvain[15] and Pietro Pavan.[16] Pius XII welcomed the conclusions in his closing address on 14 October. They expressed, he said, 'firm goodwill to extend your hand one to the other beyond national frontiers, in order to achieve in practice a full and efficacious collaboration in universal charity'.

A charter for the lay apostolate

The Pope's address was widely hailed as a charter for the lay apostolate. He recalled some 'outstanding figures' of the past, including Mary Ward, 'that incomparable woman whom, in the most sombre and bloody times, Catholic England gave to the Church'. He recalled also factors leading up to the contemporary situation. On the one hand, the Constitution of the United States of America, which was followed by a rapid growth in the life and vigour of the Church; on the other hand, the French Revolution, which also brought about the separation of Church and State, leaving the Church to rely more, for the accomplishment of her mission and the defence of her rights and freedoms, on Catholic movements of priests and laity. Then there were questions arising from the practice of the modern apostolate. His stress was more on questions than answers, foreshadowing the theological and experiential reflection that was to emerge before the World Congress of 1957 and contribute to Vatican II.

After all, the Pope asked, what is meant by apostolate?

> All the faithful without exception are members of the Mystical Body of Christ . . . Can we say [therefore] that everyone is called to the Apostolate in the strict sense of the word? God has not given to everyone either the possibility or the aptitude. It is certainly not easy to draw an exact line of demarcation showing precisely where the true apostolate of the laity begins. Must one make it embrace, for example, the conduct of the reputable and openly Catholic doctor whose conscience never wavers when there is a question of the natural and divine law? Many would be inclined to answer in the negative. We know, however, the powerful and irreplaceable value of this ordinary performance of the duties of one's state . . .
>
> It is self-evident that the apostolate of the laity is subordinated to the ecclesiastical Hierarchy . . . but the dependence admits of gradations. In decisive battles, it is often at the front that the most useful initiatives arise . . . Catholic Action must not become a litigant in party politics . . . [But] it would be blameworthy to leave the field free to persons unworthy or incapable of directing the affairs of State. Up to what point can and should the apostle keep himself at a distance from this limit? It is difficult to formulate a uniform rule . . . The circumstances, the mentality, are not the same everywhere'.[17]

In the terminology of a later generation, the Congress was a 'happening'. The second volume of the proceedings lists hundreds of press comments, of varying value. The French sociologist and journalist Joseph Folliet effectively summed up the experience for the Paris daily paper *La Croix* on 24 October 1951:

> For the first time in the annals of the Church, hundreds of lay people met at the heart of the Eternal, and universal City . . . They freely, at times hotly, discussed everything related to their apostolate. The most scrupulous equality reigned between nations, races, classes and sexes. This will leave an indelible mark on the turning-point of this half century.

The Congress, Folliet claimed, illustrated a 'sign of the times: the great process of internationalisation affecting the temporal structures of the Church'. This movement was not without its dangers: the danger of a bureaucracy 'laying down its laws from above and from afar'; of an 'abusive predominance of one or another country'; of 'a crystallisation of Catholic international organisations into anti-communist bodies'.

Folliet went on to sketch a 'geo-apostolate' — a geographical panorama of the apostolate, defining five major areas, each with its own originality: Ibero-American, Irish and Anglo-Saxon, continental European, the Iron Curtain countries, and the colonial and semi-colonial territories. 'All these have the right to exist, and none must predominate.' This concept of a geo-apostolate was to re-emerge, with variations, during the following years.

From Congress to 'COPECIAL'

Opening the Congress, Veronese had said:

> It has been clear from the beginning that we have never thought of creating a kind of world Catholic Action. The Congress is not a constituent assembly; it has been announced as what it will be: a 'study Congress'.

This declaration disappointed some, but reassured others. It was sincere. Yet on 23 January 1952, *L'Osservatore Romano* published an official

Vatican release stating that, 'in order to give lasting fruit to the good intentions expressed at the Congress by so many of his zealous sons [sic] in all countries', Pius XII was establishing the Permanent Committee for International Congresses of the Lay Apostolate (*Comitato Permanente dei Congressi Internazionali per l'Apostolato dei Laici*), of which Veronese would be the Secretary.

For the history of Italian Catholic Action and of the Church in Italy, this decision has been interpreted essentially as an elegant way of removing Veronese from the presidency of Catholic Action in favour of the Vice-President, Luigi Gedda, who had been so effective in the face of the communist threat in 1948. For the history of the universal Church, it was to prove a providential step for the promotion of the laity at world level; and, quite unpredictably, for the development of a theology of the laity that would be of service to Vatican II.

Veronese was not a man to sit down and wait for the occasion to present itself for a Second World Congress. The Vatican release had stated that the new secretariat would draw up statutes for the Permanent Committee, so Veronese, a dedicated lawyer, set to work. But one draft after another, duly submitted to the Secretariat of State, ended up where it still reposes, in a file within the archives of the present Pontifical Council for the Laity.

The Permanent Committee eventually drew up its own 'identity card', tacitly approved by the Secretariat of State. Its aims were defined as the preparation of lay apostolate congresses at world, continental or regional level, undertaking relevant studies, and gathering documentation. The 'Committee' remained a small secretariat, with no official status — and no fixed budget — until John XXIII appointed a Board of Directors in 1959. Its unmanageable title was soon reduced for practical purposes to 'COPECIAL'. In the early days of his Pontificate, Pope John, at a General Audience, turned to bestow a warm blessing on 'The Committee, the Committee . . . [a despairing gesture] . . . it ends with "laici"!'

The Committee had, however, an Ecclesiastical Commission.[18] In the press release, Cardinal Pizzardo had been named as its president. He kindly provided office space in the Palazzo San Calisto — space that had been occupied by 'Actio Catholica', an office set up in 1938 for worldwide promotion of Catholic Action but which had been inactive since the war years. One member of the Commission was appointed Ecclesiastical Assistant: at first Pietro Pavan and, when he resigned for other duties, Achille Glorieux. Glorieux, at the time editor of the French edition of *L'Osservatore Romano*, was to play an important role in Vatican II and after it.

Apart from Veronese and the ecclesiastical element, the Permanent Committee started life as an almost exclusively feminine (though not feminist) operation. Veronese had no inhibitions about giving work and responsibility to women. The driving force behind the First World Congress, and then the secretariat of COPECIAL, was Maria Vittoria Donadeo, from Milan and the Catholic Action Girls' Movement. In later years she would become the cornerstone of a small Oriental-rite Russian monastery in Rome, where her dynamism would be channelled, not only into contemplative life, but into acquiring a specialised knowledge of Russian icons and spirituality and — even before the fall of the Berlin Wall in 1989 — into making occasional discreet 'apostolic visits' to Moscow.

Italian Catholic Action also 'lent' Maria Carosi, who brought experience of pioneering work for the international involvement of Italian Catholic youth. In the administration of COPECIAL (and later of the Curial body *Consilium de Laicis*), she was professionally competent, but as far removed as possible from anything impersonally bureaucratic. Whoever met her — in the vortex of a World Congress or a UNESCO Consultation, at a World Assembly of Youth or an Ecumenical Conference of African Women — would never forget her warm friendship and her readiness to help in all eventualities (not to mention her chronic underestimation of her own capacities!). When she died in 1980, friends from around the world wrote, 'Rome will never be the same again!' (If the Vatican Administration could replace some of its clerical — and even episcopal — staff with a few women of the calibre and commitment of Maria Carosi and her assistant, Anna Matracia, it would not only benefit from their 'feminine genius' but would also, no doubt, gain in efficiency and make serious economies.)

Latin America was zealously represented on the original team by Sara Alonso from Argentina, member of a Secular Institute.[19] Later, in 1955, Marie-Ange Besson joined the staff, arriving from Paris and experience with the 'Cercle St Jean Battiste' (a missionary group founded by Jean Daniélou, SJ) and two years as a missionary in Vietnam. For the Second World Congress in 1957 there would be short-term 'loans' — especially Regina Betz, a member of the Focolare Movement sponsored by the German Bishops' Conference, and Romeo Maione from Canada, who would succeed Pat Keegan as President of the International YCW. The writer was on the spot from October 1952, invited by Veronese to be responsible for 'studies and documentation' — an assignment that proved to be anything but sedentary.

'Experts' meet

Cardijn made his first visit to COPECIAL on 21 November 1952, accompanied by Pat Keegan. There will be many biographers for Patrick Keegan, 'the first layman to address an Ecumenical Council'. The boy from 'Hindley near Wigan' started his working career as a 'little piecer' in a cotton mill. His first meeting with Joseph Cardijn, 'the dynamic little priest with bristly hair', was the start of a worldwide apostolate. He died, aged seventy-four, on 8 March 1990, commemorated as 'a man who made history' — for the Church, for the workers, for the human family. He was, as Archbishop Derek Worlock wrote, 'loved for himself, for his personal warmth, kindness, humour, outspoken courage, deep spirituality and faith'.[20]

Cardijn would have liked to find a more impressive group than 'just these women' assisting Veronese in his ground-breaking task, but he gave full cooperation from the start. Plans were mooted on the spot for laity meetings in Africa, Asia and Latin America. More immediately, an 'experts' meeting' was needed to review the First World Congress and plan for the future. Veronese's system of gathering hand-picked experts may not seem democratic but, at the time, it was the only way to ensure varied and competent input from both local and international sources.

The twenty-one experts — priests and lay people — came together in Villa Cagnola, Gazzada (Varese) in May 1953.[21] Five bishops took part, from Italy, France, Spain and Portugal, plus a representative of the Holy See. Comfortably installed in bedrooms and a meeting room overflowing with history and art, we embarked on our discussion of what to do for, and with, the laity in the modern world.

Theological discussion arising out of the World Congress was introduced by Philips and Pavan; and also by Emilio Guano, national chaplain of the Italian Graduates' Movement and previously Montini's successor in the FUCI chaplaincy. During Vatican II, as Bishop of Livorno, 'Don Guano' would be chairman of the drafting committee for *Gaudium et Spes*, the Pastoral Constitution on the Church in the Modern World.

The authentic lay viewpoint was represented by Lance Wright, an English convert, architect by profession and president of the Newman Association of Great Britain. Lance regretted the too juridical presentation of the lay apostolate in the World Congress (he refrained from naming Cardinal Caggiano), and praised a talk Philips had just given on 'The Laity in the Mystery of the Church', which responded to the lay person's need for a 'Christian mystique'. For the laity, precedence should be given to the 'indirect' apostolate, exercised in 'secular' life.

Another speaker, Raimondo Spiazzi, OP, was unlucky enough to say that the lay person's activity in the social field could only be called apostolate in a metaphorical sense. At this point Cardijn pounced: 'We have to be clear what we mean by "lay apostolate" and "Catholic Action", so that those who are in the thick of things can know where they stand. The apostolate is a life and death matter for the Church. We ask real heroism from the leaders. You can't ask that in the name of a metaphor!' — and his fist came down on the table.

The world scene was not absent from this meeting. Auguste Vanistendael (Belgium), successor to Pierre Serrarens as Secretary General of the International Federation of Christian Trade Unions, outlined the social consequences of world unification, especially in relation to Latin America, Africa and Asia. There emerged also an in-Church problem that was to remain thorny until after Vatican II: the respective fields of COPECIAL and the Conference of Catholic International Organizations (CIO). Veronese saw these as two 'centres of action': for Marie du Rostu, the French President of the World Union of Catholic Women's Organizations, the distinction was between a 'great factory' with various sections and a 'research laboratory'.

There was unanimity on the main focus for the Second World Congress: the formation of the laity for their varied roles within the mission of the Church. What this should involve was worked out in another experts' meeting, held at Castel Gandolfo in October 1954.

Formation of the laity

The question of formation inevitably brought the debate back to the nature of the apostolate and to questions of terminology: apostolate 'in the strict sense', 'in the wide sense', 'direct' or 'indirect' — distinctions that Vatican II would simply eliminate by including under the term 'lay apostolate' all forms of lay participation in the Church's mission. The state of the debate emerges from a Note drafted by COPECIAL when some twenty theologians were invited to a meeting in Rome in June 1955:

> In recent publications we find positions as far removed from one another as the stress laid by Bishop Suenens on the universal duty of 'direct religious apostolate' (as in the Legion of Mary) and, on the other hand, an almost exclusive attention to Christian witness in the modern world... While admitting a wider sense of the term 'apostolate', we might adopt a more precise terminology to distinguish, for instance, between 'witness', 'missionary action', 'Christian social action', etc.
>
> To what extent is it possible, or desirable, to define 'laity'? Defining the 'lay' person by commitment in 'secular' life is too limiting... We might stress different degrees of being 'lay' (i.e., non-clergy): from the cloistered nun to the lay man or woman in the family and professional life. We should, in any case, make a clearer distinction — at least, as to function — between lay people fully committed 'in the world' and those engaged essentially in Church-related work (those that the English call 'clerical laymen', in a rather pejorative sense).
>
> In what sense can we speak of a 'spirituality of the laity'? Is this a reaction against a supposed monopoly of spiritual life by priests and religious, or its identification with pious practices that are incompatible with the lifestyle of many lay people today?

At the suggestion of Paolo Dezza, SJ (now Cardinal), it was decided to consult Catholic Faculties of Theology and Canon Law. In November 1955, Dezza, as General Secretary of the International Federation of Catholic Universities, sent out a questionnaire (in Latin):

1. How is the notion of apostolate to be exactly defined, both as to its subject and as to its object?
2. (a) Can the Church ask from the laity any particular form of apostolate that is proper to them?
   (b) If so, what is the specific object of this form of apostolate proper to the laity?
3. In the case of an affirmative answer to 2 (a), what should be the relations between Hierarchy and laity in the different fields of the apostolate: familial, social, cultural, etc.?[22]

1. Anne Kerr, *Lanterns over Pinchgut,* Macmillan, Australia, 1988.

2. Dame Enid was a good friend of the Grail Movement and underlined her support with the comment 'All these politicians' wives are travelling, why not Rosemary!'.

3. *Vers un héroisme intégral: dans la lignée de Péguy,* Cahiers de l'Amitié Charles Péguy, Paris, 1951.

4. The words of St Augustine, 'Allargare spatia caritatis', were to become a leitmotif for Montini when he later became Pope Paul VI.

5. Montini speaking to the Preparatory Conference for the First World Congress on 19 December 1950, quoted in *Lay Apostolate,* Bulletin of COPECIAL, 1963, 2–3, p. 23. (This was the issue published after Montini became Pope Paul VI.)

6. Pius XII to the cardinals, 20 February 1946, in *Discorsi e Radiomessaggi di Sua Santità Pio XII,* VII, Vatican Polyglot Press, Rome, p. 395.

7. Pius XII, 23 July 1952, to an Italian Summer School on 'Catholics and International Life'.

8. *Growth or Decline of the Church,* Pastoral Letter, Lent 1947.

9. For Montini as university chaplain, see Peter Hebblethwaite, *Paul VI, The First Modern Pope,* HarperCollins, London, 1993, pp. 94–120. The 'Montini–Righetti tradition' was one of spiritual and intellectual seriousness, friendship, student wit and merriment (irreverent but harmless), and a resilient freedom, even in the face of violence from Fascist thugs. Montini was abruptly dismissed as chaplain in 1933 and confined to bureaucratic work. He had clashed with Jesuits over pedagogical methods and with cautious Curialists over his anti-Fascist approach.

10. *Actes du 1er Congrès Mondial pour l'Apostolat des Laïques,* Comité Permanent des Congrès Internationaux pour l'Apostolat des Laïques, Rome, 1952.

11. Cardijn said: 'During these last 25 years, while the world's population increased by 700 million, the number of Catholics only increased by 13 million . . . for one pagan [sic!] converted each year, more than 50 were born into paganism!' (*Actes,* op. cit. vol. I, pp. 153–54).

12. Count della Torre writing in the Preface to a volume of *Opera Omnia* of Giuseppe Toniolo.

13. At the ecumenical Consultation of 1974 on 'new trends in Laity Formation' (see Part III) the perennial difficulty arose. Frank Klos (United States) commented: 'Semantically, the term . . . not only sounds strange but seems to carry the connotation of a mechanical process — something done to someone else. However, the term has gained wide official acceptance. Specifically, lay formation means much more than training; and even more than education. It is the equipping of the laity to be disciples of Christ, with all that implies, in the social-cultural-political arenas of everyday life.'

14. *Actes,* op. cit., p. 309.

15. Philips (1899–1972) was one of those rare theologians whose writing reflects a habit of listening to the laity. His first book on the laity was published in English in 1956, *The Role of the Laity in the Church,* Fides Press, Chicago.

16. Pietro Pavan (1903–94), sociologist and Rector of the Lateran University, was made a cardinal in 1985. He collaborated closely with John XXIII, especially in drafting the Encyclical *Pacem in Terris.* (Cf. Franco Biffi, *Prophet of Our Times: The Social Thought of Cardinal Pietro Pavan,* New City Press, New Rochelle, NY, 1992. Translated and abridged by R. Goldie from the original *Il Cantico dell' Uomo.*)

17. *Actes*, op. cit., pp. 46–50. Experience before and since Vatican II has only proved the impossibility of uniform solutions for the kind of dilemma suggested here by Pius XII. The Council spelt out 'a clear distinction between what Christians singly and collectively do in their own name, as citizens guided by a Christian conscience, and what they do in conjunction with their pastors in the name of the Church' (*Gaudium et Spes*, 76). Paul VI, in his Apostolic Letter of 1971 on Social Problems (*Octogesima Adveniens*), in view of the diversity of situations in which Christians were living, refrained from offering solutions with 'universal validity'. He left it 'up to the Christian communities to analyse with objectivity the situation which is proper to their own country . . . and to draw principles of reflection, norms of judgment and directives for action from the social teaching of the Church' (4).

18. An Ecclesiastical Commission is a group of Ecclesiastics (bishops or priests) appointed to assist a particular body in doctrinal matters and in relations with the Holy See (at international level), the Bishops' Conference (at national level), or whatever other 'competent Church Authorities' may be concerned.

19. A Secular Institute is a form of 'consecrated life' instituted by Pius XII in 1947. The members take vows of poverty, chastity and obedience, but do not necessarily live in community. They exercise their apostolate in regular secular activity.

20. Cf. 'Layman who made history' by Austin Lyons and the Tribute from Archbishop Worlock, both in *The Universe*, 18 March 1990, p. 13. See also Edward Mitchinson, 'Patrick Keegan — An Appreciation', in *New Life*, Review of the Social Apostolate, London, 1990, pp. 2–5.

21. The proceedings of the meeting are recorded in a mimeographed report (in French) preserved in the archives of the Pontifical Council for the Laity.

22. Historical archives of the Pontifical Council for the Laity.

CHAPTER 2

In the crisis of the modern world

The Second World Congress for the Lay Apostolate was announced in May 1955. It would meet from 5 to 13 October 1957, and would have as its theme 'The Laity in the Crisis of the Modern World: Responsibilities and Formation'. National and international delegations began to be formed. In July 1957 these delegations received two theological Basic Texts and one 'sociological' Text. These had been drafted following a final meeting of about forty experts, held in the newly opened *Domus Mariae*, the conference centre of Italian Catholic Action on the Via Aurelia in Rome.

The group of theological experts was chaired by Sebastian Tromp, SJ. A Dutchman and professor at the Gregorian University, Tromp had been the main drafter of Pius XII's Encyclical on the Mystical Body of Christ (1943). He was to be Secretary of the Theological Commission of Vatican II. Ramon Sugranyes de Franch, then General Secretary of Pax Romana–ICMICA, remembers being ushered by Tromp into the theologians' sanctum with a solemn '*Ecce laicus!*' (Behold the layman!). The day of the modern Catholic lay theologian was dawning — but only just.

The theologians received, with other material, the 'consensus' emerging in the replies sent by twelve Faculties — Rome, Paris, Louvain, Lyons, Toulouse, Salamanca, Washington and St Mary's, Kansas — to

Dezza's questionnaire. Two Basic Texts were produced as a result of the theologians' work. One — *The Mission of the Church: The Mystery of the Church and of Her Mission*, a strongly biblical text — was drafted by Emilio Guano; the other was *The Nature and the Apostolic Vocation of the Laity* by Gérard Philips. After reading these Texts, it is easy to see why Roberto Tucci, SJ, reporting on the Congress, could write:[1]

> A most appreciable result of the more strictly doctrinal part of the Congress was the noteworthy contribution it made to the progressive formulation of a *doctrina communis* on the theological bases, the nature and varied forms of the laity's apostolic responsibility within the Church.

This contribution was later channelled into preparatory work for Vatican II — a destination still unknown to the experts at *Domus Mariae*.

The sociological text was drafted with the collaboration of Jean-Pierre Dubois-Dumée, editor of the French review, *Informations Catholiques Internationales*. It reflects the variegated panorama of a world become 'one': the emergence of the peoples of Asia and Africa after the Bandung Conference of April 1955; the secularisation, urbanisation and mobility of modern life; the 'sway of communism' and the spread of atheism, especially practical atheism; the spiritual longings evidenced in the striving for Christian unity among our 'separated brethren' and in the revival and renewal seen in the great non-Christian religions; the nostalgia for 'universal communion'. The response to these challenges had to be a new Christian witness, a new 'style' for Christian living, and a 'universal mentality' expressed in acts of justice and charity. This world view anticipated the Vatican II document on 'The Church in the Modern World': 'Humanity is passing from a static to a dynamic and evolutionary conception of things . . . A vast new complex of problems come to birth . . . ' (*Gaudium et Spes*, 5).[2]

Pius XII: clarifications and a 'suggestion'

Pius XII chose to speak on the opening day of the Second Congress. He wanted to clarify certain points: the relationship between Hierarchy and apostolate; the 'lay' character of the 'simple faithful' — baptised and confirmed, but not ordained — who remain 'lay' even when they receive a 'mandate' from the Hierarchy; the nature of the *consecratio mundi* (consecration of the world), which is the work of the laity, involved in social, economic and political life.³

In his address, the Pope maintained the distinctions current at the time between apostolate in the strict sense and in the wider sense, with Catholic Action as an official lay apostolate. He went on to communicate — without actually endorsing — a suggestion, that was afterwards known to have come from Leo Josef Suenens, Auxiliary Bishop of Malines:

> ... there prevails a regrettable uneasiness, originating mainly in the use of the term [Catholic Action]. This term is said to be reserved to certain types of organized lay apostolate to which it gives, in public opinion, a sort of monopoly. All organizations that do not fit into this framework remain on the fringe of the essential apostolic effort of the laity ... Two practical reforms are being considered: one of terminology, and the other, a structural reform. First, it would be necessary to restore to the term 'Catholic Action' its general meaning and apply it only to the aggregate of movements of the lay apostolate recognized as such, nationally or internationally ... The structural reform would follow. All the groups would preserve their own name and autonomy, but together they would form, as Catholic Action, a federated unity ... The eventual realization of such a plan naturally requires attentive and prolonged consideration. Your Congress may provide a favourable occasion for discussing the problem.

The delegates were unused to being consulted by the Pope, and many were disconcerted by the 'suggestion'. They passed a resolution asking COPECIAL and the CIO to gather data and seek a solution. The following year, COPECIAL sent an Enquiry to National Lay Apostolate Committees, giving examples of the situation in different cultural contexts, and asking for further information. Replies from about thirty countries revealed great diversity: for example, the Italian model was centrally coordinated with branches according to age and sex; the French-Belgian one was 'specialized' by social milieu; in Britain the term 'Catholic Action' was avoided because of its supposed political connotations. A synthesis of the replies was the first document from outside the Commission distributed to members of the Preparatory Commission on the Apostolate of the Laity set up in 1960 as part of the preparation for Vatican II. The Conciliar Decree on the Laity (n.20) attempts to meet all these situations in defining Catholic Action, with or without the name.

It all seems very remote today. But the Pope's 'suggestion' came as a bombshell that some feared would disrupt the Congress. In some countries the dogmatism of Catholic Action had gone too far. Suenens had met the problem through the Legion of Mary (founded in Dublin in 1921 by Frank Duff, which had almost a monopoly of lay apostolate in some places, while being downgraded elsewhere as not being Catholic Action. In New Zealand, the Bishops had given a Catholic Action 'mandate' only to certain youth groups, who brandished it in the face of traditional adult forms of lay activity. The rigorous application of Cardijn's formula for the YCW was the hallmark of orthodoxy for 'specialised' Catholic Action. One exasperated friend wrote to me:

> After all, 'see–judge–act' is something anybody does, but the way it reaches the community is about as comical as making a movement out of 'stop–look–listen' for traffic before automatic signalling devices came in!

Many reactions to the 'suggestion' were out of all proportion to the problems of Church and society confronting the Congress and were indicative of the unpreparedness in many sectors of clergy and laity for the Council that would soon be announced.

Hans-Ruedi Weber, Director of the Laity Department set up within the World Council of Churches (WCC) in 1954 provided an interesting commentary as the only Protestant among the 2000 and more participants. Weber had been invited — on a press ticket — through the good offices of Agostino Bea, SJ (later Cardinal President of the Secretariat for Promoting Christian Unity). In an article for *The Ecumenical Review*,[4] Weber gave 'the second thoughts of a Protestant observer who tried to listen and understand'. Apart from a number of 'competent and experienced people', he found the lay participants on the whole 'very obedient and submissive children'. This was 'no plea for anticlericalism', but only for a more questioning attitude. Among 'dangerous tendencies' was the 'excessive insistence on organization', the danger of 'institutionalism and sclerosis'.

In the gangways and corridors of the Congress building, nothing else was perhaps discussed as fervently as the short allusion, in the Pope's discourse, to the possibility of a revision of terminology with regard to Catholic Action. The 'dynamism of the Holy Spirit' was, however, at work. Its post-Conciliar fruits were highlighted by Hans-Ruedi Weber himself when, ten years later, he spoke on behalf of more than a hundred ecumenical Observers at the close of the Third World Congress.

Basic formation

The Congress workshops were devoted entirely to basic formation of the laity for the apostolate. A preparatory Enquiry had been sent to National Committees on the respective roles of family, school, parish and — complementing these educational milieux — movements of the laity. This led to a memorable exchange between Cardijn and myself. The founder of the YCW could not agree that movements were merely 'complementary'. No real formation was ever given before the age of entry into the adult world of work and the specialised lay apostolate group. I tried an argument that was difficult to refute. Had not the YCW been actively forming lay apostles for more than thirty years? Might one not hope that there were parents 'formed' in the Movement who could pass something of their formation on to their children? And how many teachers in Catholic schools had passed through the training process of the Young Catholic Students (YCS)? I am not sure that Cardijn was convinced. But, many years later, I found confirmation. When Patricia Jones, in 1987, addressed the Bishops' Synod on the Laity, she presented her credentials. She gave credit for her formation and leadership training to the YCS; but first she recalled growing up in a family 'deeply committed to the lay apostolate through the YCW and other Cardijn movements'.[5]

Speakers at the Congress

To recall the whole Congress program would involve a long list of names, many of which have already been mentioned and will be again. The main speakers developed subjects already proposed in the Basic Texts. 'The World's Need' was discussed in two lectures — in Western analysis (Joseph Folliet) and Oriental mysticism (the Chinese jurist and convert, John Wu) — and completed by presentations about concrete situations in the different world regions. The theological input was given, not only by Philips and Bishop Manuel Larrain (Chile), but also by two laymen: the Spaniard, Alfredo Lopez and the Australian writer, publisher and Hyde Park preacher, Frank Sheed. Characteristically, Sheed spoke on the lay person's role in *conveying* the truth:

> We are living in a noisy world . . . In all this uproar, how is truth to be heard, revealed truth? We have a great Pope, who utters truth profoundly, but the great mass of people never hear what he says . . . So it is with our Bishops, our great preachers and writers . . . There is only one voice that can be heard, apart from the voice of conscience, the voice of a man speaking to his friend — to the man next door, the man he works with, plays with, travels with . . . [But the lay person must be] equipped, and he is for the most part religiously illiterate.

The lecture on 'The Mission of the Church' had been entrusted to Montini, by then Archbishop of Milan. He had been uprooted abruptly from the Vatican in 1954 to lead Italy's largest diocese (a diocese different from the rest even in its liturgy which follows the rite of St Ambrose). The lecture was to have been given on the opening day but Montini was detained by his great pastoral venture, the Mission of Milan. So he spoke on 9 October, at the central point of the Congress. He may have seemed severe when he insisted on orthodoxy and a mandate as conditions for the apostolate but the audience broke into thunderous applause when he outlined his 'program':

> This is the genius of the apostolate: to know how to love . . . We will love those who are worthy of love, and those who are

unworthy...We will love our times, our community, our technical skills, our art, our sport, our world...we will love with the heart of Christ.[6]

Another speaker had close links with Montini: Aldo Moro, Italian Minister for Education. Like Veronese, he came from the FUCI of Montini–Righetti. He had been President of the FUCI and of the Graduate Movement. In 1946, he was a member of the Constituent Assembly for the Italian Republic. He was President of the Christian Democrat Party when, in May 1978, he was assassinated by the Red Brigades. The day after this premeditated crime, Paul VI recalled the friend he knew from student days: 'He was a good and wise man, incapable of harming anyone, an excellent professor, a statesman, an exemplary father and family man, with noble religious, social and human sentiments . . . '.[7] At the Congress, Aldo Moro spoke about 'The Catholic Politician in the Emergent World Community'. He saw his task, not only as an intellectual responsibility, but as 'the duty of exerting a spiritual influence in civic and political spheres'.[8]

At *the* Circolo di Roma

During the Congress a confidential meeting was held at the *Circolo di Roma* (the Roman Club for Catholic diplomats which Veronese had been influential in setting up during the Holy Year in 1950). The purpose was to take advantage of the presence of a number of 'experts', and of the arrival from Latin America of the French Dominican, Louis-Joseph Lebret, founder of the Centre in Lyons, 'Economy and Humanism' — a title that was, in itself, a philosophy and a program. Lebret had become a world traveller at the service of human development, in the great Dominican tradition of realism, mercy and justice. His name has been coupled with that of another Dominican, Bartolomeo de Las Casas, champion of the rights of the Indios during the Spanish colonisation of Latin America, beginning with the West Indies in the 16th century.[9]

The meeting discussed economic, social, political and international problems. It advocated setting up a chain of centres composed of 'complementary specialists' who would make their findings available, not only to the Catholic hierarchy and laity, but to all 'men of good will'. A number of such centres already existed in India, Japan, North Africa, Brazil, etc. The idea was that they would work in contact with a Roman Centre for documentation and study. There would be obstacles to overcome, including the lack of mutual trust between clergy and laity, a theology that was too deductive, a 'group spirit' rather than a sense of the Church, and the inability to understand non-Western peoples.

A meeting was fixed for the following month in Paris. It produced a 'provisional and strictly confidential Note'. This was intended for 'Rome', but, owing to a misunderstanding, was never actually presented to the Ecclesiastical Authorities.[10] The confidentiality seems excessive today. At the time, it was understandable. But the questions raised and the solutions proposed were soon to emerge in the discussions of Vatican II, especially in work done during the Council on the chapters of *Gaudium et Spes* concerning social and economic problems and international justice.

World Crisis and the Catholic

To bring the message of the Second World Congress to a wider public and to involve persons who had not been able to attend, Veronese approached twenty lay people, men and women, who were outstanding in their particular fields and came from widely different backgrounds. The twenty 'witnesses' consented to contribute (the question of payment was not even raised) to a volume entitled, in the original French edition, *Le monde attend l'Eglise* (The World is Waiting for the Church).[11] It was translated into English, Dutch, German, Italian, Spanish and Japanese.

The English edition, *World Crisis and the Catholic*,[12] gave pride of place to an interview given by Konrad Adenauer to Karl Bringmann. The Chancellor of the German Federal Republic saw the Christian politician's first duty was to oppose the 'active struggle against Christian principles' in 'an age remarkable for its secularization'. He regarded the unification of Europe, not only as 'a political and economic aim worth striving for, but as a real Christian obligation'.

George Meany, President of AFL–CIO (American Federation of

Labor – Congress of Industrial Organizations) — a man, it was said, who 'works in his shirt-sleeves and thinks in his shirt-sleeves' — called for a 'consensus to safeguard progress' for the true betterment of humankind.

Various fields of scientific endeavour were represented. The Italian Francesco Severi, Director of the National Institute for Higher Mathematics and successor to Einstein in the French Academy of Sciences, wanted serious consideration of 'the human and social effect of machines'. Karl Stern, Bavarian-born Chief of the Department of Psychiatry at the University of Montreal, dealt with 'Group Psychology in the Atomic Era': 'The forces of hostility and fear added up, would parallel the force of an atom bomb. There is only one thing that is stronger: that is love'. The Brazilian Gustave Corçao, specialist in astronomy and geodesy, converted to Catholicism from dreams of Marxist revolutionary idealism, expected the Church to be 'different from any other society', to be 'in the world but not of it'.

Bringing the Christian message to African and Asian peoples called for inculturation (Marga Klompé, Minister for Social Welfare in the Netherlands Government), and also for material aid (Raymond Scheyven, Belgian Member of Parliament). But Mutara III Charles Léon Pierre Rudahigwa, King of Rwanda (still a territory under Belgian trusteeship), asked: 'What does the African soul seek from the Church? — A Creator God who "made man out of love", not the divine Creator of African tradition who watches over his work "from afar"'. He also called upon the Church to respond to the African's need for moral order, true peace, respect for the national idea within the universal community; and to do so 'before technical progress has dried up the African's unsatisfied longing for the things of the spirit'.

Social and political life was seen from an international standpoint by Kotara Tanaka of Japan ('World Peace and World Law') and at the national level by John Myung Chang, Vice-President of the Republic of Korea — a country experiencing the spiritual vacuum left by the decline of religious, social and moral traditions.

The arts were represented by Ann Blyth, Hollywood film star; by the Swiss architect Hermann Baur; and by the author of *Every Man a Penny* and *All Glorious Within*, Bruce Marshall, who saw a 'tiny minority of Catholics' had come to realise that 'we cannot expect outsiders to be impressed by our claim to the truth unless its possession is seen to spur us on to right wrong' — including wrong done to animals. In the illustrated French edition, the author was shown with his arm around his cat. Times have changed, but, whatever wrongs are still inflicted, we can rejoice with Bruce Marshall that 'God's arm is round his Church'.

Christopher Dawson recalled Oriental elements in the history of Christianity: 'The Church stands neither for East nor West, but for the universal spiritual society which is destined to embrace them both'. John Ching-Hsiung Wu argued that Christianity is 'the only synthesis really possible between East and West'.

The quite unclassifiable Giorgio La Pira (1904–77) contributed a message of hope. Born of a poor Sicilian family, La Pira became Professor of Roman Law in the University of Florence and member of Italy's Constituent Assembly in 1946. As Mayor of Florence from 1951, he disconcerted some and delighted others by his Gospel-inspired economic ideas, his joyful Franciscan asceticism and his correspondence with spiritual 'power centres' (women's monasteries). He brought the world to Florence with his International Congresses for Peace and Civilisation; and, in 1959, went with a message of peace and conversion to the Kremlin.

Two French contributions gave an overall view. Count Wladimir d'Ormesson, Ambassador to the Holy See (1948–56) viewed the world crisis from a 'Roman watchtower', recalling the role played in Europe after the Second World War by parties of Christian inspiration. When the Iron Curtain collapsed, it would reveal that there were scarcely any believing communists behind it — the 'strong minorities of communist believers' being found in the 'old Latin communities'. In this changing world, 'Papal Rome', reconciling unity and diversity at the heart of the universal Church, had an irreplaceable function. Under the title, 'The Gates of Hell shall not Prevail', Joseph Folliet recalled crises through which the Church had passed in the course of her history — under a divine protection operating through human beings.

A poem specially written by Gertrud von Le Fort closed the volume: ('The Voice of the Church Speaks'): '. . . Come, my children in the world, and be my witnesses: I have blessed you and you must be a blessing'!

The end of an era

The publication of the proceedings of the Second World Congress brought to a close the pre-Conciliar stage in the life of COPECIAL. The Council announced in January 1959 was very much an unknown quantity. But this was not the only cause of uncertainty for the Permanent Committee. In October 1958 a new Pope — John XXIII — had succeeded Pius XII, founder of the Committee, which was as budget-less and statute-less as ever. And in November 1958, Vittorino Veronese was elected Director General of UNESCO. There remained the secretariat and the Ecclesiastical Commission. With an act of faith in the future, invitations were sent to some thirty experts to come to a meeting in May 1959 to review the seven years of COPECIAL's activity and look forward to a hypothetical Third World Congress.

The meeting was held at the shrine of Our Lady, 'Cause of Our Joy', on the heights of Montallegro, above Rapallo with a magnificent view over the Ligurian coast. But fog and rain greeted the experts, lifting only on the day of departure. It was appropriate for the situation of COPECIAL, but the participants were not deterred. The seven-year report was duly discussed. There was appreciation of work done, but a general desire for greater clarity as to the future. This would come within the next months, when John XXIII gave COPECIAL a Directing Board of nine members.[13] No conclusion could be reached as to a Third World Congress while the Ecumenical Council was still only an 'announcement'. But the report presented by Philips[14] on 'The present state of theological thinking on the subject of the lay apostolate' was already a contribution to the future Council. It touched on subjects that were still very new on any agenda for the laity in the Catholic Church: ecumenical involvement, the role of women and the place of public opinion in the Church. In the course of discussion, it was Sebastian Tromp who reminded the group that in the future Council, the 'voice of the people' (vox populi) would play an important role. The Council Commissions would be open to questions raised by the laity. This was to prove no mere wishful thinking.

1. Cf. the Roman Jesuit review *La Civiltà Cattolica*, Rome, 1957/4, p. 451.

2. The Basic Texts are included in the proceedings of the Congress, published by COPECIAL in 1959, in three volumes: I *Laymen in the Church*; II *Laymen Face the World*; III *Forming Apostles*.

3. The term was new in this sense, and was later the subject of much debate. Fear of undue 'sacralisation' of secular life caused it to be used only in a very attenuated sense by the Council in *Lumen Gentium*, Dogmatic Constitution on the Church of Vatican II (34). But Paul VI used it on more than one occasion in the sense intended by Pius XII (cf. General Audience of 23 April 1969).

4. Hans-Ruedi Weber, 'Rome and the Lay Apostolate', in *A Symposium on Laity*, a reprint of articles from *The Ecumenical Review*, Vol 3. Geneva, April 1958.

5. In 1992 Pat Jones was appointed Assistant General Secretary of the Bishops' Conference of England and Wales.

6. *Laymen in the Church*, op. cit., p. 90.

7. For Pope Paul's words about Aldo Moro, see *L'Osservatore Romano*, 11 May 1978, p. 1.

8. *Laymen Face the World*, op. cit., p. 160.

9. Cf. the review *Economie et Humanisme*, published by Economie et Humanisme, 14, rue Antoine-Dumont, Lyons, France, October 1986, special issue for the 20th anniversary of the death of Lebret.

10. The signers of the Note include: Louis-Joseph Lebret, François Houtart, Marga Klompé, Joaquin Ruiz-Gimenez, Patrick Keegan, Joseph Folliet, Bichara Tabbah (Lebanon), Antoine Lawrence (French Guinea), Catherine Doherty, Thom Kerstiens, Ramon Sugranyes de Franch, and Auguste Vanistendael.

11. *Le monde Attend l'Eglise*, Ed. Fleurus, Paris 1957.

12. The English edition was published by Sheed & Ward, London and New York, 1958.

13. The members of the Directing Board were: Chairman, Silvio Golzio, President of the Graduates Movement of Italian Catholic Action; Karl Furst zu Löwenstein, President of the Central Committee of German Catholics; Jean-Pierre Dubois-Dumée (France); Marguérite Fiévez (Belgian pioneer of the Young Christian Workers); Patrick Keegan; Claude Ryan (National Secretary of Catholic Action in French-speaking Canada); Ramon Sugranyes de Franch (Catalan); Juan Vazquez (Argentina); Martin Work (Executive Secretary, National Council of Catholic Men, United States). The writer was appointed Executive Secretary.

14. The text of the report was published in 1960 in the series Folia Lovaniensia of the University of Louvain.

CHAPTER 3

Living internationally as Christians

Before his election as Director General of UNESCO, Veronese had organised one last experts meeting, on 'Christian Values in International Life'. The twenty-five experts' who came to Assisi in June 1958 represented various fields of international activity: diplomacy, inter-governmental or non-governmental organisations, lay missionary activity, the academic world.[1]

Jean Daniélou, SJ introduced a theology of the international community: a basic unity of humankind, but a diversity of races, peoples, languages, habitats — inherent in the plan of creation, as evidenced in the Bible and in the works of the Church Fathers. The coming of Christ made possible a new unity as members of his Body. The theology carried implications that would be explored under the post-Conciliar categories of inculturation, interreligious dialogue, etc. and foreshadowed the problems that were beginning to explode in the decolonisation process.

Different concepts of peace were discernible (in this period of the Cold War): the peace of the diplomats ('often the only one possible'); of idealists, promoting the brotherhood of man; of evolutionary optimists, counting on technical progress to solve all problems; of imperialists, whose notion of peace would be oppression. But true peace is only possible where there are sound principles based on belief in a God of Love and on the painful exercise of pardon.

What the Christian had to do in a crisis was no problem for Giorgio La Pira:

> It's so clear and simple! — Like Ezra and Nehemiah: rebuild the Christian city . . . beginning with the reconstruction of the Temple, and coordinating with it the reconstruction of houses, shops, schools, squares, walls, the towers of Jerusalem! This is something perfectly well understood by the new nations of Asia and Africa . . .

Maria Luisa (Marisetta) Paronetto Valier warned against any complacency when non-Catholics praise us for being 'open'. Our openness could be leading into emptiness. Marisetta had ample experience of international living. Venetian by birth (with a Doge of Venice in her ancestry), she came, like Veronese, from the FUCI of Montini–Righetti. In July 1943 she married Sergio Paronetto (1911–45). In spite of ill-health, Sergio, an economist, played a leading role as a member of a group of young intellectuals who — in contact with Montini and Alcide de Gasperi — worked on a 'code' for implementing Christian social principles, nationally and internationally, in the post-war world. From 1960 to 1988, Marisetta was General Secretary of the Italian National Commission for UNESCO; she twice represented the Italian Government as member of the Organization's Executive Committee. Her in-Church commitment had been mainly in Pax Romana–ICMICA and its Italian-affiliated Movement.

Living internationally is a day-to-day affair. You cannot live only on theological and philosophical reflections. Veronese introduced discussion on the need for 'spiritual support' or, at the very least, understanding. He warned, however, against a 'pioneer complex'. Pius XII, himself a pioneer in his approach to world problems, was supportive, but few bishops had time or opportunity to grasp the relevance for the Church — and even for the diocese — of international organisations, and few theologians were interested. It is easy to forget now that, before Vatican II, there were no Assemblies of the Synod of Bishops and, with one exception — the Episcopal Council for Latin America (CELAM), set up in 1955 — no continental or regional bodies of bishops. Among the Council Fathers (apart from Papal Nuncios accustomed to being posted from one continent to another) the exceptions to the general inexperience of international matters were mostly bishops who had been chaplains or experts in Catholic international organisations.

Reflections in English

The meeting at Assisi had been French-speaking and the same subjects could look different when discussed in English. In April 1960, about thirty people came to a meeting in London organised by COPECIAL with the collaboration of the National Lay Apostolate Group for England and Wales.

Theological aspects were treated by Mgr H. F. Davis of Birmingham; 'Concepts of International Life' by John Eppstein, Director of the British Society for International Understanding and Secretary General of the Atlantic Treaty Association;[2] 'Christian Responsibility for Aid to Developing Countries' by Margaret Feeny, Secretary of the Sword of the Spirit (later Catholic Institute for International Relations). Kevin McDonnell (London University) asked: 'Are Catholics Catholic-minded?' Discussion showed how long it took for papal teaching to filter down to the faithful.

'Spiritual needs', as seen by Auguste Vanistendael, were no matter for the stratosphere:[3]

> If we are speaking of international civil servants we have to bear in mind that the majority of them are not 'apostles' by definition. Many may be practising Catholics, but they were not chosen because of their Catholic convictions . . .
> Then there are the diplomats. In 1948–49 and 1950–51, I was a member of the Belgian delegation to the United Nations and of the Commission on Human Rights. The Catholics present wanted to be the ones to propose the so-called 'Catholic articles' in the Declaration of Human Rights. But a few of us were of the opinion that it would be far better to have a Jew or a French laicist suggesting the right of parents to choose

the education of their children. Eventually we succeeded in
convincing a rabid laicist to suggest the re-phrasing of the
article; and it was passed without difficulty . . . I quote this to
show that professional difficulties can arise upon which you have
to consult your conscience; and eventually to consult a priest —
a competent priest. You cannot go to the first one you meet and
ask him what you should do. He has to know something about
the atmosphere of international conferences . . .

There are more personal problems also! In Copenhagen,
I had to buy some soap. I finally succeeded by using Flemish
dialect; but if I had had to go to confession it would have been
much more difficult.

More difficult still was to live up to what was expected of lay apostles: 'Automatically we are classified as "apostolic" laymen . . . It would be a very sad thing, if it were discovered that we are subject to the same temptations as the ordinary mortal man'. Then there is the chronic absenteeism of international living and its effects on family life:

If you are cut off from the parish, they ask your wife: 'Where is
your husband? Still travelling round?' — But with a special
smile, and an intonation that makes all the difference.

The great need is for intense personal spiritual life — in the
worst conditions possible. For humility, which is indispensable
for people exposed to public attention . . . , for dedication out
of love, not devotion to the strength of a particular organization.

Catholic International Organizations (CIO)

Who were these 'international pioneers' operating within the Church and as a 'presence' in society? At the time the Council opened, more than thirty CIO were officially recognised and members of the Conference of CIO, whose Statutes were approved by the Holy See in 1953.[4] They presented a wide variety of origins, history, membership, structure and activities. Some were mass organisations: World Union of Catholic Women's Organizations (WUCWO) grouped 36 million women from 110 organisations on five continents. Others were essentially study centres (International Catholic Child Bureau, International Union for Social Studies, etc.). Some carried on a directly religious activity (Legion of Mary); others charitable activity (Caritas Internationalis, St Vincent de Paul Society). Others again were concerned with particular social problems (migration, alcoholism, etc.), or with the use of modern communications media, and with professional and cultural activity. Some had a long history (the St Vincent de Paul Society was founded in 1833) but most were of recent creation, having come into being as part of the overall organisation of the modern world community.

For some CIO members, international life dated from the first post-war period. Veronese recalled this in 1947, in a Note for Montini:

> Since 1927, representatives of the Catholic International Organizations have been meeting annually to exchange information and consult one another on the attitude to adopt in certain cases where concerted action was needed. The initiative of the meetings was taken by the Catholic Union of International Studies, with the approval of the Bishop of Lausanne, Geneva and Fribourg, Mgr Besson, who personally took part. Since 1924, the Catholic Union had been cooperating with various bodies of the League of Nations. In 1927, eleven Organizations accepted the Union's invitation. A second session, in 1928, had on its agenda problems related to drugs and the cinema, as well as action on behalf of the Catholics persecuted in Mexico. These meetings of the 'Conference of Presidents' ceased with the League of Nations. But after the founding of the United Nations, the 'Conference' met again in Brussels in 1946.
>
> The pre-war meetings were barely tolerated by the Roman Authorities, who mistrusted the laicism of certain international groups. The second post-war period brought a new generation, eager for international contacts and enjoying the encouragement of Pius XII. The 'Conference of CIO' set up a Permanent Secretariat in Fribourg in 1951, working in contact with Catholic Centres related to UN Agencies in Geneva, Paris, New York and Rome.[5]

The Conference appointed Mieczyslaw de Habicht as Permanent Secretary. Born in Krakow, Poland, in 1918, de Habicht was serving as a diplomat outside his country when war broke out in 1939. He worked in London for the exiled Polish Catholic Action until, in 1947, he joined the staff of Pax Romana in Fribourg as Director of the Relief Department. Service in the Far East had seriously affected his health. An early memory of our friendship is that of a doleful presence interrupting my attack on my typewriter while an ailing stomach clamoured for a hot cup of tea. Pax Romana brought, however, happier moments for Mieczyslaw ('Mietek' for short or 'the Viscount' to his colleagues). In 1948, at a Pax Romana Assembly in Spa (Belgium), he met his future wife, Charlotte van Berckel, President of the Dutch Catholic Students' Union. Charlotte had resumed her law studies after Resistance activities had led to fifteen months in a Nazi concentration camp. Later, when Mietek was Under-Secretary of the Laity Council in the Roman Curia, there were many opportunities for meeting the Consultor, Cardinal Wojtyla. Since both the Cardinal and Charlotte claimed St Charles Borromeo for Patron, his feast, 4 November, became a shared festivity — a tradition that was maintained by Papa Wojtyla.

Today it is easy to be 'international'. But in the years leading up to Vatican II, almost the only occasions for serious study of world problems in all their extension and in relation to the Church's pastoral mission (if we exclude the studio of Pius XII) were the Assemblies of the Conference of CIO and the World Congresses of the Lay Apostolate. No wonder the leaders of CIO were liable to develop a 'pioneer complex'.

It is true that in the 1950s the CIO were not universal. They had all been created in Europe. But internationalisation was going ahead apace. The YCW had begun as JOC in the 1920s, a spontaneous group of young workers gathered around Father Cardijn. It was already a mass movement in Belgium and France before the Second World War. In 1957, it brought 30,000 young workers from ninety countries to a rally on St Peter's Square. Pax Romana had been set up in 1921 by Catholic student associations of three countries which had been neutral in the First World War (the Netherlands, Spain and Switzerland) and, as already noted was divided, in 1947, into two Movements — one of students and one of 'intellectuals' — representing some eighty countries from all continents.⁶

What were the CIO discussing during those years? WUCWO, in 1952, debated 'World Peace and the Responsibilities of the Christian Woman'. Pax Romana looked at 'The Universal Declaration of Human Rights' (1948); 'The Catholicity of the Church and Christian Universalism' (1949); 'Man and Nuclear Energy' (1955); and 'Culture and Cultures' (1956).

Pius XII's much-quoted address to the 1957 Assembly of Pax Romana–ICMICA⁷ foreshadows Vatican II's approach to a world in process of unification. It also reflects the hesitations of the Cold War years:

> A Christian cannot remain indifferent in the face of world evolution. If he sees an increasingly close-knit international community developing under the pressure of events, he knows that this unification, willed by the Creator, must result in a union of minds and hearts in the same faith and love . . . But is it possible to collaborate in institutions where God is not explicitly recognized as the Author and lawgiver of the Universe? Here one must distinguish the various levels of cooperation . . . The Christian will be ready to work for the relief of all material misery . . . for every undertaking directly aimed at bettering the lot of the poor and the outcast . . . Those, however, who can exert an influence on public opinion, realize that they have a still heavier task, for their participation in dubious undertakings might seem to endorse an unacceptable political or social system.

John XXIII confirmed the encouragement of his predecessor. But it was Paul VI who, on 11 November 1963 gave, not only an authoritative but also a personal endorsement to the work of the CIO. In his first Audience for the Conference of CIO, he said:

> We have been following your activity for a long time. We can say in all justice that, in accordance with the directives of Pope Pius XII of venerated memory, We were among the first to maintain

the necessity, for the movements of the Catholic laity, to
organize at the international level . . . Experience has not given
the lie to the hopes the Church placed in this new form of her
apostolate. It is with joy and pride that today she beholds nearly
40 CIO at work on a world level.

Conference of CIO and COPECIAL

The need for two international superstructures — Conference of CIO and COPECIAL — was hardly evident to the 'ordinary' parishioner, or even to most lay apostles. And the picture was further complicated by the existence of an office — housed within the premises of COPECIAL — for two-way contact between the CIO and what were still called 'mission countries' (mainly in Africa and Asia).[8] If the situation confused those at the grassroots, it also irritated some pioneers of the CIO. But, on the whole, relations were good. Mutual representation at all important events was valuable both 'vertically' (for the sectors that made up the CIO) and 'horizontally' (for COPECIAL). Specialists from the CIO could make a good contribution to World Congresses and continental meetings, while these events provided a platform for the Conference. Nevertheless, when a study of the evolution of the Conference was commissioned in February 1957 by the Continuity Committee of the Conference which operated between assemblies, its author, Ramon Sugranyes de Franch, dreamed of one overall organisation combining the aims and tasks of the two bodies in a flexible structure which might even become a Department of the Roman Curia. The report was tabled. The rest was silence. In January 1957, Veronese had called a few Roman friends together to discuss the COPECIAL–CIO problem. The move towards merging from within the Conference raised the question: where would the new organism be located? It would seem eminently natural to many that the centre of Catholic international activity should be in Rome. But there was a 'psychological difficulty': fear of the heavy hand of 'Rome' on the part of many European leaders of the CIO. This was to surface again later, during Vatican II, in the consultations that ultimately led to the creation of the *Consilium de Laicis*, now the Pontifical Council for the Laity (PCL).

1. The proceedings of this meeting exist only as a mimeographed brochure in French.

2. Cf. Eppstein's article on 'Principles of International Life' in *The British Survey*, October 1959.

3. The talk was later published in a Sword of the Spirit Pamphlet, 204, entitled *One World* (London, no date).

4. Details were given in a brochure, *Panorama of the Organized Lay Apostolate in the World*, prepared by COPECIAL and distributed in the Council Aula on 22 October 1963, during discussion of the schema on the Laity. (It was obligatorily in Latin, but vernacular editions were welcomed by many bishops.)

5. At the time of the Council, sixteen CIO members had Consultative status with ECOSOC, fourteen with UNESCO, seven with UNICEF, four with FAO, four with ILO and one with WHO.

6. The International Movement of Catholic Students (IMCS) and the International Catholic Movement for Intellectual and Cultural Affairs (ICMICA).

7. Pius XII's address to the 1957 Assembly of Pax Romana–ICMICA in *Discorsi e Radiomessaggi di Sua Santità Pio XII* (XIX), Vatican Polyglot Press, Rome, pp. 125–9.

8. The General Secretary of CIO–Missions, Emile Inglessis, was Greek. He had known the future John XXIII as the Papal Nuncio, Angelo Roncalli, in Istanbul. I attended his marriage to Eva Jung which was blessed by Pope John in the private chapel at Castel Gandolfo.

CHAPTER 4

The emerging theology

Work in progress among the experts of COPECIAL and the CIO drew largely from current thinking and writing in theological circles. We have glimpsed the role played by the Louvain theologian, Gérard Philips. No less important was the contribution of the great French Dominican (later Cardinal) Yves Congar, whose classic work, *Jalons pour une théologie du laïcat* was published in 1953.[1] But his contribution could only be made *in absentia*. Like others who were to be unquestioned experts at Vatican II, he was at the time out of favour in Rome. As a result there were parallel developments in thinking about the laity. Congar's approach: the 'priestly, prophetic, kingly' role of the lay Christian — stemming from the 'tria munera', the threefold office of Christ — provided structural elements for Chapter IV on the Laity, of the conciliar Constitution *Lumen Gentium*. The structuring developed in the lay movements and in COPECIAL is reflected more clearly in the Decree on the Lay Apostolate, *Apostolicam Actuositatem*.

One major project of theologians, for a decade or so before the Council, was to produce a 'positive definition' of the lay Christian. If *Lumen Gentium* did not give a definition, but only a 'typological description' (31),[2] it was not for want of trying. Who was the first to tackle the problem? Jan Grootaers of Louvain claimed the honour for his friend, Gérard Philips.[3] Edward Schillebeeckx, OP dates his own efforts from his article on 'The foundation of the lay person's "worldliness" in the Church' (1949).[4] Congar had written in 1957:

> Over and above the exclusively negative canonical definition of the lay person as one who is not a cleric and has no power of order or jurisdiction, there is practical agreement on a positive definition: the layman (or woman) is the Christian who contributes to the work of salvation and the advance of God's Kingdom — to the twofold task of the Church — in and through commitment in the structures of the world and temporal activity.

Congar went on to quote Karl Rahner: the lay person 'is one who, in being a Christian and as such, preserves the characteristics of his or her natural position in the world'.[5] In 1956, Rahner had said more than this. He had raised a storm of controversy by affirming that a Christian whose principal occupation was in the field of the apostolate had already passed from the ranks of the laity to those of the clergy. Rahner's theory was explicitly rejected by Pius XII in his address to the World Congress of 1957. (As a lay woman who has devoted almost all my adult life to the service of the Church I would argue that, while I am definitely not clergy, I feel I am — to say the least — not typically lay either!)

In the English-speaking world

During these same years, theologically articulate lay people in English-speaking countries were reacting against any clerical or monastic monopoly of spiritual life. In *The Layman in the Church*,[6] Michael de la Bedoyere acknowledged a debt to Yves Congar, also presenting the lay status or vocation in terms of the threefold office of priest, prophet and king. He went on to write of personal and social relationships, clergy–laity relations and a spirituality that is 'not a luxury'. He believed that, in social and political questions, it is legitimate for even the best Catholics to differ from what is generally considered the 'Catholic view'. He wanted a clergy equipped for new tasks and relationships, and a laity that would not be too 'clergy-dependent'.

John M. Todd's 'book for the Christian layman' is entitled *We are Men*.[7]

> We are Hindus, Arabs, Americans, communists, capitalists,
> Christians, monks, virgins, mothers, fathers — but we are, after
> all, men, human beings . . . [The title] includes, of course, the
> proposition 'We are women'!

The context is avowedly English — as is the humour — but the reflection ranges widely: the family in a sex-obsessed society, work and leisure, religion and prayer, organisations ('useful, [but] extra to the ordinary life of the Church'). One chapter deals with intellectuals (a 'label of disapproval' in everyday parlance). The intellectual as philosopher, 'concerned with thought about God', can contribute towards:

> . . . baptizing the good in other cultures and religions.
> Above all, Christian intellectuals have the task of being the best
> humanists, refusing either to reject or to be crushed by the weight
> of modern knowledge and its application in industrial technique.

In Australia, in 1955, a small but vocal group of Catholic intellectuals presented papers to a Conference of the Catholic University Federation. The papers were subsequently edited by Vincent Buckley and, in 1957, published under the title *The Incarnation in the University*.[8] It is doubtful whether many members of the Federation could assimilate the spiritual, theological and cultural reflection presented, but the volume signified what was maturing in the Church. It was published for the International Movement of Catholic Students, still conscious of the challenge issued by Pius XII to the Twenty-first World Congress of Pax Romana in 1950 in Amsterdam: 'The imperious necessity: presence to contemporary thought . . . at the forefront of the combat of the intelligence'.[9]

American approaches to the apostolate

Very different in style, but also indicative of the period, was a volume published in Chicago in 1954: *The Apostolic Itch* by Vincent J. Giese.[10] The 'Itch' referred to what Giese called 'a whole new breed of Catholics, roaming the highways and byways . . . Let me call them "Apostles Anonymous" '. A breed of 'tourists', wanting to drop in on every new form of lay apostolate, from the Catholic Worker (CW) (founded by Dorothy Day and Peter Maurin in 1933) to the Christian Family Movement (CFM) or YCS — but committed to none.

In successive chapters, Giese spelt out what genuine commitment means: lay spirituality; Christian friendship; poverty, taking his intellectual cue from France — Cardinal Suhard, Yves Congar, Henri de Lubac. He did not see any original intellectual contribution from Catholics in the United States, but acknowledged their characteristic role in bringing to the *practice* of the lay apostolate their 'know-how' and healthy approach to clergy/laity relations — the fresh energies of a young Church. In spite of the Cold War and McCarthyism, he asked:

> Is America preparing to assume the spiritual leadership
> of a world grown weary with war and the threat of war? This
> question has been on the minds of many serious-minded people
> who have been watching apprehensively as the US makes her bid
> for the political and economic leadership of Western civilization.

Surprisingly, while saying there had been much talk about Catholic Action (almost equated with lay apostolate), Giese makes no explicit mention of the official organisations: the National Council of Catholic Men (NCCM) and National Council of Catholic Women (NCCW) that federated thousands of lay groups at diocesan level. NCCM and NCCW were, in fact, the equivalent of Catholic Action in their relation to the Hierarchy, whereas the newer apostolic ventures were more or less marginal institutionally, in spite of their real impact, not only on 'itchy tourists', but also on the development of action and reflection within the American Church.

A similarly selective view of the Catholic laity in the United States emerges from an article by Dorothy Dohen:[11] the 'action of the laity' is essentially that of the avant-garde movements. *Commonweal*[12] of 23 August 1957 recalls these movements as being originally the fruit of the depression years. The founding of CW in 1933 had marked the beginning of the modern lay apostolate in the United States. Shocking the consciences of both clerical and lay Catholics, the CW set in operation the spiritual and corporal works of mercy in the Skid Rows and Boweries of an economically depressed America. When volunteers came to live Christianity, they were given a dish cloth or a peeling knife instead of an English translation of the *Summa Contra Gentiles* of St Thomas Aquinas. During the same years the social action apostolate began, with its educational effort and its approach to the root causes of poverty.

Attempts had been made to develop the apostolate to the social milieu of Cardijn's Young Christian Workers. The YCW was brought to the United States when Paul McGuire came to issue his 'call to Catholic Action'. Mary Irene Zotti told the story of several hundred young men and women crowded into a parish hall in Chicago in May 1939, and stirred to their depths by a 'dapper, 40-year-old gentleman with an attractive Australian accent'.[13] He introduced them to specialised Catholic Action; and described the 65,000 young workers from twenty-four countries who had gathered for a rally in Paris in 1937. He could not know of the experiences that many of these young workers would share with priests during the war in Europe[14] and the new relationships which would be created. After the war: 'in the euphoria of refound freedom, the question of the status and role of the laity in the Church took on a new urgency'.[15]

In the United States, the post-war period brought significant changes of a different kind: the economic boom, with the 'upward mobility' of American Catholics and the subsequent migration to suburbia. The growth of the CFM and the YCW was conditioned by this context of a prosperous economy and a better-educated laity but the storefront and Skid Row apostolate remained as a constant reminder of the demands of justice for the new poor and racial minorities.[16]

Coming of age

'The Emerging Theology' (1957) was the title of an article by Louis J. Putz, CSC, in the issue of *Commonweal* already quoted, with the subtitle: 'It will need a team of scholars, priests and laymen, to effect the Christian synthesis of the modern world'. The theology emerging was that of Guardini in German, of Suhard, de Montcheuil, de Lubac, Congar and Philips in French. The stress was on the need for an 'adult and responsible laity', active in a contemporary society with its emphasis on world conquest through science and industry to liberate humanity from economic and political servitude. While the same reflection was being developed on both sides of the Atlantic, the lay apostolate in the United States was seen as a pioneering enterprise with 'the advantage of working in virgin territory. We do not have to live down sins of the past, like the mass of the working class in Europe'.

A few years later, when the Council was in preparation, the election campaign that brought John F. Kennedy to the Presidency gave American Catholics an unprecedented opportunity for developing relationships between their ecclesial and civic commitments. Among books reflecting this experience was *The Emerging Layman: The Role of the Catholic Layman in America* (1962) written by Donald J. Thorman, Director of the Institute for the Development of Spiritual Life.[17] Thorman heralded 'a new and exciting era':

> When Pope Pius XII spoke to the First World Congress for the Lay Apostolate in Rome in 1951, anyone who would have predicted what has actually happened between then and now would have been regarded as a dreamer.

It might be true that 'in the minds of many, a lay apostle is still regarded as a kind of frustrated priest, a hanger-on at the fringe of the clerical ranks', but a new mutual respect was emerging between clergy and laity. The experience of the YCW, YCS and CFM had brought the Church's social teaching to life; taking an active part in liturgy was considered part of the lay apostolate; the ghetto mentality was giving way, in a democratic, pluralistic society, to an appreciation of religious freedom and the opportunity to express personal views, with a new approach to the race problem and the beginnings of ecumenism. A year later, in 1963, Daniel Callahan, associate editor of *Commonweal*, working from a solid historical background, treated the same themes in *The Mind of the Catholic Layman*.[18] John Cogley[19] commented (on the jacket of the book):

> Baffled bishops, puzzled priests, uncertain laymen, and all who are interested in the present mood of the Church in America, can learn from this volume. Mr Callahan is the voice of a new Catholic generation . . . American Catholicism has come of age.

The new maturity was evident in a series of talks given in the early 1960s by Martin H. Work. A month before Kennedy's election, Work said:

> We don't want the Church in politics — we don't want the Church involved in the work of the State — nor do we want the State intruding in Church affairs. But we want, and our country needs, men in public life whose consciences have been formed on Christian principles and who will place the dictates of their conscience above all man-made laws.[20]

In August 1961, in a different context, Martin told chaplains of the CFM:

> If lay people have a myopic vision of the Church, and of their own role, are they altogether to blame? We were educated as 'pew-sitters', then shoved into the aisle as collectors and ushers, hired as sacristans . . . and now we are being pushed into the jungle of the temporal world, where we should have been all along.

Who is Martin Work? When he was appointed to the Directing Board of COPECIAL in 1960, we were told by NCCM: 'Martin never lets you forget two things about himself: he is a first generation Irishman (H. is for Haverty) and a native-born Californian'. After graduating in Arts and Law, his career took him from broadcasting to service as a military consultant, to advertising and, finally, to full-time service of the Church — all with the help of his supportive wife Maria and their three children. In 1970, he left the national scene to help construct a 'post-Conciliar archdiocese'. On the invitation of the Archbishop of Denver, James V. Casey, he took up work as Director of Planning and Administration for the Archdiocese, a post he held until his retirement in 1984.

The layman and the Council

In 1964, when Vatican II was well on its way, a small volume entitled *The Layman and the Council* appeared.[21] Anticipating the Council Decree on the lay apostolate, it brought into focus the questioning of the preceding years and the tensions emerging in the excitement of Vatican II. With the help of the editor, Michael J. Greene, authors John Cogley, Daniel

Callahan, Donald Thorman and Martin Work welded together a series of 'conversations' as 'a candid assessment of the American layman's past and an outline for his future'.

Thorman's 'great fear' was 'that laymen will fail to accept the challenge of the Council' once they discover that lay apostolate can be hard work, that it means change: 'People want to talk about problems, but they apparently don't want to do anything specific about them'. Callahan, however, was convinced that results could be obtained by a 'pragmatic approach'. The Church is not a democracy, but the American layman 'knows at first hand, what it means to participate in decisions, to make his views known in the community, to be consulted'. Results will be obtained, Martin Work pointed out, not by giving the layman 'authority and jurisdiction' (something which would be impossible), but by building on the 'common priesthood', shared by every member of the Church. This could only be done, Thorman insisted, if people are helped to understand what they are expected to do as Christians in the parish or the secular community. And you cannot expect people to change overnight.

Cogley's opening chapter on the (not entirely fictional) caricature of 'Miss L' makes a real point: the vast majority of lay people could not be forerunners of the Council. Let us meet 'Miss L' (incidentally, the only lay*woman* we are presented with in the book):

> In Miss L's view, the 'good Catholics' valued obedience, loyalty to the group and earnest conformity above all else. Her idea of the Church, in fact, was uncompromisingly military. At the top, the Pope — a Generalissimo leading embattled troops in a last-ditch fight; below the Holy Father, the bishops — executing papal orders as line-officers working in perfect harmony according to a master-plan; below them, the clergy and religious — harried NCO's keeping order and discipline in the ranks; finally, the laity — tough, disciplined battalions of subservient Christians, with no responsibility for anything but unquestioning obedience. Theirs not to reason why.

But even 'Miss L' — Martin Work was convinced — would be moved a little to the left of her position when the Council had completed its work on defining the nature of the Church.

'Well, what do laymen want?' is one chapter heading. 'They want a positive identity', Cogley answers. 'Too much attention has been focused on the role of the layman in the Church and not enough on the role of the Christian in the world'. Beware of a 'kind of pseudo-hierarchy of professional laymen whose preoccupations are overwhelmingly ecclesiastical in the narrow sense!' Thorman is not so convinced about a caste system developing among the laity. He recognised the potential danger but dismissed it as a reality in the majority of American dioceses. He was more concerned about the possible divisive effect of insisting too much on apostolate in the secular world which could result in a separation of clergy and laity:

> I am thinking of dozens of priests and lay people who are intimately involved in the needs of the Church as a whole as well as with such secular matters as civil rights, nuclear warfare, poverty, social services and human relations generally.

Yes, Cogley responded, but you need to stress the distinctive roles of clergy and laity in relation to this secular world. The Council was, in fact, already spelling out what the Church — through both clergy and laity — *gives* to the world, and what, as Church, she *receives* from the world's 'secularity': 'the experience of past ages, the march of science, the treasures hidden in the various cultural traditions'.[22]

Callahan asked the question Where are we? . . . 'with wonder and dismay, confidence and uncertainty, hope and anxiety, joy and misgivings'. Cogley voiced *one* layman's hopes: 'a larger role for the laity'; 'less sectarianism and separatism among us'; 'the acceptance of modernity' together with many things that have since become normal in the life of the Church. Martin Work reflected that, in the mind of John XXIII, Vatican II was a Council for unity and that a new awareness of 'ecumenical responsibility' was also growing among the laity.

The text was introduced by Charles H. Helmsing, Bishop of Kansas City (home of the *National Catholic Reporter*). As was indicated by his comment to a group of laymen before leaving for Rome, he was very much at one with the writers and their hopes: 'My great concern was, and still is, that the accomplishments of the Council be made effective'.

1. Les Éditions du Cerf, Paris. A revised edition, with addenda, was published in 1964. The English translation of the revised edition by Donald Attwater, *Lay People in the Church. A Study for the Theology of the Laity*, published by Geoffrey Chapman, 1965, was reissued in 1985 by Geoffrey Chapman, London, and Christian Classics, Inc., Westminister, Maryland.

2. Cf. the report of the amended text, *Relatio super caput IV textus emendati Schematis Constitutionis de Ecclesia*, Vatican Polyglot Press, Rome, 1964, p. 5.

3. Cf. the article on the role of Gérard Philips in Vatican II, in the volume offered to Philips, gathered by a committee of theologians of the University of Louvain, *Ecclesia a Spiritu Sancto edocta. Mélanges théologiques*, J. Duculot, Gembloux, Belgium, 1970, p. 347.

4. Cf. *La Missione della Chiesa*, Edizioni Paoline, Roma 1971, p. 126. (Original title: *De zending van de kerk*, Ed. H. Nelissen, Bilthoven, Netherlands.)

5. Yves Congar, 'Esquisse d'une théologie de l'action Catholique', August-September 1958.
    Cf. K. Rahner, 'L'apostolat des laïcs', in *Nouvelle Revue Théologique*, Jesuit College of Philosophy & Theology, St Albert's Louvain, t. 78, 1956, pp. 3–32.

6. Burns & Oates, London, 1954.

7. Sheed & Ward, London and New York, 1955.

8. Geoffrey Chapman, Great Britain, 1957. Among the authors were John Dormer, Ian Howells, Brian Buckley, Terence Mahony and William Ginnane.

9. *Pax Romana*, New Series, Pax Romana, Fribourg, Switzerland, October–November 1950, p. 1.

10. Giese was at the time Editorial Director of Fides Press. He became a priest in 1965.

11. Dorothy Dohen, 'L'action des laïques catholiques aux U.S.A.', published in the French review, *Actualité Religieuse dans le Monde*, Malesherbes Publications, Paris, 1 April 1955, pp. 25–6.

12. Published by The Commonweal Publishing Co. Inc., New York. (Now Commonweal Foundation, 15 Dutch St., New York 10038)

13. *A Time of Awakening: The Young Christian Worker Story in the United States, 1938 to 1970*, Loyola University Press, Chicago, 1991.

14. Marcel Callo, a French 'Jocist' who died heroically in one of the death camps in 1945, was declared Blessed by John Paul II on 4 October 1987.

15. Cf. Yves Congar in *Ministères et Communion ecclésiale*, Editions du Cerf, Paris, 1971, p. 14. Congar himself shared the experience of the prison camps.

16. Cf. Denis J. Geaney, OSA, 'Social Action in America', in *Commonweal*, 23 August 1957, pp. 513–16.

17. Doubleday & Company Inc., Garden City, New York, 1962.

18. Charles Scribners Sons, New York, 1963.

19. John Cogley, former Executive Editor of *Commonweal*, was a member of the Center for the Study of Democratic Institutions, Santa Barbara, California.

20. This talk on 'The Role of American Catholic Laymen in Public Life' was given in the parish auditorium, Chevy Chase Circle, Washington DC, on 4 October 1960.

21. Templegate, Springfield, Illinois, 1964.

22. Cf. the Pastoral Constitution on the Church in the Modern World, *Gaudium et Spes*, 41–5.

Part 2
AT LAST... VATICAN II

'The church must enter into dialogue with the world.
The Church becomes word; the church becomes message;
the church becomes communication.'
    Paul VI: Encyclical *Ecclesesiam Suam*, 6 August 1964.

CHAPTER 5

An Ecumenical Council

In the Catholic Church Councils are meetings composed mainly of bishops and are held in order to discuss affairs of the Church, make decisions and promulgate decrees. They can be held at different levels: local, provincial, etc. A meeting of representatives of the whole Church is an Ecumenical Council. According to the current Latin Canon Law (Can.338) only the Pope can summon an Ecumenical Council, preside over it personally or through others and approve its decrees. An Ecumenical Council can infallibly define a dogma of faith. Historically, it may be difficult to decide which Councils were 'Ecumenical', but Vatican II is generally held to be the 21st — the first being the Council of Nicaea in 325, which pronounced against the Arian heresy that denied the divinity of Christ. (The Orthodox Churches recognise only Councils held during the first millennium as 'Ecumenical'.) Long before that, however, there was the 'Council of Jerusalem', referred to in Chapter 15 of the Acts of the Apostles, during which the apostles and disciples, with Peter as their Head, decreed that converted pagans were not to be bound by all the prescriptions of Judaism.

Traditionally, lay people — other than kings and princes — did not take part in Councils, although they could be asked for information and express consent. Vatican II was the first Ecumenical Council to deal specifically with Laity, and the first to which lay people were officially invited as Auditors — equated with periti (experts).

The First Vatican Council — which defined the doctrine of papal infallibility — had been interrupted in 1870 by the Franco-Prussian War and the withdrawal of French troops from Rome which brought an end to the Papal States and achieved the unity of Italy. There had been talk of another Council — or a continuation of Vatican I — during the Pontificate of Pius XII, but the idea had been abandoned. It was John XXIII who made the dramatic announcement of Vatican II in St Paul's-without-the-Walls, on 25 January 1959. In the ante-preparatory phase, which started immediately, the bishops of the whole world were consulted on the agenda. Real preparation began at Pentecost 1960, with the setting up of ten Preparatory Commissions — the tenth being on the lay apostolate. The task of the commissions was to draft texts (schemas) for submission to a Central Commission.

The Council 'Fathers' — cardinals, patriarchs, archbishops, bishops and superiors general of (male) religious congregations — were nearly 3,000 in number. They met during four periods, each of about eight or nine weeks, from September to December of the years 1962 to 1965. Plenary Assemblies (called Congregations)[1] were normally held every morning, except Sunday. They were closed to the public and to the press with '*Exeant omnes*' (All out!) proclaimed after the Mass. The Commissions met in the afternoons, and during the months between the periods of Council deliberation. Public Sessions, which as their name suggests were open to the public, were Plenary Assemblies for the promulgation of documents after the final vote had been taken. In all, sixteen documents were promulgated: four Constitutions (on the Church, Divine Revelation, Liturgy, and The Church in the Modern World); nine Decrees (on communications, ecumenism, Eastern Catholic Churches, bishops, priestly formation, religious life, laity, priests, and missionary activity); three Declarations (on Christian education, relations with non-Christians, and religious freedom). No dogmas were defined and no 'anathemas'[2] pronounced. This was to be seen as a Pastoral Council for the renewal of the Church — an 'aggiornamento' (updating or 'todaying'). It was also — as Pope John had expressly provided — an ecumenical council in a special sense: During each period of discussion, nearly 100 Delegated Observers were present from other Christian communions (Orthodox, Anglican, Protestant), as well as a number of 'ecumenical' guests.

I make no attempt to relate the Council. There are libraries filled with memories, reflections and even scientifically conducted research on almost every minute of Vatican II. What I wish to recall here are experiences or aspects that concerned the involvement of lay people.

The atmosphere of the Council

The Second Vatican Council opened on 11 October 1962. The enthusiasm and the wonderment that greeted the solemn procession of more than 2500 bishops from the Vatican's Bronze Door to St Peter's Basilica survived, with varying intensity, through its four periods to the closing Mass in front of the Basilica on 8 December 1965.

In March 1965, I was invited to Turin to speak on 'The Council seen by a lay person'. I tried to give some idea of the teaching that was emerging on the whole 'People of God' — lay and non-lay — and on 'The Church in the Modern World'.[3] I also tried to give some idea of the

> ... fascinating spectacle the tourists come to admire when the 'Fathers' arrive in the morning for the General Congregation. Many, like schoolboys, thirty to a coach, others on foot or at the wheel of a '2 chevaux', full of French bishops, already arguing with their theologians . . . Or the other spectacle, when they emerge at mid-day, and the Square becomes a multi-coloured garden with every shade of red and purple, bright against the black, grey or brown of the Friars, the non-Catholic observers and, here or there, a lay person or a nun . . . This may not be a profound view of the Council, but photographers have, at least, a sense of witnessing something important . . .

The universality of the Council was not spectacular only for the tourists:

> For the first time in history, the Successors of the Apostles are meeting from all parts of the world. They are of every race and speak all languages. Even the Council Latin, spoken with so many accents, becomes, no 'dead' language, but 20 foreign tongues.

In 1962, if you asked any bishop for first impressions, nine times out of ten he would begin by saying: 'Wonderful! In front of me in the Aula there is a Chinese bishop, to the right a German, on the left a Brazilian or a Congolese . . .' Our Bishops — and not only those generally invited to speak at international congresses — were discovering, concretely, the catholicity of the Church.[4]

But universality was not the only first impression. The Council was a curious mixture of liturgical solemnity and — especially as time went on — familiar simplicity, particularly when the 'Fathers' slipped away to foregather in one of the bars (Bar Abbas or Bar Jonah, as one Council wit named them).

The Council was also a great act of prayer. Entering the Basilica by St Martha's Door, you could see many bishops in the side chapel where the Blessed Sacrament was reserved. And liturgically, there was a steady progress from the pre- to the post-Conciliar phase. In 1965 I could say:

> We need only think of the Concelebration in dialogue with the vast assembly at the close of the third period, and remember the Pontifical Opening Mass of 1962, when more than 2500 Successors of the Apostles listened in silence to the polyphonic singing of the Credo.

Living the Council

At the Extraordinary Synod[5] of 1985, I was one of a group of 'Special Guests', all of whom had taken part in one way or another in the Second Vatican Council. The group included nine cardinals, a bishop from Eastern Europe, three eminent theologians — Hans Urs von Balthasar, Gustave Martelet, SJ and Max Thurian of Taizé — and a lay professor of the Catholic University of Lublin. I had been invited as one exemplar of a category forever closed: a woman Auditor at Vatican II — a category which had included ten religious and thirteen lay women appointed by Paul VI.

The appointment of lay Auditors — thirteen men in 1963, and the women in 1964 — was an historical first that made the front pages even of the secular press. But the account of the laity given so far will suggest that it was not altogether unexpected. From the time the Council was announced by John XXIII on 25 January 1959, we had been living 'in a state of Council'. Lay journalists of high calibre had been explaining its significance. Jean-Pierre Dubois-Dumée, a member of the COPECIAL Directing Board, had given more than a hundred lectures to packed audiences up and down France. The Conference of CIO had been busy drafting memoranda for the Preparatory Commission on the Lay Apostolate, as well as providing an information service and organising a Campaign of Prayer. COPECIAL, taking its cue from Pope John's Encyclical *Ad Petri Cathedram*,[6] had launched a worldwide study on unity — between people, between Christians, between Catholics. In some countries (for example, Belgium and the Netherlands) preparation was invited by bishops at diocesan level.

This form of lay involvement was to continue throughout the Council. In Canada, twenty-five lay men and women — housewives, university professors, lawyers, business executives, trade unionists — 'spoke their minds' in a volume published in 1965 in response to a general invitation issued by their bishops. This was a constructive dialogue on subjects ranging from political and labour problems to sexual ethics and ecumenism. The text included three approaches to the role of women in Church and society. The laity met with a receptive hearing. In a Foreword to *Brief to the Bishops* Philip Pocock, Coadjutor Archbishop of Toronto, wrote:

> The essays came to us as a brief at a time when we knew that upon our return to Rome our main deliberations and decisions would affect the laity directly and intimately; we knew that we were going to be called upon to state in unequivocal terms the Church's posture towards the modern world. With such . . . fearsome challenges before us, we welcomed the opinions contained in the essays presented to us'.[7]

In the French-speaking diocese of Saint-Jean, a hundred lay people had responded to an invitation from their Bishop, Gérard Coderre, to meet in January 1962. It was therefore no coincidence that the

Canadian bishops were among those who advocated 'declericalisation' and less emphasis on the authority of the hierarchy in the schema on the laity. Bishop Alexander Carter of Sault Ste Marie complained that lay people had been consulted 'too little, too late' and that the schema had been 'conceived in the original sin of clericalism'.[8] On 28 October 1964, during debate on Schema 13 (The Church in the Modern World), Coderre made the first substantial statement concerning women in Church and society.

During the first period of the Council (October–December 1962), the Conciliar Commission on the Lay Apostolate met without the laity. The Secretary, Achille Glorieux, had to explain to the members the steps that had been taken during the preparatory period to make up, to some extent, for the absence of the laity: consultation, circulation of documents from lay groups, and indirect contact through 'periti' from the Preparatory Commission. Later, when the schema on the Lay Apostolate was introduced in the Council Aula on 6 October 1964, the President of the Commission, Cardinal Fernando Cento, stressed the contribution that had effectively been made by lay men and women.

The lay 'Auditors'

The importance for the Council of lay people's international experience, which was acknowledged in the appointment of the lay Auditors, was stressed by Paul VI when he received, for the first time, representatives of the CIO:[9]

> At this historic moment when the Church, gathered in Council, is making, as it were, her examination of conscience and a vast stocktaking of her apostolic forces, We felt that a few qualified representatives of the laity could and should be associated, as Auditors, with this great 'review of life' and admitted to attend the Council. And We turned in the first place towards the movements which represented the laity in the most authoritative and ample fashion: the Catholic International Organizations.

There were many women in these movements. Among the CIO there was, for instance, WUCWO, which claimed to group 36 million women from all parts of the world. Shortly before the appointment of the female Auditors, I explained to one interviewer:

> When the men were appointed as Auditors, Catholic women rejoiced. They saw this as a 'symbolic' gesture which was mainly important for the promise it gave of a more effective and more fully recognized presence of the laity in the apostolate of the Church. Inevitably, however, the women asked themselves (as did lay men, priests, bishops ... even cardinals) why there was no woman in this little group. There is reason to believe that the omission is only temporary (the Fathers need not fear a 'march on the Council' of enraged suffragettes!).

The omission was soon remedied. It seems that delay was not due to reluctance on the part of Pope Paul. There had been a 'campaign' for the presence of women after Cardinal Leo Josef Suenens and the Melkite Bishop of Akka (Israel), Mgr Hakim, had pointed out the surprising silence in the draft Constitution on the Church regarding 'the other half of humanity'. However, there would have been resistance to overcome (the fearful to reassure); the Pope could not seem simply to yield to a pressure group. This would explain also the restrictive terms in which Paul VI announced his intentions during a Mass celebrated at Castel Gandolfo on 8 September 1964:[10]

> We have given instructions that some qualified and dedicated women should assist, as Auditors, at several solemn functions and General Congregations of the forthcoming Third Session of the Second Vatican Council: at those Congregations which will be discussing matters of special interest for the life of women. In this way, for the first time perhaps, women will be represented in an Ecumenical Council. The women present will, naturally, be few in number; but it will be a significant and, as it were, a 'symbolical' representation.

We could not help wondering what aspects of the Church's life are *not* of interest to women. Surely women are also 'the Church'? However, in reality, there was no distinction made between the male and female Auditors. We attended the General Congregations every morning, received Holy Communion at the daily Council Mass and took an active part in the Commissions to which Auditors were invited in the afternoons and between the Council periods. All the Auditors, both men and women, were well aware of the symbolic nature of their participation.

The first woman to enter the Council was Marie-Louise Monnet, the French foundress of the International Movement for Apostolate in Independent Social Milieux (MIAMSI). She was the sister of Jean Monnet, initiator of the Economic Plan for Europe. On 20 September 1964, the members of the constituent Assembly of MIAMSI were attending the Pope's Mass in St Peter's Basilica. In his address[11] Paul VI referred to the importance of lay participation in the Council. He added: 'In confidence, We can tell you that your President is on the list of the persons We intend to invite to the Council as Auditors'. On the strength of this 'confidence', Monnet was admitted to the Council the next day. According to the Bulletin of St Joan's International Alliance[12] one of the Fathers greeted her entry with the words: 'At last, the flowers have appeared in our land!'. I have not been able to verify this 'intervention'. The rest of us made our appearance, armed with the Council 'passport', a few days later.

The spectacular effect of the feminine presence was short-lived. After the first days, cardinals and bishops no longer came simply to look at these Council 'Mothers' who were sitting — demurely veiled — on the plush chairs of St Andrew's tribune, alongside the male Auditors and the theologians. Fewer speakers, when greeting the Assembly, expressly included the *'carissimae sorores'* (beloved sisters) or *'pulcherrimae auditrices'* (beautiful Auditresses) and photographers began to look elsewhere for something of public interest. By the end of the Council, our presence was — happily! — part of the normal scene and our contributions were taken seriously in commission meetings. We had come to feel at home in our tribune and in the special bar arranged for our use just through the Porta Rezzonico, behind the main altar. Our waiter is now a very senior member of the group of Sanpietrini — the group of men who permanently staff the Basilica. (Stairs led down from the bar to a reserved toilet — a much appreciated novelty for St Peter's!)

There is now a major work on the *Auditrices*.[13] Carmel E. McEnroy, an American Sister of Mercy and Professor of Theology at St Meinrad's College, Indiana, undertook a research project on the women at the Council: their background as religious or lay women; their experience of the Council and what they did with it; their frustrations in dealing with bishops not schooled in dialogue, especially with women. The project took her from America (United States and Mexico) to Europe (Rome, Madrid, Germany and elsewhere). Where personal contact was not possible, she used the files I had put together in Rome. Reading Carmel's book, I 'discovered' the women religious. During the hectic days of the Council, there was no time to get to know one another well. The exception was Mary Luke Tobin, SL, at the time President of the Conference of Major Religious Superiors of Women in the United States. With her I shared most of my Council experience and I have followed with interest her post-Conciliar activities: supporting every major justice issue and promoting cooperation between religious and lay women in new fields of apostolate.

Not only symbolic

Following their appointment in 1963, the group of thirteen male Auditors met regularly to study subjects on the Council agenda with the help of competent periti. Certain interventions prepared during these meetings were authorised to be presented in the Aula. The first lay person to address the Council in this way was Patrick Keegan. He spoke (in English) on 13 October 1964, during the 100th General Congregation, at the close of the debate on the lay apostolate.[14] The 'schema', he said, reflected 'the progressive discovery by men and women of their responsibility and role within the whole apostolate of the Church'. The apostolate of the laity was 'no luxury or passing fashion' — no cleric could ever again treat it as a 'hobby' for some interfering lay people.

In November 1964, there were two interventions. Juan Vazquez[15] (Argentina) spoke on the responsibility of the laity in relation to the problems treated in Schema 13 (The Church in the Modern World). James Norris,[16] of United States Catholic Relief Services and President of the International Catholic Commission on Migrations, made (in Latin) a personal appeal for action to overcome world poverty; an appeal which contributed to the decision to set up what is now the Pontifical Council for Justice and Peace. During the fourth period, Eusèbe Adjakpley[17] (Togo) addressed what was to become the Decree *Ad Gentes* on the Church's Missionary Activity, stressing its ecumenical dimension.

Two Auditors had addressed Pope Paul VI, on 3 December 1963, during a Public Session commemorating the IVth Centenary of the Council of Trent. One was the French writer, Jean Guitton, first layman at the Council. Invited personally by John XXIII and 'belonging' nowhere, he had been seated with the Ecumenical Observers. He spoke now of his experience of ecumenism. The other layman was Vittorino Veronese. On behalf of the Auditors, he thanked Paul VI for the privilege of their participation in the Council, a privilege that was 'worth a lifetime'.

The Auditors hoped that, at least once, their spokesperson could be a woman. For the intervention on Schema 13, they proposed the name of Pilar Bellosillo (Spain), President of WUCWO. Without result. When the Council was nearing its end, they wrote to the Pope requesting an opportunity to express, in the General Congregation, their gratitude for the privilege granted them. As speaker, they again proposed Pilar Bellosillo. There may have been no time to grant the request, although we were later told (not by the Pope) that it had been thought premature to let a woman's voice be heard in the Aula. This was no doubt also the reason why the famous economist, Barbara Ward (Lady Jackson), was not allowed to make the personal appeal on behalf of the 'economically underdeveloped', the poor of the world.

A Roman secretariat

A subject of much consultation during the Council was the proposal — which had emerged already in the ante-preparatory phase of Vatican II — to set up a special secretariat at the Holy See for the service and promotion of the lay apostolate. This was to lead, finally, to the creation of the *Consilium de Laicis* in 1967, now the Pontifical Council for the Laity. The CIO and their Conference and COPECIAL were both vitally concerned; the former because of the relations they would have to establish with any office of the Holy See dealing with lay action at international level, the latter because it would probably be integrated into any such official body.

In June 1964 Cardinal Cento convened a meeting of five bishops, two priests and eight lay people to draw up plans for the future secretariat. This was followed, early in 1965, by a worldwide consultation of Bishops' Conferences and lay organisations. Replies were received from seventeen Bishops' Conferences and thirty-six international groups. A report was submitted from an ad hoc assembly of the Conference of CIO. The results of the whole consultation were studied by a small group similar to that convened in June 1964.

Debate in the Aula during the last Council period led to the adoption of N.26 of the Decree on the Lay Apostolate;[18] but discussion was to continue in the Post-Conciliar Commission (1966) and until the creation of the *Consilium de Laicis*, which was to become a 'Dicastery' of the Roman Curia. Some of the lay people involved in this whole process would have preferred the Roman secretariat to be consultative rather than directive, a Dicastery. They wanted lay opinion and experience taken into account in the government of the Church but they feared too much 'direction' where lay responsibility was involved.[19]

The laity and Schema 13

In January 1963, a 'Mixed Commission', composed of the Theological Commission and the Commission on the Lay Apostolate, was instructed to prepare a new schema on 'The Principles and the Action of the Church for the Promotion of the Welfare of Society'. This was Schema 17, later Schema 13, and would become the Pastoral Constitution on 'The Church in the Modern World', *Gaudium et Spes*.

During the first months of 1963, five laymen were consulted over the initial drafting. In April, fourteen laymen took part in a meeting for the new schema — the first such official invitation issued to lay people.

When a central sub-commission was set up in December 1963, with Emilio Guano, Bishop of Livorno, as Chairman, the collaboration of lay people became normal procedure. The high point of the consultation was the meeting held at Ariccia, near Rome, from 31 January to 6 February 1965. Thirty Council 'Fathers' and about fifty periti took part, with ten laymen (not all Auditors), four laywomen and two women religious.[20]

The schema drafted during the intersession 1964–65 was presented to the Council on 21 September 1965 and debated until 8 October. Redrafting began during the discussion in ten sub-commissions. Lay people collaborated actively in all of these, often with decisive impact (for example, the chapters on marriage, economic life and the political community). This participation was inevitably spread rather thin, and, during the final stages, the rhythm of work was constantly accelerated. To propose any change in the draft, a 'modus' (amendment) had to be hastily presented through a Council 'Father' or a more influential peritus during Commission work, or in a rapid conversation in the 'coulisses' (transepts of the Basilica) of the Aula. Vigorous signs of disapproval when an unpalatable proposal was under discussion at the Commission table could also be effective — especially if made by someone like Luz Alvarez Icaza.[21] Under these circumstances, it is difficult, if not impossible, to trace the source of certain changes. It is all the more remarkable that, in the two fascicules of the *Textus recognitus* (Amended Text), the Mixed Commission notes at least twelve instances of the position taken by lay people — their insistence being sometimes the only justification for including or excluding a particular idea.

Tensions were inevitably many and varied, particularly with regard to the worldwide political community (economic problems, nuclear deterrents, conscientious objection, etc.) and — notoriously — the issue of birth control. It was imperative that no formulation be introduced into the schema that might seem to prejudge a question that was still under study in the special Commission created by John XXIII and enlarged by Paul VI. The lay people were as worried as some of the bishops. On 25 November 1965, with the encouragement of a specially competent peritus — Bernard Häring, C.SS.R. — a letter was drafted, signed by a group of Auditors, and delivered to the Pope by Cardinal Maurice Roy.

The Auditors wrote (in French):

> ... We feel it our duty in conscience to express to Your Holiness our great anxiety since the reading in yesterday's session of a letter from the Cardinal Secretary of State, proposing certain 'modi' on the chapter about Marriage. These deal with questions about which — rightly or wrongly — public opinion is extremely sensitive. Questions which have not been discussed by the Council because it was understood that they were of the competence of the special Commission created by Your Holiness, and the answer would be given at the time and in the terms Your Holiness would consider opportune . . . It seems to us of the first importance that the answer should be adequately developed and given in conditions that would facilitate confident reception by the faithful and respectful understanding from a watching world. Such a reception would be gravely compromised by a partial and unexpected response in the form of last-minute modifications of a text which, in its general terms is already known to the public . . . Your Holiness understands the spirit of submission and of love for the Church and for Your Person in which we venture to formulate these remarks . . . [22]

Next day, this initiative was mentioned in the report from the Council published in the Catholic daily paper, *L'Avvenire d'Italia*[23] (certainly with the knowledge of the Pope). The initiative was seen as responding to 'the proper role of the laity in the Church, especially with regard to the Council'; it had been 'objectively evaluated' (in Italian: 'avrebbe incontrato un sereno apprezzamento').

Should the Council speak about women?

During work on Schema 13, Claude Dupuy, Archbishop of Albi (France) asked us: Should we speak about women? The approach of the women Auditors — lay and religious — was to encourage all statements against discrimination, but to oppose any attempt to define strictly (or even poetically) 'woman's role', whether in society or in the Church. The danger was not imaginary. The schema on the Lay Apostolate distributed in 1963[24] contained two articles: on men (*de viris*) and on women (*de mulieribus*); but this schema was reduced and the articles eliminated. The article on women had called for development of 'the natural and supernatural values of [woman's] personality'. It also exhorted the faithful to make known 'the Church's doctrine on woman, especially on her dignity, her rights and duties'. This was thought 'dangerous' because it supposed that the Church had a ready-made doctrine, a model of femininity. In the end, all that remained was the general principle:

> 'Since in our days women are taking an increasingly active share in the whole life of society, it is very important that their participation in the various sectors of the Church's apostolate should likewise develop'. (Decree *Apostolicam Actuositatem*, 9).[25]

Nevertheless, everything said about lay participation in the Church's mission was unequivocally intended to refer to both men and women. In *Gaudium et Spes*, there was stress on 'non-discrimination' in society (29); and, most importantly, in Part 1, introduction of the scarcely explored field of theological anthropology, the biblical vision of the relationship of man and woman, created in the image of God, as 'the first form of communion between persons' (12).

On these and other points emerging in the development of Schema 13, there were contributions from the laity: but there were also at least twenty-five interventions in the Aula. The first substantial intervention — that of Bishop Gérard Coderre (Canada) on 28 October 1964 — referred to recognition of the equal dignity of men and women as a 'sign of the times'.[26] It raised a murmur of assent from the women in St Andrew's tribune, who sent a letter of thanks by messenger across the Council. It was supported by Augustin Frotz, Auxiliary Bishop of Köln who, in October 1965, spoke on women's contribution to culture (cf. *Gaudium et Spes*, 60). Several African bishops referred, not only to women's 'full human dignity', but also to problems specific to Africa (polygamy, abuse of bride-price, marriage without full consent of the bride, etc.).

Paul Hallinan, Archbishop of Atlanta (United States), made a written intervention[27] that was released to the press in October 1965, but which reached the Commission working on Schema 13 too late to be taken into account. He wrote: 'We must not continue to be latecomers in the social, political and economic development that has today reached climactic conditions'. Most of his proposals for women in the Church sounded revolutionary at the time and not all have yet been put into effect. Women are now acting as lectors and acolytes in liturgical functions (although not with a recognised Ministry); they are encouraged to become competent as theologians; women religious are consulted and represented in matters concerning them; but women are not serving as 'Deaconesses'. What sounded revolutionary in 1965 may seem very tame in the 1990s (nevertheless it took thirty years before girls were allowed to become altar servers!). In any case the Council could not be expected to give answers to questions that had not yet arisen, or were emerging only in marginal groups. The question of the ordained ministry, for instance — which we shall see rapidly escalating after the Bishops' Synod of 1971 — was, at the time of the Council, a concern only of a few Catholic feminists or 'progressive' theologians.[28] But Vatican II invited the people of God to take a new look at their Church and to be open for a change of mentality, for a 'conversion of heart' regarding women's full human and Christian dignity.

A letter from Bishop Albino Luciani

A few days after being admitted as an Auditor, I was invited to speak to the French-speaking bishops of Africa about work in progress for the future Decree on the Lay Apostolate. The other members of the panel were Achille Glorieux and Roberto Tucci, SJ. I commented positively on various aspects of the schema. Finally, I picked up some criticisms that were circulating inside and outside the Aula, summed up by a Canadian bishop: 'This schema was conceived in the sin of clericalism!' Naturally, my critical remarks were reflected in the press — with repercussions as I discovered many years later.

On 29 August 1978, after the election of John Paul I, *L'Avvenire* (successor to *L'Avvenire d'Italia*) published a letter of the new Pope. Under the title, 'Women too at the Council!' it was addressed by Albino Luciani, Bishop of Vittorio Veneto, in September 1964, to the chaplains of women's Catholic Action in his diocese. He related the recent appointment of the women Auditors to the 'prophetesses' of the Old Testament and the early Church, and to the historic role of the 'courage, enterprising spirit and breadth of vision of Teresa d'Avila, Francesca Saveria Cabrini, Catherine of Siena . . . ', ending with a treatise on holiness in marriage. But, in case his enthusiasm might be misunderstood, he reassured his priests:

> Don't let it so much as pass through your mind that my references to prophesy mean sympathy for a Church of charisms as opposed to a hierarchical Church, at the expense of Authority and in favour of an exaggerated independence of the laity! . . . And let no one feel his heart sink, like that of a parish priest I know who read in the newspaper that Rosemary Goldie, from being an 'Auditor' at the Council, had become a 'speaker', expressing to a group of bishops a certain reticence about the schema on the laity, which she would like to see less paternalistic, less clerical and less juridical . . . 'It will come to this', said the shocked priest, 'that for these good women, Catholic Action will be, not the collaboration of the laity with the apostolate of the Hierarchy, but the collaboration of the Hierarchy with the apostolate of the laity'. I reassured him. The laity, if they refuse 'paternalism', accept and respect the priests' spiritual 'paternity'; they ask to be guided in spiritual matters, but they think it exaggeration ('clericalism') that absolutely everything in the Church has to come from the bishops and the priests, with the committed laity acting as mere 'fuel for the ecclesiastical locomotive'; finally, whether in speaking or acting, they would like the emphasis to be rather less on rights and powers (legalism), and everyone to remember a little more that we are a family, practising charity, fraternity, service. That was the style of St Augustine, who almost apologized for making use of his episcopal rights.[29]

I had no idea that I had been defended with such authority. On 7 September 1978, I wrote to thank Pope John Paul I and to ask his blessing for all women working at the service of the Church. The 'paternal' reply — signed by Cardinal Villot, Secretary of State — was dated 27 September, the day before the Pope's death.

Ecumenical meetings

The Auditors' Conciliar experience had an ecumenical dimension — a novelty for the majority of the laity. The Decree on Ecumenism opened up a whole new area in renewal of the Church (at times, an area of some confusion!).

For the women Auditors, direct involvement was not limited to the enjoyable occasion when a tea was arranged, on 12 October 1964, with all available wives of the Delegated Observers (there were never women among the official Observers). This was held at Foyer Unitas, the ecumenical centre of the Ladies of Bethany.[30] In September a memorandum[31] had been sent from Geneva and Rome to a carefully selected group:

> Agenda and plans are being developed for a meeting between a group of Roman Catholic women, including some of the Auditors of the Vatican Council, and a group of women from the constituency of the World Council of Churches. The theme: 'Forms of service for women in our Churches'.
>
> The meeting will have a strictly *unofficial* and informal character with *minimum publicity*. It will be sponsored by the Secretariat for Promoting Christian Unity in cooperation with COPECIAL on the one side, and the Department for Cooperation of Men and Women in Church, Family and Society and the Division of Ecumenical Action of the World Council of Churches [WCC] on the other.

The meeting was to be held 23–24 October in a retreat centre at Vicarello, Bracciano (outside Rome), followed by a visit to Rome.

The initiative for the meeting had come from Mgr (now Cardinal)

Johannes Willebrands, Secretary of the Secretariat for Promoting Christian Unity, and from Madeleine Barot,[32] Executive Secretary of the WCC Department. According to the Memorandum, Madeleine and I were 'jointly responsible for the agenda and physical arrangements'. We were very conscious that this was a pioneering venture which could have unforeseen results.

In the WCC group there were Orthodox, Anglican and Protestant women: deaconesses, religious and laity. Three participants were to be future members of the WCC Presidency: Cynthia Wedel, of the Episcopal Church, Associate General Secretary of the National Council of Churches of Christ in the United States; Marga Buhrig of the Reformed Church of Switzerland, and the theological Observer for the WCC, Fr Paul Verghese.[33] The Roman Catholic 'Observer' was Bernard Häring. After the meeting, Cynthia Wedel wrote:[34]

> ... It was amazing to see our surprise as we discovered over and over again how much we have in common. All of us share in concern for missions, for social action, for young people and better family life. All are seeking more vital forms of prayer and devotional life. All want better education and training for the laity. All have an increasing number of women studying theology. All feel a dangerous gap between the leadership of the Church and the average lay person in the local congregation. All feel restive under the restrictions placed upon women by the Church at a time when the secular world is rapidly removing such restrictions ... Any suspicion of one another with which we may have come to the meeting evaporated in the understanding and mutual affection which quickly grew ...

Two somewhat formal presentations were discussed. Sister Mary Luke told of the changes taking place in the religious orders. One of these was presented visually when she and Sister Ann Richard appeared in attractive new habits, with short skirts, loose jackets and short head-dresses ... She quoted Pope Paul, who had told the nuns they had been too marginal to the currents of thought in the Church and the world ...

In the other formal presentation — biblical and theological — Marga Buhrig stressed the fact that subordination of women in the Church can be traced, not to the Biblical record, but to its later interpretation. Bernard Häring and Paul Verghese made appreciative comments.

Final suggestions included the need for further study on the image of woman — as person, wife, mother, worker — and her 'maximum contribution' to Church and society in religious orders and Secular Institutes, in the organised life of the Church, and in meeting the needs of the human community.

On Monday, 25 October, the group departed for Rome: a visit to Cardinal Bea, a reception at Foyer Unitas and briefing on the Council. The climax was attendance, on 28 October, at a Public Session for the promulgation of five decrees. Elizabeth Souttar, Head Deaconess of the Anglican Diocese of London, later described the ceremonial:

> ... glittering chandeliers, more than two thousand bishops in white mitres, Cardinals in scarlet, Swiss Guards with halberds, officials in black velvet with white ruffs and gold chains, the diplomatic corps in evening dress and orders, ladies in mantillas, the Knights of Malta, and at last, the Pope himself. Then, after the concelebrated Mass and the promulgation, the Pope passing close to us and giving us his blessing. I think none of us will ever forget the feeling of love and unity in those moments of fellowship in which we knelt together — Roman Catholic, Anglican and Protestant — as true friends, sharing (though, alas, not yet fully).[35]

Returning home, Ann Porter Brown, General Secretary of the Board of Missions of the Methodist Church in the United States, wrote: 'I am still in somewhat of a dream world thinking of the experience together at Lake Bracciano ... I am sure that I shall never be quite the same again'.[36]

Dream world or not, Vicarello had its follow-up. Ecumenical links were developed in Europe and the United States. A second meeting at Cret-Bérard (Switzerland) was jointly sponsored, in 1966, by the WCC and the Conference of CIO. When a more ambitious meeting was held at Taizé, 19–24 June 1967, over a hundred women took part, with male consultants and, as speaker, the Rev. André Dumas, of the College of Protestant Theology, Paris. Concluding the Conference report — 'The Christian Woman, co-artisan in a changing society' — Pilar Bellosillo, President of the Conference of CIO, wrote:

> Our international gatherings already have a history. We have experienced the difficulties, the pains and the joys of our journey . . . We shall continue to bear the same suffering together, to pray the same prayer together, and to hope the same hope together.[37]

Laity questions

A few participants at Vicarello had already worked together in relation to the Council.

In January 1964, a confidential meeting on issues related to the laity had been held at Glion (Montreux, Switzerland) between a group formed by the WCC and another formed by COPECIAL with the help of the Secretariat for Promoting Christian Unity. The meeting was 'confidential' — only a brief and uninformative press release was ever published — because the Catholic group included bishops and priests Johannes Willebrands, Emilio Guano, Jerome Hamer (later a cardinal), Charles Moeller, who were involved at the time in drafting the Conciliar texts on the Church, the Laity, the Church in the Modern World, and Ecumenism. On the WCC side there were also well-known names: Lukas Vischer, Nikos Nissiotis, Proto-presbyter Vitaly Borovoi (all Delegated Observers to the Council). Co-Chairmen were Klaus von Bismarck, Director of West German Radio and Ramon Sugranyes de Franch. Among the lay people present were Madeleine Barot, Maria (Rie) Vendrik and myself. Another lay participant, Birgit Rodhe of the Church of Sweden, commented:

> Sitting here like a layman [sic!] makes you feel as if you were being discovered . . . like the Red Indians when Columbus discovered America. But the Indians were there already . . . We

are groping from both sides to discover what we are and where we are... We must keep together a theology of the Church and a theology of the world... If lay people are to recognize themselves, theology must take into account the fact that they live in a world where certain tasks are not strictly the mission of the Church.[38]

In September 1965 another WCC–COPECIAL Consultation was held at Gazzada (Varese) which did not require the same confidentiality. The Council was still in progress, but it had already formulated, in the Constitution *Lumen Gentium*, its 'ecclesiology of communion' and it had declared ecumenism to be the responsibility of the whole People of God (Decree *Unitatis Redintegratio*, 5). At Gazzada, the subject was laity formation, and lay men and women were the main actors. Two participants who were shortly to play an important role at Vicarello were also there: Mary Luke Tobin and Paul Verghese.

1. Plenary Assemblies were meetings of all the bishops in the Aula (Council Hall in St Peter's Basilica) for debate on the texts and other general business.

2. The *Standard Dictionary of the Encyclopaedia Britannica* (Chicago), 1962, defines anathema as 'A formal ecclesiastical ban or curse, excommunicating a person or damning something, as a book or heresy'.

3. Papers in the possession of the author.

4. The full text of the conference was never published, but the conference was reported, with a summary of the text, in an (unsigned) article in *L'Italia*, 28 March 1965, p. 8, under the title 'Cronaca di Torino'.

5. An Extraordinary Assembly of the Synod of Bishops is convened by the Pope to discuss matters which need rapid solution. The Episcopal Conferences are represented only by their Presidents, instead of by an elected group of bishops, as in the Ordinary Synod. The Assembly of 1985 was called — twenty years after the close of Vatican II — to commemorate, confirm and 'promote' the Council.

6. The Encyclical *Ad Petri Cathedram* of John XXIII, 29 June 1959. An English version, under the title 'Truth, Unity and Peace', is published by St Paul Publications, Sydney (undated).

7. *Brief to the Bishops: Canadian Catholic Laymen Speak Their Minds*, Ed. Paul T. Harris, Longmans Canada Limited, Toronto, 1965, p. 1.

8. Intervention of Bishop Alexander Carter, 9 October 1964, reported in French, *Documentation Catholique*, Maison de la Bonne Presse, Paris, 15.XI.1964, p. 1469. (Intervention is the term generally used for a statement made in the course of the debate.)

9. 11 November 1963.

10. Address to the women religious of the diocese of Albano, *Insegnamenti di Paolo IV*, II, 8 September 1964, p. 529.

11. *Insegnamenti de Paolo IV*, II, p. 551.

12. *The Catholic Citizen*, Journal of St Joan's International Alliance, Paris, 15 January 1965.

13. Carmel E. McEnroy, *Guests in Their Own House: The Women of Vatican II*, The Crossroad Publishing Company, New York, 1996.

Inevitably, in such a mine of information — gathered often in hasty interviews — not every view will be shared (Carmel's views can be more negative than mine); but, as Bernard Häring says in the Foreword, the book is not only fascinating, but historically 'important and necessary'.

14. Pat Keegan's address to the Council was published in *Lay Apostolate*, Bulletin of COPECIAL, 1, 1965, pp. 9–10.

15. Juan Vazquez spoke on 10 November 1964 in Spanish. The text is summarised in English in *Lay Apostolate*, 1, 1965, pp. 8–9.

16. James Norris addressed the Council on 5 November 1964. The English text of his address in Latin is given in *Lay Apostolate*, 1.

17. Eusèbe Adjakpley spoke in French on 3 October 1965. The English text is given in *Lay Apostolate*, 3, 1965, pp. 8–9.

18. 'A special secretariat should be established at the Holy See for the service and promotion of the lay apostolate. It should serve as a well-equipped centre, supplying information about the

various apostolic programmes of the laity, promoting research into modern problems arising in this field and assisting the Hierarchy and laity in their apostolic works with its advice. The various movements and projects of the lay apostolate throughout the world should be represented in this secretariat; and clergy and religious should cooperate also with the laity', N.26 of the Schema *Apostolicam Actuositatem* on the Laity, as adopted on 18 November 1965.

19. In the Decree on the Pastoral Office of Bishops, *Christus Dominus*, the 'Fathers of the Council' recommend simply that the Departments of the Roman Curia 'listen more attentively to laymen outstanding for their virtue, knowledge and experience, allowing the latter in this way to have an appropriate share in Church affairs' (10) Austin Flannery, *Vatican Council II: The Conciliar and Post-Conciliar Documents*, 1975. , p. 568.

20. In his book, *Crossing the Threshold of Hope*, Jonathan Cape, London, 1984, John Paul II recalls his participation in this meeting as Archbishop of Krakow.

Roberto Tucci, SJ gives the names of all those who took part in the different phases of the drafting of *Gaudium et Spes* in his history of the constitution: *L'Eglise dans le monde de ce temps*, Tome II, Editions du Cerf, Paris, 1967, pp. 33–127.

During the week following the meeting at Ariccia, the work done was revised by a group meeting in the Vatican. Two laymen were invited and three women: Mary Luke Tobin, Pilar Bellosillo, and myself.

21. Luz and José, the Mexican presidents of the CFM for Latin America, were the only married couple invited to be Auditors at the Council. Both as members of the CFM and parents of fourteen children, they had experience to offer for the chapter on marriage and family.

22. The Auditors' letter was not published at the time. In 1986, I quoted the original French in an intervention made during an international Colloquium of the Istituto Paolo VI, Brescia, on Paul VI and the Ecclesiological Problems of the Council. I was speaking about Paul VI and lay participation in the Council.

23. *L'Avvenire d'Italia*, 27 November 1965, p. 2.

24. These documents are now being made available for research through the Archives of the Second Vatican Council.

25. For the Council documents, see SOURCES of this volume.

In 1996, Flannery published a new version: *The Basic Sixteen Documents: Vatican Council II. Constitutions Decrees Declarations. A Completely Revised Translation in Inclusive Language* (Costello Publishing Company, Northport, New York; Dominican Publications, Dublin, Ireland).

26. Cf. The Encyclical of John XXIII, *Pacem in Terris*, 11 April 1963: *On Establishing Universal peace in truth, justice, charity and liberty*, Vatican Polyglot Press, Rome, 1963.

27. Paul Hallinan's written intervention was distributed by him to the press in English. The official Latin text is published in the Council Proceedings: *Acta Concilii Vaticani secundi — periodus IV*, pp. 754–8.

28. A Swiss lawyer, Gertrud Heinzelmann, issued a petition explicitly demanding priesthood for women. It was published after the Council: *Die getrennten Schwestern: Frauen nach dem Konzil*, Interfeminas-Verlag, Zurich, 1967. St Joan's International Alliance — originally a Catholic Suffragette movement in England — entered the field in 1963.

29. The full text of the letter is published in Italian in the volume, Albino Luciani, *Un vescovo al Concilio*, Città Nuova, Roma, 1983, pp. 79–89.

30. A community of women religious (in lay dress) founded in Holland, in the 1920s, by Jacques

van Ginneken, SJ. In the Holy Year 1950 they opened a 'Foyer' to receive non-Catholic visitors to Rome. Their work was especially important during the Council. The history of their ecumenical activity is told in the volume, *Hearth of Unity: Ladies of Bethany and Ecumenism in Rome*, by Josefa Koet, Leideke Galema, Marion M. van Assendelft, Fratelli Palombi Editori, Rome, 1996.

31. The archives of the World Council of Churches and the Pontifical Council for Promoting Christian Unity.

32. A volume in French, *Madeleine Barot* (Éditions du Cerf, Paris, and Labor et Fides, Geneva, 1989), signed by André Jacques, but written in collaboration with Madeleine herself, recounts her long life of courageous Christian witness: her action in aid of refugees, Jews and resisters during the Second World War and later as President of Christian Action for the Abolition of Torture (ACAT) and her years as a world traveller for the WCC.

33. Later Metropolitan Paulus Mar Gregorios, of the Malankara Syrian Orthodox Church of India, until his death in 1996.

34. In an article, 'Church Women and Christian Unity', published in *Catholic World*, New York, October 1965, pp. 279–80.

35. Susannah Herzel, *A Voice for Women*, World Council of Churches, Geneva, 1981, p. 56.

36. Letter from Ann Porter Brown to the writer, 1 November 1965.

37. *Report of the Women's International Ecumenical Conference: The Christian Woman co-artisan in a changing society, Taizé, France, 19–24 July 1967*, p. 101 (printed in France, no date available).

38. Birgit Rodhe's words are from the unpublished, mimeographed report of the meeting in Glion, p. 15 (Archives of COPECIAL).

CHAPTER 6

The post-Conciliar Congress

> The Council has awakened in the Church a new awareness of her nature and her mission... The preparation of the Third World Congress will now afford a providential opportunity, enabling the Catholic laity, in their diversity of race, culture, social position and state of life, to discern more clearly the vocation to the apostolate of every baptized person... For it is not only a matter of receiving and spreading the teachings of the Council, but also of being transformed in the likeness of the Conciliar Church — a Church renewed in her prayer, in the expression of her faith and hope, and in the charity of her dialogue with all Christians, with all mankind...[1]

Paul VI was speaking on 8 March 1966, to the COPECIAL Directing Board, which was meeting to prepare for the Congress that would take place from 11 to 18 October 1967 under the title, 'God's People on Man's Journey'.

It had been clear since 1959 that the next World Congress of the Laity would be post-Conciliar. In 1951, there had been the post-war coming together of a cross-section of the whole People of God in a 'world becoming one', a new experience of the fact that the laity also are the Church. In 1957, the Second Congress gathered the fruits of regional developments and the work of theologians and other experts that were to lead into Vatican II. It was more a stocktaking; a Congress for teaching and stimulation than debating. The stock would be later reflected in the Conciliar Decree on the Lay Apostolate. Even the 'storm in a tea-cup' over what was or was not Catholic Action produced clarification in N.20 of the Decree (afterwards largely forgotten until movements again became a talking-point in the Church).

The Congress of 1967 met at a time when the world was accelerating at a hitherto unprecedented pace. With the end of the colonial era, there were more actors on the world scene rather than new solutions for the escalating problems of poverty, under-development, demographic pressure, international and national conflict. There were sensational technological developments. The Congress of 1957 had opened the day after Sputnik 1 — the first artificial earth satellite — was launched into orbit by the Russians. The Congress of 1967 had, among its invited witnesses, the Commandant of *Gemini IV*, Colonel James McDivitt, who presented Pope Paul with a model of his spaceship.

In preparing for the Third World Congress, lay people had been, since 1959, in 'a state of Council'. They had also experienced intensely the brief Pontificate of John XXIII. The keynote of Pope John's magisterium was *unity*. Inspired by the Pope's first Encyclical, *Ad Petri Cathedram*, COPECIAL announced in 1961 that Congress preparation would take for its theme, '*Ut unum sint . . . ut mundus credat*': 'That they may be one . . . that the world may believe' (Jn 17:21). A study guide was prepared entitled *What helps and what hinders unity: between men — between Christians — between Catholics?* A biblical and theological text was written by Gérard Philips: 'Unity among Christians in a world seeking unity: a gift and a mission'.

An itinerant preparation

Very few of those who would come to Rome in October 1967 could prepare for the event by imbibing the atmosphere of the Council. 'Rome' must go to them. The limited workforce of COPECIAL and the Conference of CIO was once more sent out on mission, to take the message of the future Congress to laity and clergy, while updating our knowledge of the post-Conciliar Church. We who had already visited groups in many countries knew from experience that these visits could provide an occasion — perhaps a first occasion — for these local groups to come together and get to know one another.

The prize for the pre-Congress marathon must go to Marie-Ange Besson. In January 1964, she journeyed through West Africa: Dakar (Senegal); Conakry (Guinea); Abidjan (Ivory Coast); Accra (Ghana); Cotonou (Dahomey, now Benin); Lagos and Enugu (Nigeria). There were meetings with bishops, chaplains, lay groups. There were unexpected hazards — and not only from local air travel. In Guinea, Archbishop Tchidimbo had warned her that, since there were no associations, she would have 'nothing to do'; no 'apostolic' visiting, but a three-day initiation into African life in a country where the Church was struggling to keep alive in a hostile political situation. Her visits from family to family, from office to presbytery were punctuated by a hospitality that a guest *must* accept. The Archbishop merely warned her not to mix her drinks. So, having started by accepting whisky, she spent the morning going from whisky to whisky, trying to remain relatively lucid!

In 1966, Marie-Ange completed a two-month tour of fifteen countries of Western, Central and Northern Africa. And in 1967, she went on three months of visits to thirteen Asian countries, in a tour that began in Lebanon and ended in Cairo. By the time she reached Indonesia her passport was so full of 'suspicious' stamps that the authorities checked to make sure none of her interests were more subversive than the good works of the Catholic women of 'Wanita Katholik'.

I completed the itinerant Asian consultation in February 1967 by making a detour to Sydney via Seoul, Tokyo and New Zealand. In Seoul an historic meeting took place. Some sixty representatives from seven Korean dioceses inaugurated a National Association of lay movements together with a Preparatory Committee for the World Congress. I thought of my first visit to Korea after the Asian meeting in Manila in December 1955: the touch-down at Seoul airport — little more than a few wooden barracks; the contacts arranged by the Korean delegate to Manila, Hainam Lee; Midnight Mass with the Columban

Sisters at the '38th parallel'; lunch with a group of Korean Catholic women, with whom I exchanged cordial sentiments in sign language. (I was informed afterwards that the Bishop had not yet allowed them to form any organised group.)

I had been invited by the Catholic Women's League of New South Wales to meet lay groups and the general Catholic public in all capital cities of Australia, with a few extra stops for good measure. My whirlwind tour, from 1 to 17 March, ended before a public audience of more than 2,000 people in Sydney's Trocadero, in the presence of Cardinal Gilroy and a representative of the Apostolic Delegate. It would have been more intimidating if it had not been such a 'family' gathering. There were people who had known me as a small child, as a student of Our Lady of Mercy College, Parramatta and of Sydney University, as a member of the Grail in the war years and as a visitor from Rome in 1954. They gave a heart-warming welcome to the local phenomenon — after attending the Ecumenical Council, I had just become the first woman in the Curia. I could only hope they were also interested in the message of the Third World Congress.

The Americas were not forgotten in these itineraries. In October 1966, a North American Preparatory Meeting was organised by the NCCM and the NCCW in the United States, together with French-speaking Canada. Seventy people met at Villa Cortona, a retreat centre in the wooded suburbia of Bethesda (Maryland), including Observer-Consultants from United Church Men and United Church Women of the United States. Apart from planning for the World Congress, the meeting also considered 'Poverty in the national and international order'; 'Mobility: the transition of American Catholicism from an immigrant urban Church to a middle-class suburban Church'; and 'The participation of laity in the structures of the Church'. The papers were challenging but, as I remember it, the refrain at the meeting was: 'At the Congress, will we be able to say what we think?'

From Bethesda, Mieczyslaw de Habicht set off to 'preach' the Congress during a Latin American Lay Apostolate Meeting in Buenos Aires, as well as visiting groups in Montevideo, Lima, Bogota and Mexico. Rie Vendrik took the message to Cuba, where her visit was greatly welcomed.

God's people on man's journey

In July 1964, in a meeting held at the Retreat Centre where the Preparatory Conference for the First World Congress had been held in 1950, the process of integrating the findings of the Unity theme with the orientations emerging from Vatican II began. The COPECIAL bulletin, *Lay Apostolate*, which appeared three times a year between 1960 and 1967, records COPECIAL Board and staff, leaders of the CIO and Council periti commuting from Commissions and Sub-Commissions of the Council to these planning meetings for the post-Conciliar Congress.

In 1966 it was at last announced that the Congress would be held from 11 to 18 October 1967. It was a significant gesture of Paul VI that the dates were made to coincide with the first convocation of the Synod of Bishops, created in 1965. As a result of long hours of discussion the Congress theme had emerged as '*Le Peuple de Dieu dans l'itinéraire des hommes*' (God's People on Man's Journey).[2]

As a further step in preparation, an Enquiry had been sent out to all regular correspondents of COPECIAL and the CIO in October 1966 to gauge response to Vatican II, insofar as it could be evaluated at such an early stage. The replies indicated the tentative nature of the responce and the predictability of many reactions. Not all local churches had flourishing publishing houses to disseminate the Council texts, nor any adequate means of overcoming language difficulties (apart from the inevitable difficulty of ecclesiastical language). Not all parishes could claim they were 'an obvious example of the apostolate on the community level' (Decree on Lay Apostolate, 10). Asked whether the Council had brought 'greater awareness of belonging to a diocese', many tended to relate this to the personality of the Bishop. The faithful in Senegal saw 'their' Bishop leaving for Rome; they read 'his' statements in the press; when he came back, they welcomed him 'with pride and enthusiasm'. In several countries lay people were reported to be already active in Pastoral Councils — but it was doubtful that real responsibility was involved. From the Netherlands came news of the experiment of their National Pastoral Council, whose outspokenness and democratic tendencies were soon to cause concern in Rome. There, as in other countries where anything coming from 'Rome' had been virtually unquestionable, once questions began to be asked — even about the slightest points of custom or devotion — it seemed almost anything might be called into question. Catholic education had not been strong on distinguishing the essential from the non-essential.

A question about experiments in dialogue revealed great confusion about the nature of dialogue. It could be seen as an exercise in 'sounding out what the Bishop is thinking'. 'Tremendous confusion' was reported between 'mission' (evangelising activity) and 'development' (action against poverty, illiteracy, etc.): 'It is absolutely necessary to rethink the Church's missionary activity'. On ecumenism — a new field for most of the Catholic community — reaction to the Council was 'almost invariably favourable, and often enthusiastic'. But a seminary instructor in the United States was quoted as saying: 'What people think the Council said about ecumenism is widely diffused; what the Council said, not so widely'. Overall, the replies throw light on the state of preparedness — and unpreparedness — for Vatican II among God's People. The unpreparedness was to produce much of the post-Conciliar confusion.

The organisational maze

I doubt that anyone will look to this account in search of a model for organising future World Congresses of the Laity. There has not been another such Congress, and it is unlikely that there will be. The post-Conciliar Congress belonged to a particular moment in the life of the Church. But, if anyone should be so misled as to look here for lessons in method, I would issue a solemn warning: simplify organisation and keep your lines of communication clear. In many ways the Third World Congress was a success — the grace of God was with it — but its organisation was a maze!

In November 1966, the COPECIAL Directing Board made itself into an Organising Committee, with several coopted members and Sugranyes as Chairman. Vice-Chairpersons were Rie Vendrik, Vittorio Bachelet and Pat Keegan. Within the Committee, an Executive Group of seven persons was formed, with Sugranyes as Chairman. Rie Vendrik was Vice-Chair of this group and Chairperson of a Program Group responsible for the workshops. There was a separate Liturgical Committee (which did some of the best work of the whole Congress). A Technical Secretariat was opened near the Auditorium under the able charge of Alma Herger, 'lent' by the NCCW of the United States. Overall responsibility during the Congress would be taken by a Steering Committee, with Sugranyes as Chairman, which included, with the whole Organising Committee, five international Presidents (Veronese was First President) and five Vice-Presidents. The Steering Committee had its own Secretary: Thom Kerstiens (Netherlands), with three Assistants. The Assembly of Heads of Delegations had its own Chairpersons. A Resolutions Committee was chosen from among Heads of Delegations and from the Steering Committee.

As Executive Secretary of COPECIAL, I was — nominally — General Secretary of the Congress, assisted by staff from COPECIAL. Having followed the intricacies of the long preparation, I might have been the obvious person to draw together the threads of the Congress operation, although it was probably better that I was not asked to do so. I was weary and the previous three months of preparation had coincided with an unbroken spell of Rome's humid summer heat. The fact remains that this was one of the very few times when I have felt that, had I been a man, responsibility would not have been given elsewhere. (This is not a criticism of Thom Kerstiens: a good friend, who left us all too soon when he died on 1 August 1990.)

The proceedings[3]

Of the eight Congress days, five were devoted mainly to workshops. This did not mean the Congress was a closed event, shunning the public eye. Day after day, the great doors of the Auditorium were thrown open to admit, not only the 2,000-plus official participants — national and international delegations, experts and Observer–Consultants — but also fluctuating numbers of nearly 900 'Auditors' who were admitted to public sessions and ceremonies.

On 11 October (the fifth anniversary of the Opening of the Second Vatican Council), Vittorino Veronese declared the Congress open. Few places were reserved for Authorities but Cardinal Cento, President of the Conciliar Commission for Lay Apostolate, was there, with some eighty bishops, and the Italian Prime Minister, Aldo Moro.

At the First World Congress in 1951, Cardijn had set the tone with the challenge of his world-sweeping panorama. In 1967, shortly after his death, a Mass was offered commemorating all that Cardijn's life and work had meant for the Church and, especially, for the laity. The Introductory Lecture was given by Thom Kerstiens (at the time, General Secretary of the International Christian Union of Business Executives, UNIAPAC). Thom recognised the participants as 'committed Christians' in a world whose mood was for change, for service of God through service to the world. In a 'climate of liberty', there must also be a right relationship between clerics and laity:[4]

> If, in former times, in certain areas our habit was to put our priests on pedestals so that they would not be too contaminated by the world, which allowed us to complain that they did not know the realities of modern life, and were too paternalistic, it now looks as if we only want them to be completely and utterly immersed in worldly things, which will consequently allow us to complain that we no longer hear the word of God in any sermon, or that priests, because they dress as laymen, want to run everything as clergymen.

But the problems were not only within the Church community. Committed Christians had to be ready to answer the key questions that were asked in *Gaudium et Spes*, and in Pope Paul's Encyclical *Populorum Progressio*, on the Development of Peoples: What ideals does Christianity offer to modern youth? If there is no alternative to peace and development is the new name for peace, what do we do to ensure the conditions for such a peace?

The workshops, where questions were meant to find answers, were divided into two series. The first, 'Man Today', considered spiritual attitudes; the family; cooperation between men and women; tensions between generations; social communication; development in a planetary society; peace and world community; migration. The second series, 'Renewal of the Church', looked at presenting the Christian message;

Christian education; new methods of formation; dialogue within the Church; Church communities; lay organisations; missionary activity; ecumenical dialogue and collaboration.

Public sessions of 'witness' accompanied the workshops. Chairing a session on 'Man Today', Klaus van Bismarck, a Lutheran, defined its subject with the opening words of *Gaudium et Spes*: 'The joys and the hopes, the griefs and the anxieties of the men of this age'. The panel that followed — as Barbara Ward Jackson explained — wanted to pick out 'new facts' of a 'new history', beginning with the developments in science and technology; accumulated riches in the world where two-thirds of humanity were living in sub-human conditions. What answer must Christians give to the question: Am I my brother's keeper?

A former student leader from India, P. T. Kuriakose, directed attention to conflicting frustrations in the younger generation. Youth of 'poor' countries were looking enviously towards affluent post-Christian societies, from which young people in revolt were flocking to India in search of Oriental mysticism. (This was a year before the student riots of May 1968 in Paris.)

The astronaut, James A. McDivitt, showed film of what 'one world' looked like viewed from space; but pointed also to another 'one world' emerging through peaceful cooperation in space programs — specifically between Americans and Russians.

There was consideration of the problems of racism; the scandal of continuing war (Vietnam); the ratio of food to population; the bribery and corruption affecting developing countries. But there was also the promise of great hope for the future: a new awareness of values; a sense of human dignity; equality; freedom; the search for an authentically contemplative life in some of the worst conditions of modern existence. New challenges arose also in the field of education: the need to create in 'new elites' able to cope with change. Kathleen Bliss, former General Secretary of the Board of Education of the Church of England, spoke of this — in the Symposium on 'Man Today' — from her experience among the silk-weavers of South India, whose whole world had fallen apart with the introduction of industrial technology.

The second series of workshops also had an accompanying symposium on 'Faith Today'. (Paul VI had proclaimed a Year of Faith, from June 1967 to June 1968, for the 19th centenary of the Martyrdom of SS Peter and Paul.) Among the speakers were Mgr Charles Moeller, Under-secretary of the Congregation for the Doctrine of Faith, and Margaret Shannon, Executive Director of Church Women United (United States). The Moderator James O'Gara, editor of *Commonweal*, reminded his hearers that:

> for many unbelievers the mediocrity of Christians is at least a justification if not a cause, of unbelief . . . the institutional Church . . . often feudal, medieval, baroque [bears its part of blame.] Obviously we need institutions, but we need also to purify the Church in the light of the Gospel . . . to take on again the character of the suffering servant.[5]

On Sunday, 15 October, at the heart of the Congress, the Fathers of the Synod joined the Congress participants at the Mass concelebrated in St Peter's Basilica by Paul VI and twenty-four bishops. After Mass, Rienzie Rupasinghe (Sri Lanka, International President of YCW) addressed the Pope — at considerable length — outlining what the Congress had done and still had to do: 'Within the Church . . . the Hierarchy and the clergy are called upon to listen to those who are immersed in the world'! The Holy Father then pronounced an allocution in five parts,[6] each in a different language, summing up the Council's teaching on the laity. The passage pointing to the special role of pastors, and to the absurdity of any supposition that there could be 'two parallel hierarchies' in the Church, was read in English. This may have been a response, not to any pretensions on the part of those present, but rather to a press that seemed determined to detect a power-seeking laity attacking the hierarchical bastion of Rome.

In the conclusion of his address, Paul VI announced his intention of proclaiming St Teresa of Avila and St Catherine of Siena, Doctors of the Church. October 15 is the Feast of the Saint of Avila. And 'who', the Pope asked, 'was ever more involved with the world than the great St Teresa?'

In the afternoon the Congress heard the lecture, 'God's Call', prepared by Yves Congar, who was unfortunately prevented by ill-health from presenting it in person. It was a text of great depth and wide vision:[7]

> The world or history are not for the Church just a changing scene, in front of which she performs her age-old chant; they are not even like a simple audience to which a prepared message is addressed in a more or less adapted form. The world and history furnish the Church with the matter for her own life and the conditions, one might say the determining factors for the carrying out of her mission, the matter and conditions of the 'today of God', which she must live day after day. Complex questions were clarified in relation to the 'temporal actions' of Christians, simply 'as Christians', and to the involvement of lay Christians in an 'action of the Church'. There was a penetration from the inside of the work of Vatican II, even of its 'limitations': Vatican II has not done for ethics what it has done for ecclesiology, for the laity or for ecumenism. This is an area which calls for new formulations . . .

The closing talk, 'Towards the Future', was given by Joaquin Ruiz-Gimenez,[8] Professor of Law in the University of Madrid, President of Pax Romana–ICMICA, member of the newly created *Consilium de Laicis* of the Holy See. It was a vibrant address expressing (in Spanish) 'the vibrant life of the Congress', its universality, its excitement, its impatience to 'speak in the name of people unable to speak', its straining towards 'an ever more witnessing Church'. The guide chosen for this rapid journey in faith was that 'extraordinary woman' recalled by Paul VI: 'Teresa of Jesus, the woman who, for love of God and humankind, tirelessly walked the ways of earth and heaven'.

In this same session, six young people, each from a different continent, were asked for their 'impressions'. Predictably, they spoke enthusiastically of universality and diversity, of prayer and fellowship. But Michael Barry from the United States — he and his wife had arrived on a 'kind of honeymoon' — regretted that youth were 'poorly represented' at the Congress, not always by people really youthful, and that there was no opportunity to express together their 'deep agony at the situation in the world today'. (Perhaps, nearly thirty years later, he witnessed the VIII World Youth Day which brought more than half a million young people from all over the world to meet the Pope in Denver in 1993, to voice their joy but also their distress.) Therese Shak,[9] from Hong Kong, registered the hope of many that such a Congress could be held outside Europe; particularly in lands where the majority of the people have been 'prepared by God through other religions to be ready and white for the harvest'. Should we not be equally eager to fill God's barns with rice as much as with wheat?

It had been hoped that Paul VI would have a greater physical presence in the Congress but he had already postponed necessary surgery in order to be available for the Synod. Had he been present — as were many bishops from the Synod — at the close of the Congress, his heart would have been warmed by the Credo sung by all the participants before they set out to resume their 'journey'.

In addition to the concelebrated Eucharist and his allocution, Pope Paul was, however, also present in a prayer,[10] specially written for the occasion and used as Prayer of the Faithful in the Mass of 15 October. For the First World Congress, Pius XII had composed a prayer,[11] which he knelt to recite at the Audience of 14 October 1951: a prayer for grace to carry out the 'holy mission' of lay people called 'to the honour of making [our] humble contribution to the work of the apostolate of the hierarchy'. In 1967, even members of Catholic Action might have found that restricting (more restrictive than Pius XII himself was towards the lay apostolate). Paul VI prayed with the 'laity of the People of God' to Jesus Christ, 'Lord, Master and Saviour of Humanity', asking also 'how to unite our efforts with all men of good will, to realize fully the good of humanity in truth, liberty, justice and love'.

An ecumenical event

More than any other aspect of the Congress, its ecumenical dimension was a prolongation of the mood of Vatican II.[12]

The ecumenical Observers had been invited to the Council through the Secretariat for Promoting Christian Unity, set up by Pope John in 1960. It was through the Secretariat also that COPECIAL was able to invite Observer–Consultants from all the Orthodox Churches, from all communions of 'other Christians', from the World Council of Churches, the World Student Christian Federation, the Young Men's Christian Association (YMCA) and the Young Women's Christian Association (YWCA), and other international bodies. All responded by sending officially delegated Observers. Even the Baptist World Alliance, which had not been represented at the Council, delegated two members. In addition, national delegations were authorised to associate 'other Christian' friends with their preparation for the Congress, and invite them to accompany their Catholic friends to Rome. Altogether eighty-eight Observer–Consultants took part in the Congress. A liaison group, coordinated by Ruth Reardon Slade, facilitated their participation. A pre-Congress orientation and a post-Congress evaluation were programmed. Gerhart M. Riegner, Secretary General of the World Jewish Congress, was invited as a special guest.

Messages

At the opening session, a Message from the Ecumenical Patriarch, His Holiness Athenagoras I of Constantinople,[13] was read by His Eminence Metropolitan Emilianos:

> In all the Churches, there is concern about the present spiritual crisis. An effort is being made to find out why many people are keeping away from the practice of religion. The only explanation tendered has been an extremely facile and over-simplified one. It consisted in proclaiming that the mass of non-practising people was made up of unbelievers or of insignificant believers whose opinion was not worth taking into account.
>
> Your Conference . . . will attempt a deeper diagnosis that will prove meaningful for all Christians. You have rightly pointed out that one of the main reasons for this deficiency is the abdication of the laity or the fact that they play too marginal a role in the general Mission of the Body of Christ. We too, in the Orthodox Church, are anxious, like yourselves, to make our faithful more aware of their duty and of the active share they must take in the

apostolate, in accordance with the teachings of the Church
Fathers, to spread the saving Message of the Gospel . . .

I offer my greetings in Christ and my warm wishes for the
success of your work, in order that new and effective solutions
may be found for the good and unity of all the Churches: that
all may believe, 'ut omnes unum sint'.

The Message from His Grace Michael Ramsay, Archbishop of Canterbury,[14] was delayed in the mail, but later communicated to all taking part in the Congress:

> I greet all of you who have been gathered in Rome for the
> Third World Congress for the Lay Apostolate. This has been the
> first major Congress since the recent Vatican Council, and all
> of us who have been watching it from a distance, have been
> encouraged by the mutual good will and willingness to work
> together that have brought into one place so many delegates
> from all over the world. If the Church of the present and future
> is to be strong and united, lay people must play their full part,
> remembering that it is they as much as the clergy, who are *sent
> out* by the Lord in the mission of His Church. I pray that God
> may have guided your deliberations and that He may abundantly
> bless you as you return to your homes in His service.

A workshop on ecumenism brought together, in four language groups, about 100 participants, including thirty-six Observers. One burning topic of the day was 'mixed marriages' and a Resolution on the issue was communicated to the Synod of Bishops. There was also a public symposium, introduced by Madeleine Barot of the Reformed Church of France. Commenting on her outline of the history and practice of the WCC, Thomas Stransky, CSP, from the Secretariat for Promoting Christian Unity, pointed to a difference in the origins of the ecumenical movement. Among Anglicans and Protestants, the movement developed mainly from the pressure of world mission, also among the laity; in the Roman Catholic Church, it came largely from theological reflection — notably that of Yves Congar. Stransky continued:[15]

> While the ecumenical movement was growing within the
> Protestant tradition and gradually reaching out to the Orthodox
> Churches, the Roman Catholic Church *officially* kept very much
> aloof. Suddenly it entered the movement, and the entrance is
> causing new problems for both itself and the other Christian
> Communions. I use the example of a huge, clumsy elephant outside
> a delicate garden, with his long trunk hanging over the wall, sniffing
> and seeing whether it was worthwhile to change his posture.
> Suddenly the elephant decides 'yes' and bursts through the walls.
> The result: an ecumenical garden that had been cultivated delicately
> and prudently for fifty years now finds this huge animal of 500
> million members sniffing and walking around *inside* the walls.[16]

Other speakers included Chakko George, Director of the Medical Mission of the Syrian Orthodox Church in India and John Littleton, of the Church of England in Australia. Introducing himself as a 'liberal' and impatient young Anglican, Littleton told of positive developments, but called for more pressure from the grassroots: 'Let us act and see what happens . . . Maybe, as individuals, we can drag our Church into unity, that we may be one'.

Annie Jiagge, a Justice of the High Court of Ghana and member of the Evangelical Presbyterian Church, if not impatient, was concerned:[17]

> I wonder whether our spiritual leaders in the Protestant
> Churches and in the Roman Catholic Church are prepared for
> the results of this Conference. If they are not, it looks as if there
> might be frustration . . . Enthusiasm may carry some people
> away so that they start running before they can crawl . . .

For Stransky, the tensions did not all come from the same source:[18]

> You find bishops that are very much enthused, and who
> are worried that the laity are not supporting them enough in
> ecumenism. You find pastors who say the same thing about
> their congregation. You find laity saying it about their pastors.

Madeleine Barot added a word of hope:[19]

> We must go step by step, listening as well as we can to the Holy Spirit... The graces we have received in this field during the last few years are so great that we cannot help feeling a very great hope.

Impressions

Enthusiasm, hope and prudence also emerged in the impressions registered by other ecumenical Observers after the Congress.[20]

Hamilcar Alivisatos of Athens, Observer–Consultant for the Church of Greece, sent a substantial report to the Church's Holy Synod:

> The administrated Church (the people) is fully cognizant of its rights within the ecclesiastical organization and of its Christian responsibilities. It is for this reason that it is asking for immediate rectification of what had been distorted, not in any spirit of hostility towards the Hierarchy, but in close cooperation with it, for the purpose of completely restoring the Church to its true place, and not a Utopian place, in the very heart of society.[21]

The experience of the Congress augured well, he thought, for future developments in Roman Catholic–Orthodox dialogue.

Two comments by Observers accompanying the Scottish National Delegation capture something of the joy and the thought-provoking novelty of the experience. Ian Fraser, Warden of Scottish Churches' House, Dunblane, wrote in *The Scotsman* (25 October 1967):

> In Rome one was aware of a struggle taking place. At times it seemed to be between the hierarchy and the rest of the Church; at times between reactionary and forward-looking thinking.

For the Countess of Mar and Kellie, Presbyterian and social worker among youth:

The world was certainly at the Congress — we were every shape, size and shade ... The Scots had included us in all their briefing meetings ... We arrived in Rome feeling part of the party; so much so that I heard myself saying: 'There goes our Bishop'. I found it difficult to pray in St Peter's — only elephant's tusks are missing from the décor! Yet, when the Pope stopped his chair opposite our tribune, one felt such a tremendous sense of being *en rapport* that I found myself clapping — shades of John Knox! I was jealous of your solidarity when, as one man, 3000 said the Credo together — then I saw the point of Latin![22]

The most comprehensive ecumenical comment came in the 'Impressions of an Observer–Consultant', presented at the closing session by Hans-Ruedi Weber under the title, 'A foretaste of things to come'. Weber compared this experience of the renewal stemming from the Second Vatican Council with his previous experience at the Second World Congress, 'disguised as a journalist, feeling utterly lost as the only non-Catholic among more than 2,000 Roman Catholics'. He continued:

This time, we Observer–Consultants, have felt almost totally at home, so much so that we speak no more about *your* Congress, but about *our* Congress ... You have now accepted us fully as participants and brothers in Christ. This time, the world has provided the agenda: the 'oikoumene' in the original sense of the term: 'the whole inhabited world'. This is an essential mark of true ecumenicity ... This time, nothing has impressed me more than our worship ... The most precious gift we take home from Rome is this set of liturgies. We have been taught how to bring in worship the hopes and anxieties of modern man before God, how to receive forgiveness for the concrete individual and social sins of our time, and how to be guided by the Word of God.

Weber, however, felt the lack of the corporate Bible study, so important in meetings of the WCC and so necessary for the growth of a 'mature laity'. Finally, he offered a plea:

> The challenge of our existence as Orthodox and Protestant Churches and our ecumenical experience has perhaps helped you a little in the renewal of your Church. Now I plead: Be patient with us and help us in our renewal.[23]

The culmination of the ecumenical experience was the Ecumenical Service held at St Paul's-without-the-walls on 17 October. Cardinal Bea joined the Congress in prayer. The liturgy booklet pointed out that:

> This should not be a service of prayer for Christian unity, but rather a service in which representatives of the various Christian communities would actively participate, and which would be focussed on the common mission of proclaiming the Gospel.

In the Invocation, Ian Thomson (Anglican Communion in England) prayed:[24]

> O God, our Father, God of all goodness and grace . . .
> Thank you for bringing us together, and for opening our eyes to a greater vision of our unity and mission in Christ.
> Prepare us that we may become instruments of your purpose, so that your kingdom may grow in the hearts of all men everywhere.
> We ask this in the name of Jesus Christ our Lord and Saviour.

A 'democratic' Church?

The safety-valve for the 'democratic' spirit of the Congress was the Assembly of the Heads of Delegations: 107 national and about sixty International delegations.[25] The Assembly met four times during the Congress week. The first three meetings were largely devoted to adoption of the Memorandum that was presented to the Synod of Bishops, on 15 October. The fourth meeting received twenty-four draft resolutions for debate. Three were adopted: two — on 'The

Handicapped' and 'Racism' — unanimously; one, 'Women in the Church', with two against and sixteen abstentions. This Resolution had been introduced by St Joan's International Alliance. A contested passage read:

> The World Congress for the Lay Apostolate wishes to express its desire that women be granted by the Church full rights and responsibilities as Christians, *both as regards the laity and the priesthood*.

An amendment introduced by the delegation of England and Wales led to the words in italics being changed to read: 'and a serious doctrinal study be pursued on the place of woman within the sacramental order and within the Church'.

The meeting resumed on 17 October and went from 9 p.m. to 2 a.m. the following morning. Five Resolutions were adopted: 'The Fight against Oppression'; 'Peace and World Community'; 'Development'; 'Mass Media'; 'Follow-up to the Congress'. The hardest nut to crack was the Resolution on Development. It summed up excellent work done in the workshop on Development, but included a formulation concerning responsible parenthood which originated from the workshops on the Family. After an arduous debate it was adopted:[26]

> In view of the agonizing problem of demographic expansion [the Congress recalls] the very strong feeling among Christian lay people that there is need for a clear stand by the teaching authorities of the Church which would focus on fundamental moral and spiritual values, while leaving the choice of scientific and technical means for achieving responsible parenthood to parents acting in accordance with their Christian faith and on the basis of medical and scientific consultation.

This took place several months before the publication of *Humanae Vitae*. When the Encyclical appeared in July 1968 the Congress proceedings were about to emerge from the press. 'Higher Authorities' decided to leave the Congress record as it was indicating that, given the date, it could not be understood as a disclaimer of the teaching of the Encyclical.

In accordance with a ruling of this Assembly, all draft resolutions — whether or not there had been time to discuss them — were published in the Proceedings. This was rash. Whatever the good will and the sense of urgency, it is always unwise — at times, almost immoral — to present, as the considered opinion of a group of serious people, formulations reached in the stress of protracted and generally nocturnal debate. Fortunately, the regulations of the Congress allowed a certain margin for revision and for the role of the Ecclesiastical Commission, presided over by Cardinal Maurice Roy.

This role had been vociferously contested at the beginning of the Congress when some enterprising persons (identity forever unknown) leaked a summary of remarks made by Cardinal Roy to the bishops accompanying delegations. They were not to block free speech in the Workshops:

> It may happen, in the heat of discussion, that one or another of the laity may speak in a manner that to us seems inexact from the point of view of the Church's doctrine . . . In his own diocese a Bishop might feel obliged to make a correction. But here the situation is different. If a lay person errs, there will surely be another lay person to express a more exact opinion. In addition, in each Workshop there is an Ecclesiastical Assistant who can help in replying to theological questions.

Years later I learned that this reasonable statement had been interpreted as an 'attempt to rig' the Congress, that it had caused a 'multilingual furore' while 'a dark cloud hovered over the Congress'; not even dispelled by a statement from Cardinal Roy given to the press later the same day. My quotations are from a review by Peter Hebbelthwaite in *The National Catholic Reporter* (18 September 1981) of a book by Jean-Guy Vaillancourt, *Papal Power: A Study of Vatican Control over Lay Catholic Elites* (University of California Press).[27] I regret that the reviewer, explaining that he did not share Vaillancourt's 'sense of shock' at the Cardinal's speech, added:

> Whoever heard of a Vatican event that was not preplanned? It would seem the height of folly to Roman curialists to embark on a congress without having its resolutions prepared.

If ever anything in a 'Roman' meeting was unprepared by the Curia, it was the Resolutions of the Third World Congress! After the Congress, we received hundreds of paper clippings from a Press Service (mostly from the United States), giving the impression that the lay people coming to the Congress had only two preoccupations: affirm the laity against the hierarchy, and obtain legitimisation of artificial birth control. If it had been true — which it was not — it was hardly something the Roman organisers would have pre-planned.

The other Resolution that may have inspired the comments of the daily press was on 'Follow-up to the Congress'. This 'respectfully requested' the Holy Father to enlarge the newly created *Consilium de Laicis*, 'in accordance with democratic processes' (not just by Papal appointment), as a step towards accelerating 'the democratic establishment of structures of the laity at all levels across the world'. It further urged the delegates to 'labour consistently for the democratic implementation at all levels' of the purposes of the 'proposed lay councils'.[28]

This was also the purport of the Memorandum adopted by the Assembly and presented to the Synod of Bishops by Mrs John Shields, President of the United States NCCW. Veronese had always returned to the distinction — more easily made in English than in other languages — between decision *making* and decision *taking*. Even when decisions to be taken are of the competence of the pastors, lay Christians can, and should as a general rule, be involved in their making. But the laity cannot always be represented by formal election. The call for 'democratic' structures during the Congress was useful if it meant structures operated in a 'democratic spirit', with consultation and dialogue. Nevertheless it was largely unrealistic. Not only must the pastors' freedom be respected, but election as a general rule at world level would suppose the existence, at all other levels, of democratically elected bodies representing the whole People of God. Much has since been attempted, but universal suffrage in a political sense cannot be the answer to the problem of coresponsibility in the life of the Church.

It was encouraging, in any case, to note that a post-mortem on the Congress held by the *Consilium de Laicis* revealed that, in Martin Work's words,[29] whereas:

> the delegation of the United States had been somewhat 'feverish' when they came to Rome, they left in much better health: their temperature had gone down . . . The remedy came especially from the free speech in the workshops and from the Assembly of Heads of delegations. ('It would have been a catastrophe', Martin Work said, 'if the Assembly had not existed'.) The delegation left without any complexes, knowing that they are active members of God's People.

'A responsible laity'

In his Christmas Address to the Cardinals, 23 December 1967, Paul VI recalled the event:[30]

> Among the events of the last six months which concern the Church's internal life and activity, the Third World Congress for the Lay Apostolate — held in Rome from 11 to 18 October last — has an outstanding place, for the subjects dealt with, for the number and quality of the participants and for its future consequences and its repercussion throughout the world . . .
>
> Many things were said at this meeting, and much has been written about it, and very well written, even if everything cannot be given unreserved approval and agreement. Among the many good things which emerged, We should like to mention one in particular: the sense of responsibility and of availability for the Church among the Catholic laity. The laity — and this is without doubt a most encouraging sign — feel responsible, both for the whole of mankind, to whom they want to show that the Church is involved in the spiritual penetration of temporal reality, and with respect to the Hierarchy and clergy, to whom they want to offer their own cooperation in the work of salvation and of 'service' to which the whole Church is called among men by her Founder's will.

We should like all these sons and daughters . . . to keep engraven in their hearts one impression: the Pope's love for them, the trust he places in them, and the invitation he addresses to them to work always in loyal harmony with the Church's magisterium and with the Hierarchy, whose only desire is to see them carrying out the tasks assigned to them by the recent Council.

1. *Insegnamenti di Paolo VI*, IV, pp. 98–101.

2. Only the Italian version managed to avoid exclusive language: 'Il Popolo di Dio nel cammino dell'umanità'.

3. The *Proceedings* was published by COPECIAL in 1968, in three volumes: I *God's People on Man's Journey*; II *Man Today*; III *The Laity in the Renewal of the Church*.

4. Thom Kerstiens, Introductory Lecture, in *Proceedings of the Third World Congress for the Lay Apostolate. I: God's People on Man's Journey,* vol. 1, pp. 43–63.

5. The full text of this part of O'Gara's concluding remarks is: For many unbelievers, the mediocrity of Christians is at least a justification, if not a cause, of unbelief. But this much is perhaps almost a cliché. I think that those of us who are Catholics must go further. We must say that the institutional Church must bear a large part of the blame for the increasing unbelief in the modern world. We have to admit, I think, that the Church has too often clung to the forms of the past, has failed to explore what is new. The style of the institutional Church is very often feudal, medieval, baroque. Authority and obedience are too often conceived in these feudal terms, and the men who arouse most suspicion are precisely those who want to explore what is new. Obviously we need institutions, but we need also to purify the Church in the light of the Gospel, to put away all the forms of princely splendour, to take on again the character of the suffering servant (*Proceedings*, Vol.2, op. cit., p. 55).

6. *Proceedings. I: God's People on Man's Journey*, op. cit., pp. 28–30.

7. Ibid, pp. 111–34.

8. Ibid, pp. 153–69.

9. Ibid, p. 152.

10. Paul VI's Prayer: *Proceedings of the Third World Congress for the Lay Apostolate*, Vol.1, Rome, 1968. Printed in photo section, between pp. 24 and 25.

11. Pius XII's Prayer: *Proceedings of the First World Congress for the Apostolate of the Laity*, Rome, 1968, p. 8.

12. Regrettably, this 'ecumenical happening' has been given little recognition. No ecumenical history of the past thirty years seems to have taken note of it. The Council's insistence that the effort to bring Christian unity closer concerns the *whole* Church (cf. Decree on Ecumenism, 5) is not often quoted; nor the reference to Ecumenism in the Decree on the Laity (27). And yet, Prayer for Unity and the 'ecumenism of collaboration' are, in practice, flourishing in many local situations and groups.

13. *Proceedings I: God's People on Man's Journey*, op. cit., pp. 40–2.

14. Ibid, p. 42.

15. Fr. Thomas Stransky CSP (USA) was a staff member of the Secretariat for Promoting Christian Unity from the foundation of the Secretariat in 1960. In 1970 he became Superior General of the Paulist Fathers. Today he is Director of the Ecumenical Institute of Tantur, Jerusalem.

16. *Proceedings III: The Laity in the Renewal of the Church*, pp. 165–7.

17. Ibid, p. 175.

18. Ibid, p. 175.

19. Ibid.

20. Cf. the review *The Laity Today*, Pontifical Council for the Laity, Vatican City, 4/5, December 1967.

21. *Ekklisia*, XLV, 1968; and, in a French translation, in the review *Proche Orient Chrétien*, Saint-Anne, Jerusalem (no date).

22. *Pax Romana Journal*, 6, Pax Romana, Fribourg, Switzerland, 1967, pp. 10–11.

23. 'A Foretaste of Things to Come', in *Proceedings II: God's People on Man's Journey*, pp. 138–44.

24. *Proceedings III: The Laity in the Renewal of the Church*, p. 193.

25. The texts adopted and a summary of the work done by the Assembly are published in *Proceedings II: Man Today*, pp. 223–39.

26. *Proceedings III: The Laity in the Renewal of the Church*, p. 288.

27. Vaillancourt had been given permission to make a sociological survey among Congress delegates as part of his research for Berkeley University. He was given every facility for his research. The results were never communicated to the organisers of the Congress.

28. *Proceedings II: Man Today*, p. 231.

29. Meeting of the *Consilium de Laicis* (no date).

30. *Insegnamenti di Paolo VI*, V, op. cit., pp. 637–8.

Part 3
LAITY IN THE POST-CONCILIAR CHURCH

'God writes straight with crooked lines'
(Portuguese proverb)

CHAPTER 7

Why speak about 'laity'?

A 'theology of the laity' had been gradually emerging during the years leading up to Vatican II although Yves Congar had already pointed out that 'there can be only one sound and sufficient theology of laity, and that is a "total ecclesiology" '.¹ Meanwhile, theologians — particularly Congar, Rahner, Schillebeeckx, Philips — vied with one another in a search for a positive definition of the laity, something more than the negative canonical definition (that is, neither clergy nor religious). In the Basic Text for the Congress of 1957, Philips defined the lay person as 'the Christian in the world' (without wishing to exclude clergy from the world!). In the preparation for Vatican II, these theologians were among the most influential 'periti'.

In the event, the Council stopped short of any 'positive definition' of the lay Christian. It simply completed the negative definition with: '[The lay Christian is called] to seek the Kingdom of God by engaging in temporal affairs and ordering them according to the plan of God' (*Lumen Gentium*, 31).² By virtue of his or her baptism the lay person is a member of the People of God, incorporated into the Body of Christ; of equal dignity — if not identical function — with the ordained minister.

Paradoxically, it is at this point in our history that we meet the question: Since all the baptised are full members of God's People, should we bother speaking about laity at all? The post-Conciliar Congress was hardly over when theological debate about laity disappeared almost completely. Bibliographies that had been growing apace suddenly showed signs of arrested development. The WCC noted symptoms also among its own constituency.³ Christians had new concerns in the turbulent years following 1968 and during the 'angry seventies' which brought new urgencies for the Churches: 'liberation' in its different forms, poverty and justice, development and peace, radical feminism, new nationalisms, inculturation and, overall, the secularisation — and secularism — accompanying the growth worldwide of a technological civilisation.

Attention to Vatican II was, at times, focused exclusively on *Gaudium et Spes*,⁴ on the Church in solidarity with the world. Scarcely remarked was the stress in *Gaudium et Spes* (43) on the approach to 'human affairs' that is specific for pastors of the Church who are to 'shed the light of the Gospel' in their dialogue with the world. Lay people, for their part, are to act, with attention to the Church's teaching, but on their own responsibility, not expecting expert solutions from their pastors for every problem but also not claiming the Church's authority for their own views.

Focus on the notion of laity as such was also diverted by a new attention to what came to be called coresponsibility. This expression, not found in the Council, was introduced by Cardinal Léon-Joseph Suenens.⁵ Although *Lumen Gentium*,⁶ in its chapter on the laity, reminds Pastors that:

> they were not established by Christ to undertake alone the
> whole salvific mission of the Church to the world, but . . .
> to be shepherds of the faithful and to recognize the latter's
> contribution and charisms so that everyone in his or her own
> way will, with one mind, cooperate in the common task. (30)

One form of coresponsibility that aroused much initial enthusiasm was that recommended in the Decree on Bishops, *Christus Dominus*⁷ (27): 'Every diocese should have a "Pastoral Council", presided over by the diocesan Bishop, in which clergy, religious and laity specially chosen for the purpose will participate'. The enthusiasm was often short-lived. Inadequate preparation and the inexperience of available lay people brought inevitable setbacks. In many cases, a fresh start gave better results.

Post-Conciliar coresponsibility also took the form of ministries exercised by lay people. 'In the Church there is diversity of ministry, but unity of mission', stated the Decree on the Lay Apostolate (2)[8]. Ministry here, however, was used in the wide sense of service. Only in the Decree on Missionary Activity is there any reference to a 'lay ministry' for catechists or for Catholic Action.

It was the Synod of Bishops of 1971 that introduced the subject, 'Diversity of Ministries'. This was followed by debate on the role — or roles — of women in the Church which accelerated, especially after the publication, in August 1972, of the document *Ministeria Quaedam*[9] which replaced 'Minor Orders' for the clergy by the 'Instituted Ministries' of acolyte and lector, open to the laity — but (scandal!) to lay*men* only. To increase confusion, in January 1973, came the Instruction *Immensae Caritatis*[10] from the Congregation for Divine Worship, authorising lay men *and* women to act as 'Extraordinary Ministers' for the distribution of the Eucharist. Finally, in November 1973, the French bishops, at their annual Assembly in Lourdes, received a report, 'The Ministry of Priests in a Church that is Wholly Ministerial'. What did this 'ministeriality' mean? Could every service in the Church be termed a ministry? Taking up the collection or making coffee? To clarify matters, Yves Congar gave, in Lourdes, a definition of non-ordained ministries that has since been widely used:

> Ministries are particular services of vital importance, that are necessary for the life of the Church, in any case for the Church's well-being . . . involving real responsibility . . . recognized by the local Church . . . instituted, for instance, by a liturgical act . . . Finally, implying a certain duration.[11]

These different, if not divergent, enthusiasms — solidarity with the world and pastoral responsibility in the Church — combined with the crisis of all institutions after the student uprisings in 1968, led to a serious decline in lay organisations. Groups appeared and disappeared. There was a polarisation between groups for social activism and those concentrating on spirituality. The situation is reflected in the last major document of Paul VI, *Evangelii Nuntiandi*[12] (Evangelization in the Modern World'), published 8 December 1975. 'Small communities' (*communautés de base*) were the new thing at the time and the Pope's document states that they can be 'a hope for the universal Church', but only if they:

> do not allow themselves to be ensnared by political polarization or fashionable ideologies; if they avoid the ever present temptation of systematic protest and a hypercritical attitude; if they do not isolate themselves and are never sectarian. (58)

In the same document Paul VI defined the 'primary and immediate task' of lay Christians: 'to put to use every Christian and evangelical possibility latent but already present and active in the affairs of the world'(70). We are told, however, not to forget 'the other dimension: the laity can also feel called, or be called, to work with their Pastors in the service of ecclesial community ... by exercising a great variety of ministries ... ' (73)

The identification of laicity or secularity, not only as a dimension of the whole Church, but as specific for lay Christians was called into question in a heated controversy among Italian theologians in the 1980s. One of the better-known young theologians, Bruno Forte, crossed swords with a veteran: Giuseppe Lazzati had been, for more than thirty years, writing and speaking on the laity and their 'Christian commitment in temporal reality', including political reality.[13]

Perhaps the simplest and clearest approach to the vexed question of whether — or how — to speak of laity was given by another Italian theologian, Tullio Citrini: *layman is a 'pastoral concept'*, not a theological category. 'There are as many lay vocations as there are lay people'.[14] This was also the approach taken some ten years later by Avery Dulles:

> Unfortunate though the name *laity* may be, we nevertheless need a term to designate Christians who are not members of the clergy or religious institutes, and no other term seems to be available.[15]

The term may be unfortunate because, in common parlance, lay means lacking in expertise. In other contexts it can have political overtones. (In Italy, a *partito laico* is a party without religious reference, and possibly anticlerical).

In the same address, Avery Dulles questioned the terminology of the word ministry:

> In Vatican II, the secular activities of Christians, whether clerical or lay, were generally designated by the more general term *apostolate*. For some reason the term has recently fallen out of favor, but I hope that it may be salvaged or restored. The term *ministry* is being used in so many different senses that confusion is created. I do not find it helpful to describe professional services such as psychiatry or legal aid, even though given to the poor free of charge, as 'ministries'.

Congar's definition, if adhered to, could be the solution. Congar's own post-Conciliar reflection, on the 'ecclesiology of communion', gave special importance to ministries; to a 'community based on ministries and charisms'.[16] What we need would seem to be a good synthesis of Congar's pre-Council insights on lay secularity and his post-Council approach to a diversity of ministries within the Church as communion.[17]

In the Catholic Church, the temporary eclipse of laity has, in any case, been relative. Paul VI and his successors have continued to speak the language of Vatican II. And in many cultural contexts — especially among the 'younger' Churches in Africa and Asia — the lay apostolate has continued to be promoted in Conciliar (at times, even pre-Conciliar) terms.

The question of semantic change, with special reference to the meaning of ministry, was addressed by Dolores R. Leckey in her book *Laity Stirring the Church: Prophetic Questions*.[18] Leckey brings her experience as Executive Director of the United States Bishops Committee on the laity — more a nationwide 'dialogue ministry' than a desk job, one gathers — as well as her personal experience, her wit and wisdom. She did not convert me to the current use of the term ministry; but her thinking on spirituality; marriage and the family; women; changes and challenges; the world of work; call to co-creation; community, suggested great hope for the Church both in and beyond the United States of America.

1. *Lay People in the Church*, translated by David Attwater, Geoffrey Chapman, London, 1985, p. xvi.

2. Cf. Austin Flannery, *Vatican Council II: The Conciliar and Post-Conciliar Documents*, The Liturgical Press, Collegeville, Minnesota, 1975.

3. Discussion on the laity only returned to the WCC agenda in 1993, following the First World Convention of Christian Lay Centres and Movements (Montreat, NC, USA, September 1993). Cf. *The Ecumenical Review*, WCC, Geneva, 4, October 1993: 'Reopening the ecumenical discussion of the laity'.

4. Austin Flannery, *Vatican Council II: More Post-Conciliar Documents*, New York, 1982.

5. Cf. L. J. Suenens, *La coresponsabilité dans l'Eglise d'aujourd'hui*, Desclée de Brouwer, Paris, 1968.

6. Austin Flannery, *Vatican Council II: The Conciliar and Post-Conciliar Documents*, op. cit.

7. Ibid.

8. Ibid.

9. Ibid.

10. Ibid.

11. Congar's quote from Lourdes: *Tous responsables dans L'Eglise*, Centurion, Paris, 1973, pp. 58–60.

12. Austin Flannery, *Vatican Council II: The Conciliar and Post-Conciliar Documents*, op. cit.

13. Cf. The review *Regno Attualità*, 12, 1985, p. 339.
   Lazzati (1909–86), historian of the early centuries of Christian literature, served in an Alpine regiment at the beginning of the war, before maturing his reflection and his personal holiness in a German concentration camp. After the war he was a member of the Constituent Assembly of the Italian Republic in 1946 and later Rector of the Catholic University of Milan.

14. Cf. his article on the theological basis of laicity in the light of Conciliar ecclesiology, in *Presenza pastorale*, Rome, March–April, 1978.

15. 'Can the Word Laity Be Defined?' — an address to the Catholic League for Civil and Religious Rights, published in *Origins*, vol. 18, 29, Catholic News Service, Washington DC, 29 December 1988, p. 71.

16. Cf. Congar's 'Itinerary in the Theology of the Laity and of Ministries', in *Ministères et Communion ecclésiale*, Editions du Cerf, Paris, 1971.

17. To explain the phrase 'the church as communion' adequately would require another book! It expresses the unity that makes the Church 'one in Christ'; 'communion' between all baptised members of the Church; between local Churches and the universal Church; 'communion' with the Pope. It includes participation, interdependence, coresponsibility. It is typical of the thinking that prepared Vatican II and emerged from Vatican II. The best reference might be the Encyclical of John Paul II on 'Commitment to Ecumenism', *Ut Unum Sint* (That they may be one), 25 May 1995.

18. Laity Exchange Books, Fortress Press, Philadelphia, 1987.

CHAPTER 8

Associations, movements, communities, 'charisms'

Before Vatican II, any reference to lay apostolate would have suggested to most people *organised* forms of Christian witness and apostolic activity. This is reflected in the Decree on the Lay Apostolate. Chapter IV, 'The Various Forms of Apostolate' begins, however, with the individual apostolate, 'the origin and condition of the whole Lay Apostolate ... which admits of no substitute'; and which, in certain 'special circumstances', can be the only possible form of apostolate. The circumstances could refer to Catholics living in a diaspora situation — 'few in number and widely dispersed'; or to 'professional' commitments (political life or international civil service) where mutual support could be given in small informal groups rather than in recognised associations; but especially to situations 'where the freedom of the Church is seriously hindered'.[1]

In 1966, during the Second European Lay Apostolate Meeting, the Polish delegation explained their own situation. In the 1930s, in response to the call to Catholic Action issued by Pius XI, a vast network of associations had been set up, more or less modelled on what existed in Italy. However, war and occupation had swept everything away. The only organisations now authorised by the regime were clubs of 'intellectuals' in several cities; so pastoral activity had to be reconstructed on the basis of parish and diocese. There were advantages in such a situation, as Archbishop (later Cardinal) Bolislao Kominek pointed out on one occasion. There was no danger of clinging to obsolete forms of association. But the situation was certainly limiting. In 1967, the Consultor, Cardinal Karol Wojtyla, explained to members of the *Consilium de Laicis* the approach that had been adopted in Poland by the competent Bishops' Commission. They recognised an *organised* apostolate in the parish (catechesis, liturgy, charitable activity, pastoral action in the university); an *organic* apostolate in the family; an *individual* apostolate for the professions. The work of the *Consilium* was to bring the future John Paul II in contact with many other forms of organised lay activity.

The greater part of Chapter IV of the Conciliar Decree[2] stresses the 'importance of the *organized* Apostolate and the wide variety of its forms'. The 'group apostolate' corresponds to a human need for community. Together with family, parish and diocese, it also 'signifies the community and unity of the Church in Christ'. From a pragmatic standpoint, 'only the pooling of resources can make it possible fully to achieve the aims of the modern apostolate'. The 'wide variety' of associations comes from diversity of aims, but also from the variety of situations. 'Nor will it always be fitting to transfer indiscriminately forms of the apostolate that have been used in one nation to other nations'. The voice of experience can be heard here. Specialised Catholic Action movements (YCW, YCS, etc.) had come in for criticism from bishops in the younger Churches for their calm assumption that their programs were applicable everywhere without adaptation to local needs and pastoral planning.

N.20 of the Decree defines the four characteristics that together constitute Catholic Action, with or without the name: a 'general' apostolic aim; effective lay responsibility; organic unity; cooperation with the hierarchy. For Paul VI, Catholic Action understood in this way was 'part of the constitutional design and the operative programme of the Church'[3] and 'a singular form of lay ministeriality'.[4]

Chapter V of the Decree further spells out lessons from experience: the importance of unity and coordination among groups, always tempted to rivalry; different relationships to the hierarchy according to the nature of the groups concerned; the supporting roles of clergy and religious; etc. One last section, reflecting experience of the Council, recommends 'dynamic and prudent cooperation' with other Christians on the basis of the 'common heritage of the Gospel and the common duty of Christian witness'. On the basis of 'common human values' there can also be cooperation with 'those who do not profess Christ's name, but acknowledge these values'(27).

After such careful attention to the organised apostolate, one might have expected, after the Council, a great flowering, together with judicious pruning, of the whole sector. Problems had emerged in the course of debate but no one could have foreseen the upheaval that was to come; the crisis of organisations generally that swept through the economically developed countries, compounded with the crisis of authority in the Church that followed the publication of *Humanae Vitae* in 1968.

In the years following Vatican II small informal groups tended to take the place of formal associations. Political commitment — often tinged with Marxist ideology — clashed with the relationship to the hierarchy of specialised Catholic Action, especially among workers and rural youth. In France, where 'the apostolate in the social milieu' was the most characteristic form of Catholic Action, the bishops met the crisis with a liberating action. They decided, in 1975, to withdraw the much discussed hierarchical 'mandate' from the Catholic Action movements, leaving them freer to adopt 'temporal options' consistent with their faith, but which might not be those of the Church nor of other Catholic movements.

In Italy, the post-Conciliar crisis was followed by the emergence of new movements, but also by a radical renewal of Italian Catholic Action, responsive to changes taking place in society. The Association kept its unitary structure, but old divisions — men/women and young men/young women — were done away with (with some loss of efficacy in sectors where women had always been the most active elements). There remained two sectors — adults and youth — with a movement for children, and specialised movements for university students, 'intellectuals', workers, etc. More difficult than these structural changes, was the defining and implementation of what was called the religious or pastoral option. This was sometimes understood as taking lay people away from their 'primary tasks' in social, economic, cultural and political life. In reality, the aim — and the effect — was, and still is, to equip for these tasks, with an evangelical perspective, in collaboration with pastoral approaches of the bishops and without involving the Association in party politics. New statutes were adopted in 1969. This complex process was carried out under the guidance of Paul VI. Its principal agent was Vittorio Bachelet — President of Italian Catholic Action from 1964–73, assisted by the Vice-President, Sitia (Teresa) Sassudelli.

On 12 February 1980, Bachelet was to pay for his commitment to the social responsibility of the Catholic intellectual with his life. As a student he was an active member of the FUCI, and later of the *Movimento Laureati* (Graduate Movement of Italian Catholic Action). From 1976 he was Vice-President of the Supreme Law Council (whose President is the President of the Italian Republic). All who knew Bachelet counted on him, not only for the warm smile of friendship, but for a calm, reflective wisdom, rooted in faith. It was only after he died that many of us discovered that 'our Vittorio' was a recognised authority in the legal field, his death as deeply regretted by the agnostic or the unbeliever among his colleagues. He was coming away from the University of Rome, where he was Professor of Administrative Law, when he was shot down by terrorists from the Red Brigades.

The new era of group endeavour

New movements emerged as centres of interest in many countries, especially in Europe and North America where traditional associations were on the wane or struggling for renewal. These movements were not all particularly 'new', but they did show new energy and adopt new approaches. They were sometimes described together as 'charismatic'. This could but did not necessarily refer to the Catholic Charismatic Renewal (CCR) or 'Renewal in the Spirit'. CCR originated in Pittsburgh, United States, in 1967 and spread rapidly — seemingly by spontaneous generation — in the form of prayer groups, where healing, 'speaking in tongues' and 'baptism in the Spirit' were practised. Lay leadership was normal — at least, the leadership of lay *men*, women being more often assigned a subordinate role. Theological problems inevitably arose, and were confronted at the highest level. A turning point was the Catholic Charismatic Conference held in Rome in the Holy Year 1975. Pope Paul gave prudent encouragement to members, thousands strong, who thronged St Peter's Basilica, after a Mass celebrated by Cardinal Suenens.

Other movements, hitherto known as movements for spirituality, also took as reference the Council's teaching on charisms (gifts):

> It is not only through sacraments and the ministrations of the Church that the Holy Spirit makes holy the People, leads them and enriches them with his virtues. Allotting his gifts according as he wills (cf. 1 Cor 12:11), he also distributes special graces among the faithful of every rank . . . Those who have charge over the Church should judge the genuineness and proper use of these gifts, through their office, not indeed to extinguish the Spirit, but to test all things and hold fast to what is good (cf. 1 Thess 5:12 & 19–21). (*Lumen Gentium*, 12)[5]

Among these Movements are the Focolarini, founded in 1943 by Chiara Lubich, and now present worldwide, spreading their charism of unity.[6] In Italy, the Movement, Communion and Liberation (*Comunione e Liberazione*, CL) grew out of the experience of its founder, Luigi Giussani. In the 1950s, he had been chaplain to the Student Movement of Catholic Action. In the crisis of the 1960s, the Movement moved into the university context, where its militant approach to anti-communism and anti-secularism had divisive effects. Its leaders went on to develop a complex network of social, cultural, journalistic and even political activities, as well as organising the spectacular annual meeting held at Rimini on the Adriatic coast. Thousands of members were rallied through community catechesis and concrete tasks that called at times for courage and radical commitment. As adults members formed the Association of the Fraternity of CL. At the heart of the Movement a group, *Memores Domini* of consecrated laity, lay people who have taken vows of poverty, chastity and obedience, acted as a spiritual powerhouse. Today the Movement also has its own Missionary Seminary, which has sent priests to serve in various European countries. One team (ordained ministers and laity) is at work in Novosibirsk, capital of Siberia. This whole complex of ideas and activities defies definition. What is the charism of CL? It is clear, at least, that Giussani is a charismatic personality, who is able to stir enormous enthusiasm among young people.

A panorama

At the Synod of Bishops of 1987 on the 'Vocation and Mission of the Laity', Guzman Carriquiry from Uruguay, Under-Secretary of the Pontifical Council for the Laity, presented a panorama of Associations of the Faithful.[7] In an historical overview, he recalled expressions of community and 'spiritual affinity' arising in 'periods of critical cultural transition': the first monastic groups during the crisis of the Roman–Christian Empire; the Mendicant movements arising from urban life in the Middle Ages; the groups formed around the first Jesuits during the Counter-Reformation; and those stemming from the missionary thrust of the Church in the 19th century.

Today, the new ecclesial movements coexist with the centuries-old witness of Confraternities, Third Orders, Christian Life Communities (formerly Sodalities of Our lady). The Conferences of St Vincent de Paul (founded in 1833 by Frederick Ozanam), and the women's International Association of Charities (founded by St Vincent himself in 1617) are adapting to the demands of new forms of poverty. The pioneering work of St Vincent Pallotti (1795–1850), St John Bosco (1815–88) and Adolph Kolping (1813–65) is still bearing fruit. In recent years also, more and more lay movements have been formed in association with religious communities of long standing — seeking to share the particular charism of the Institute. We have, not only the lay Cooperators of the Salesians of Don Bosco, but the Lassallian Family (related to the De La Salle Brothers), the Canossian Laity (associated with the Congregations founded by St Magdalen of Canossa), the Carmelite Family, and so on.[8]

From new movements can grow new communities. These are ecclesial rather than specifically lay. Their members are priests, religious and lay people, married or single, in relationships that are not hierarchical. Their charism may imply particular forms of evangelisation; but it is their community life of praise, prayer and fraternal charity that specifies them rather than any particular task.

These various forms of association differ from Catholic Action, created to collaborate with the pastoral action of the local Church. And they are even more different from the CIO that, with expertise in particular fields, allow the voice of organised public opinion to be heard, from a Christian standpoint, in relevant debates at the level of the United Nations and its specialised agencies. In the 1950s, the peak time of the Conference of CIO, the Organizations were jealous of their lay character. They counted priests among their members, but generally as experts in scientific fields, mass media, etc. The World Federation of Sodalities of Our Lady was admitted to membership only after lengthy debate and in recognition of their commitment to the betterment of society, in their assistance to those in poverty and their promotion of justice and peace. It required the direct intervention of the Holy See to gain admittance for the worldwide Legion of Mary.

Seeking recognition

Like other associations with a claim to internationality, the 'new ecclesial movements seeking recognition at this level must apply to the Pontifical Council for the Laity'.[9] They are expected to conform to the 'criteria of ecclesiality' that were first formulated by the Italian Bishops' Conference in 1981, and later taken up in the post-Synodal Exhortation *Christifideles Laici* (30).[10] The criteria concern the 'call to holiness', profession of faith, communion with Pope and Bishop, willingness to cooperate with other groups, and a 'presence in society' in the light of the Church's social teaching.

Associations can be approved as public, if established by the hierarchy; otherwise they are private.[11] Catholic Action (in the sense intended by the Council) is a Public Association. So also is the Community of St Egidio — called after the little church where, since 1969, young people have been meeting for evening prayer and organising themselves to help poor children, lonely old people, the sick, the homeless, in the picturesque, but grubby, back streets of this ancient Roman district, where St Paul may have lived and St Francis came to visit his Little Brothers. Today the Community has spread to other cities, even other continents. Their spiritual leader, Vincenzo Paglia, parish priest of the Basilica of Santa Maria in Trastevere, has written on Medieval Confraternities and their modern resurgence. The President, Andrea Riccardi, is also an historian. 'St Egidio' has entered in spectacular ways into *modern* history. With representatives of the Italian Government, it has taken part in mediation to end the struggle between Government and rebels in Mozambique. As a follow-up to the historic interreligious meeting convoked by John Paul II at Assisi in 1986, it has organised annually a colourful and prayerful series of similar meetings for peace in Warsaw, Bari, Malta, Brussels, Milan, Rome. Like CL, 'St Egidio' defies all attempts at classification.

The movements meet

The new movements have come together in a series of meetings of a special kind. In 1981, CL took the initiative — in association with the Polish Movement 'Light and Life' — of bringing together, in Rome, movements differing in history, size and spirituality. John Paul II celebrated Mass for the group at his summer residence at Castel Gandolfo. He greeted them enthusiastically:

> The Church herself is a movement and, above all, a mystery . . . a movement within the history of humankind and of human communities. The Movements in the Church must mirror the mystery of the love from which the Church was born and continues to be born . . .

Seen as a 'source of hope' for the Church, the Movements were also greeted by Bishop Paul Cordes, Vice-president of the Pontifical Council for the Laity. He was to become successor to Cardinal Suenens as delegate of John Paul II for contact with the CCR worldwide. In April 1991, he presided over a further meeting in Bratislava (Czechoslovakia). Following the events of 1989, the majority of the movements represented were from Eastern Europe and were answering the call to a new evangelisation. This could invite the question: What is the greater need for the local Churches of countries emerging from ideological oppression, denial of religious freedom and practical atheism? New movements fostering particular charisms, or help in mobilising and equipping lay collaboration for the reconstruction of normal pastoral activity adapted to the new cultural and social situations?

New (religious) movements — sects and cults

In the 1980s, the proliferation of sects, cults or — more neutrally — new religious movements, had become a major concern of mainstream Churches worldwide. Their origins were diverse: Christian, non-Christian, Hindu, 'Afro', humanistic. Their beliefs ranged from the traditional to the fantastic; their methods from the conventional to the sinister; their aims from the idealistic to the purely economic. But, in the name of religion, all managed to attract, even to entrap, seekers after truth or consolation, happiness or success. Latin America was their happy hunting-ground, but no continent was exempt.

In February 1984, in response to urgent appeals from Bishops' Conferences, the Holy See began to gather information worldwide and, in 1986, published a document, *Sects or New Religious Movements: Pastoral Challenge*.[12] The aim was not to anathematise, but to give a summary glance at this many-sided reality, inducing a Christian attitude and a pastoral approach to those who felt — or were — threatened.

The 1980s were also the years of an upsurge of movements within the Catholic Church. A research project of the International Federation of Catholic Universities showed that certain factors which were drawing people to the sects and away from the Churches could also account in part for the attraction exerted by some Christian movements: warmth, colour and spontaneity in religion; ready answers to complex questions; the chance to participate in something 'special'; the fascination of a charismatic leader. Reflection on experience within the Church did not identify movements with sects or cults, but it did reveal the sectarian tendencies that can develop whenever group experience is deeply felt. The movement can become for its members the only way of 'being the

Church', of following Christ. A strongly doctrinal approach can become fundamentalist; charismatic leadership can be exercised as power.[13]

Voices from the Synod

The whole question of movements and associations was the focus of considerable interest and some heated debate during the 1987 Synod of Bishops on the Laity. Four interventions give some idea of the underlying tensions:[14]

> The various movements are capable of awakening faith and helping people to rediscover Christ. Still they must be perfected: by *a decisive insertion into the overall apostolate of the local Churches*; by sincere obedience to and communion with the Pastor of the local Church ... *No movement can ... judge itself self-sufficient, or think that those who do not belong to it are not authentic Christians ...*
> Aloisio Lorscheider, Archbishop of Fortaleza (Brazil)
> 8 October

> Ecclesial movements are historical forms with which the Spirit helps the mission of the Church today ... Two factors are necessary: The first: total openness of the charism to the ecclesial institution and therefore *obedience to the Bishop.* The second: *freedom, through which the fatherhood of the Bishop, beyond his own opinions and expectations, knows how to respect the identity of the charism,* and welcome as a constructive factor ... the concreteness of forms which the charism assumes in the diocese ... *in the living Communion with the Successor of Peter,* place of ultimate peace for each member of the faithful.
> Luigi Giussani, Founder of CL and 'expert' at the Synod,
> 9 October

> On the possible problems facing spiritual movements, the Pastor cannot give a 'political' response ... He would deprive himself of his own legitimacy if he scorned in others the same Spirit which gives him power. *The antagonism between individual Church*

*and universal Church is held in balance by the Chair of Peter
. . . Spiritual movements bring tensions here and there,
but 'new wine' has always put old wineskins into crisis.*
> Bishop Paul J. Cordes, Vice-president of the Pontifical
> Council for the Laity, 10 October

The Church in Italy can count on many lively forces. Besides 'traditional' associations (e.g. Catholic Action, Scouts), there are many groups, organized and not, whose action is efficacious . . .

There are also many associations that are referred to as 'new', in so far as they were born or have grown in recent decades . . . They are committed and capable of arousing enthusiasm. *Our principal pastoral duty before these new realities is discernment, which means not only evaluation, but also accompaniment over time . . . The particular Church, in the communion of the Churches, is the natural place for discernment of the path chosen by a movement.*
> Cardinal Carlo Maria Martini, Archbishop of Milan,
> 12 October

Clearly, the relation of the 'fatherhood of the Bishop' to communion with the Bishop of Rome was not always interpreted for the movements in quite the same way. The post-Synodal Exhortation, *Christifideles Laici*, when presenting the 'new era of group endeavour', rather than resolving the problem, seems to suggest that it is already resolved: 'The communion with Pope and Bishop must be expressed in loyal readiness to embrace the doctrinal teachings and pastoral initiatives of both Pope and Bishop'.[15]

Questioning the movements

The complexity of the whole situation in which the new movements developed was reflected in a seminar organised at the Pastoral Institute of the Pontifical Lateran University in 1991. The students invited key representatives from a number of movements (Focolarini, CL, neo-catechumenal communities) and also from traditional associations (Catholic Action, Catholic Scouting, Christian Life Communities).

Discussion after the presentations made by the visitors produced a number of questions.

Does the generic use of the term 'movement' take into account the diversity that is involved? What does the term mean in an ecclesial context? It can refer to the dynamism of the Spirit in the Church ('The Church is a movement', John Paul II said); to biblical, liturgical, ecumenical, charismatic movements; to movements — old and new — for spirituality or social activism. It can even be used to describe a community — like the Emmanuel Community which, in several countries, 'evangelises' the family, the neighbourhood, the workplace, the passers-by on city streets and squares.

The phenomena involved, besides being highly diversified, can be extremely *fluid*. A spontaneous group can become a movement — at local, national and even international level — and then become a structured association, with statutes defining its nature and aims. Or it can simply disappear (especially if it is a youth movement) as charismatic leaders 'move' elsewhere.

Another questionmark can be attached to the current ubiquity of the term 'charism'. (There is an inflation of 'charisms' within the Church!) After Vatican II made the theology of charisms more widely known, pre-Conciliar movements for spirituality (or for one of the great 'spiritualities' that have grown within the history of the Church: Benedictine, Franciscan, Dominican, Carmelite etc.) began to define themselves as founded on a charism. Was this a mere change of terminology? A theological reinterpretation? A new experience of the action of the Spirit? And what is meant when members claim to share the charism of their Founder?

John Paul II, laity and movements

Every Pope brings to the Petrine ministry his background, his gifts — and his limitations, responding in his own way to the burdens and the joys of his office, and to the situation of the world in which he is called to live.

From the beginning of his Pontificate, John Paul II has wanted his doctrinal and pastoral approach to the laity — the *Christifideles laici* —

to be in continuity with that of Paul VI and, above all, in fidelity to Vatican II with stress on the teachings of *Lumen Gentium*, *Gaudium et Spes* and the Decree on the Lay Apostolate. As well as innumerable talks to groups of all kinds on every continent, there have been major post-Conciliar documents on what are specifically lay concerns: the Exhortation *Familiaris Consortio*[16] (the Family) and the Encyclical *Laborem Exercens*[17] (Work) both published in 1981. The teaching is summed up in *Christifideles Laici* (1988), which develops themes from Vatican II in the light of the 1987 Synod of Bishops on Laity.

The post-Conciliar situation is clearly reflected in three sections of the post-Synodal document: firstly in the chapter entitled 'Women and Men' (49–52), which deals with positive developments for women in the Church (ordination excluded); secondly in the section on ministries entrusted to the laity (23). The latter marks a certain development, since John Paul II has always been wary of the term 'ministry' applied to lay people — fearing confusion with the ordained ministry. Nevertheless, after a general introduction on 'ministries, offices and roles of the lay faithful', the whole question is referred to a Commission set up after the Synod, but whose findings have not yet been made public. A third area, concentrating on group forms of participation (29) is not only post-Conciliar, but belongs specifically to the Pontificate of John Paul II. It greets 'a new era of group endeavour'.

If there are elements of continuity with the Pontificate of Paul VI,[18] there are evident differences of background and approach. We have seen 'Pope Wojtyla' coming from a situation where the possibilities of organised apostolate were extremely limited. Giovanni Battista Montini had grown up with Catholic Action — its merits and its problems — as part of the Italian scene. He had helped to build its ethos of Christian secular responsibility as chaplain to the FUCI: a responsibility of 'authentic' lay people, expressed in a particular form of cooperation with the pastoral ministry of bishop and priest. He suffered deeply from dissent; he demanded fidelity and obedience — but in a climate of dialogue.[19] He found a similar blend of secularity and ecclesial spirit among the CIO, whose growth he had fostered.

John Paul II appreciated the heritage of organised lay commitment stemming from Vatican II. He was ready to encourage the post-

Conciliar approaches of Italian Catholic Action and other traditional associations, but he also had his own priorities. After the institutional crisis of the 1970s, new movements were claiming attention — movements which corresponded to some of his deep concerns: direct evangelisation; missionary drive; fostering of priestly and religious vocations; unwavering adherence to 'sound' doctrine (38). There were movements that tended to seek affirmation of their charism by direct appeal to the Pope — to the Petrine principle, the supreme authority of the Pope as successor to St Peter — often without much reference to the local Church. There movements which responded enthusiastically — to his repeated calls to youth, reflected in the Letter to Youth of 1985, and the series of Messages which recall, without being able to recapture, the spiritual dynamism of the World Youth Days.[20, 21]

1. Austin Flannery, *Vatican Council II: The Conciliar and Post-Conciliar Documents*, op. cit.

2. Ibid.

3. All of Pope Paul VI's addresses to Italian Catholic Action are published in the volume *L'ACI nel magistero di Paolo VI*, Editrice AVE, Rome, 1980.

4. Ibid.

5. Austin Flannery, *Vatican Council II: The Conciliar and Post-Conciliar Documents*, op. cit.

6. The Publishing House of the Focolarini produces material on the Movement, its history and spirituality: Città Nuova, Roma; New City Press, New Rochelle, New York.

7. *Lay Voices at the Synod*, 19, Documentation Service of the Pontifical Council for the Laity, Vatican City, 1988, pp. 141–51.

8. Cf. Aquilino Bocos Merino, CMF, 'Lay associations created under the inspiration of institutes of consecrated life', in *All Branches of the One Vine*, 28, Documentation Service of the Pontifical Council for the Laity, Vatican City, 1984, pp. 92–101.

9. Cf. *Christifideles laici*, 31, Post-Synodal Apostolic Exhortation of John Paul II on the Vocation and Mission of the Lay Faithful in the Church and in the World, 30 December 1988, in *Insegnamenti di Giovanni Paolo II*, XI.4, 1988, pp. 1967–2082.

10. Ibid.

11. Cf. Canon Law Society of Great Britain & Ireland, in association with the Canon Law Societies of Australia, New Zealand and Canada, *Code of Canon Law*, Collins Liturgical, London, 1983, Can. 312 and 322.

12. The full text is published by the Information Service of the Secretariat for Promoting Christian Unity, Vatican City, 61, 1986, III.

13. This challenge to Pastors to exercise *their* charism of *discernment* with regard to movements that are 'new' or not so new: cf. Gordon Urquhart, *The Pope's Armada*, Bantam Press, London & New York, 1995.

14. The interventions are quoted from the summaries published in the English edition of *L'Osservatore Romano* (19 & 26 October 1987). The italics are mine.

15. *Christifideles Laici*, (30), op. cit.

16. *Familiaris Consortio*, Post-Synodal Apostolic Exhortation on the Christian Family in the Modern World, 22 November 1981. English text in Austin Flannery, OP, *Vatican Council II. More Post-Conciliar Documents*, Dominican Publications, Dublin, 1982, pp. 815–98.

17. Encyclical *Laborem Exercens* on Human Work, 14 September 1981, in *Insegnamenti di Giovanni Paolo II*, IV.2, pp. 154–266.

18. Cf. Peter Hebblethwaite, *Paul VI. The First Modern Pope*, HarperCollins*Religious*, London, 1993.

19. Cf. the first Encyclical of Paul VI: *Ecclesiam Suam*, 6 August 1964.

20. These traits are also found in *Opus Dei*, which is sometimes quoted among the movements. Opus Dei did indeed start life as a 'Pious Union', for the Christian formation and professional apostolate of lay men. As such it was recognised in 1941 under the Canon Law current at the time. After the promulgation by Pius XII of the Apostolic Constitution *Provida Mater Ecclesia*, in

1947, *Opus Dei* found a new status; it became a Secular Institute, with a male branch (priests and laity) and a female branch. Finally, in 1982, it became a *Personal Prelature*: a status made to measure to ensure freedom of action for the vast and varied commitments of its lay members. Under the *Code of Canon Law* of 1983 (Can.294–97), a Personal Prelature is composed of 'deacons and priests of the secular clergy', and 'presided over by a Prelate as its proper Ordinary'. 'Lay people can dedicate themselves to the apostolic work of a personal prelature by way of agreements made with the prelature.' It is subject only to the authority of the Pope.

21. The first World Youth Day was convened by John Paul II on the occasion of the International Youth Year proclaimed by the United Nations for 1985. Since then it has become an annual event in Rome (and every diocese) on Palm Sunday, and in every other year, also in a different city at a date to be fixed and with the presence of the Pope. Youth have gathered in great numbers in Buenos Aires, Santiago de Compostela, Czestochowa, Denver, Manila and Paris, to pray and celebrate, and reflect on a message from the Pope, sent out beforehand. For the young people it can be an unforgettable experience, as well as for John Paul II, who enters into it with all his authentic charism!

CHAPTER 9

Council 'on', 'of' or 'for' the Laity

On 14 July 1966, the Australian News and Information Bureau in Canberra published an item from Associated Press of America:

> Pope Paul has named an Australian woman to a special committee to mobilize the Roman Catholic Church for an active role in the war on hunger.

Well, not exactly! I was the woman concerned and the special committee was the final stage in a long process of consultation, begun during the preparatory phase of Vatican II, to determine the future role of the Secretariat that the Decree *Apostolicam Actuositatem*[1] (26) recommended 'should be established at the Holy See for the service and promotion of the lay apostolate'. The Committee's terms of reference concerned, however, not only this N.26, but also recommendations for implementing 90 of *Gaudium et Spes*, which suggested the creation of 'some organization of the universal Church whose task it would be to arouse the Catholic community to promote the progress of areas which are in want and foster social justice between nations'.[2]

Confusion about the nature of the Committee was not surprising. Even Vatican Radio referred to it as a 'Provisional Committee for the Lay Apostolate' — lending colour to fears that only one body was to be created, in which world problems treated in *Gaudium et Spes* would be seen only as laity problems in a narrow sense.

The Committee itself was in no doubt about its task. Nor about its provisional status. Pope Paul wanted no delay and a small group should be able to work rapidly. The President was Maurice Roy, Archbishop of Quebec, the Secretary, Achille Glorieux, the members, four lay people: Vittorino Veronese, Auguste Vanistendael, Johannes Schauff (West Germany) and 'the Australian woman'. But work could only begin after the summer vacation break when the Committee held just one session, from September 29 to October 12. Input from a wider group of competent people was provided through a series of 'hearings'.

Among those consulted were Barbara Ward Jackson, James Norris and others who had taken part in a Working Group that met in Rome in May 1966 to make proposals for implementing N.90 of *Gaudium et Spes*. Co-Chairmen of the Working Group were Bishop Edward E. Swanstrom, Executive Director of the United States Catholic Relief Services and Mgr Jean Rodhain (France), President of Caritas Internationalis, with Mgr Joseph Gremillion, from the United States Catholic Relief Services as Secretary. Those heard included Archbishop Benelli, soon to be Substitute in the Secretariat of State, and later Cardinal Archbishop of Florence; Mgr Luigi Ligutti, Observer of the Holy See to the Food and Agriculture Organization (FAO); and Presidents of CIO.

What were the options to be considered? The Post-Conciliar Commission on Lay Apostolate — meeting from January to June 1966 — had received a proposal for a Sacred Congregation for the Laity. The proposal was rejected. It was to re-emerge ten years later when the time came to give the organism for the laity a definitive form; and twenty years later, when John Paul II was preparing the Apostolic Constitution on the Roman Curia, *Pastor Bonus* (June 1988). From the point of view of the Curia, it was suggested that a Congregation would give more prestige to lay participation. But was that what the laity needed? The members of a Congregation are cardinals and a few residential bishops. Lay people could only be consultors (and how often would they be consulted?). A Congregation has jurisdiction over persons (bishops, priests, religious) or a particular sector (doctrine, worship, etc.) for which it is created. But lay people do not form a category or a sector in the Church. They are baptised people whose Christian life is governed by the beliefs, principles and norms common to the whole People of God. The juridical approach and style of operation of a Congregation would be inappropriate, given lay people's experience of Christian living.

The status finally proposed by the Provisional Committee — a Council (Consilium) — was confirmed when, at long last, on 6 January 1967, Paul VI, by his *Motu Proprio*,[3] *Catholicam Christi Ecclesiam*,[4] created two new organisms of the Curia: the *Consilium de Laicis* (literally, Council *on* the Laity) and the Pontifical Commission for Justice and Peace. They were united at the top by their President, Maurice Roy and their Vice-President, Archbishop Alberto Castelli, but had distinct tasks entrusted to them. The *Consilium's* first aim was to 'work for the service and promotion of the lay apostolate', very much along the lines of the task that had been undertaken by COPECIAL. The possibility of some limited jurisdiction was suggested by an obscure reference to 'fostering the faithful observance of the ecclesiastical laws concerning the laity'. This was confirmed when, in August 1967, the Apostolic Constitution *Regimini Ecclesiae Universae*[5] included the *Consilium de Laicis* among the dicasteries of the Roman Curia — a dicastery being an office of the Curia that has some share in the ordinary jurisdiction of the Pope as universal Pastor. The juridical competence of the *Consilium* was to concern mainly the Associations of the faithful and formal recognition of international associations.

The Pontifical Commission for Justice and Peace was defined as a Study Commission, whose aim was to arouse the whole People of God to the Church's responsibility in promoting international social justice, and in helping underdeveloped nations to work for their own development. In the first audience he gave to the new Commission, on 21 April 1967,[6] Paul VI imaginatively spelt out the task of arousing the People of God:

Formerly, and even today, when a church or a steeple is finished, the figure of a cock is placed on top of the roof as a symbol of watchfulness for the faith and for the whole course of Christian life. In like manner, this Commission has been placed on the spiritual building of the Council with the specific role of keeping the eye of the Church alert, her heart open and her hand outstretched for the work of love she is called upon to give to the world so as to promote the development of the poorest peoples and to foster social justice among nations.

Joseph Gremillion, as first Secretary of the Commission, gave an enthusiastic welcome to the cock as its mascot. During his years in office, he collected cocks of every stuff and size and colour, adorning shelves and keeping the staff 'alert'. Before coming to Rome, Gremillion had been Director of Socio-Economic Development for the United States Catholic Relief Services. In July 1966, with Veronese, he was one of the Roman Catholic observers at the World Conference on Church and Society of the WCC. After the WCC Assembly in Uppsala in 1968, he became Co-Chairman of the Committee on Society, Development and Peace (SODEPAX), jointly set up by the Pontifical Commission and the WCC.

It is impossible to know whether the dynamism of Gremillion was too much for the Curia, or whether the Curia was too much for Gremillion. In 1974, he resigned from the Pontifical Commission after seven years of fruitful service. He retired to the University of Notre Dame to reflect, research and write and died there in 1994.[7]

Lay people in the Curia

Not all the proposals from the *Coetus ad exsequendos* were retained. It had seemed natural to suggest that, with a Cardinal President, lay people could fill the roles of Vice-President or Secretary, or both, for the *Consilium*. But the Vice-President was a bishop and the Secretary a priest. There was still a novelty that made the headlines: the appointment of two lay Under-Secretaries: a lay man, Mieczyslaw de Habicht, and . . . a lay woman. A woman in the Roman Curia! Before the Council, not only were there no women but there were scarcely any lay people at all in the Curial offices. Even typing or filing was normally done by ecclesiastics (unless an enterprising cardinal smuggled in some clandestine female labour in order to get things done).

The initial members of the *Consilium* were all lay people — twelve men and two women; the consultors: eight ecclesiastics (including Cardinal Wojtyla) and five lay people, (including one woman: Pilar Bellosillo, President of WUCWO).

Receiving the *Consilium* during the first Assembly, on 18 April 1967,[8] Paul VI greeted the group joyfully: 'Difficulties', he said, 'were not lacking when it came to setting up this modern cooperation demanded by new times'. (The sinister-minded will see dark Curial plots to sabotage the new venture!) Two years later (15 March 1969) he identified the Council as a place of 'listening' and 'dialogue'.[9] Dialogue also with the Pope, bringing to him the voice of the laity at a time of 'vast questionings' and 'multiple contestations', and taking back to the laity from the Pope 'the echo of his worries as a Pastor'. The members of the *Consilium* were his 'experts on life'.

The nature of the *Consilium* was, however, to remain a problem for many of its members. Should it not be *of* the laity or *for* the laity rather than Council *on* the Laity? During the first five years, much time and many reams of paper had been devoted to defining and redefining operational aspects, relationships with other bodies in the Curia, with the Conference of CIO, with Bishops' Conferences, with lay people generally. Its internal working presented a particular problem. The lay members and Consultors were almost all leaders of international or national organisations. They were accustomed to having a secretariat at their disposal, and an influential, if not final voice on all matters with which they were dealing. As members of a dicastery of the Curia, they had to relate to a Presidency and Secretariat that, besides implementing decisions or recommendations of the Assembly, must at all times be available for any service the Holy Father or the Secretariat of State might require of them. Years later, looking back on this experimental period, Rie Vendrik mused: 'We sometimes thought that the Pope might come here himself to listen to us. It seemed that was impracticable. After all, one can wonder why . . . '

Curial customs nearly produced a minor revolution when, at the first meeting, members were asked to take an oath of secrecy. They were indignant. Were they not responsible persons who knew the importance of professional secrecy or discretion? Cardinal Roy did not press the point.

If members and consultors had some difficulty in adjusting to their roles, the executive lay staff[10] had to discover — or invent — modes of operation appropriate to the daily life of the Curia. This was facilitated by excellent personal relations. The President presented only one drawback — as Archbishop of Quebec he was very often absent. Alberto Castelli was a wise and helpful Vice-President, but left initiative mainly to the Secretariat.[11] The Secretary and Under-Secretaries were three such totally different personalities that they could work together in harmony. Considering the problem of relations between COPECIAL and the Conference of CIO before the Council, it was a master stroke to appoint as Under-Secretaries the Permanent Secretary of the Conference and the Executive Secretary of COPECIAL!

Achille Glorieux brought to the *Consilium* journalistic experience and the meticulous efficiency of his work as Secretary to the Preparatory, Conciliar and Post-Conciliar Commissions on the Lay Apostolate. He brought also qualities we had appreciated in his position as Ecclesiastical Assistant of COPECIAL: a discreet, but genuine priestly presence, and a scrupulous respect for the responsibility of the laity. In October 1969, he left us to become Papal Nuncio, first in Damascus and then in Cairo. He was no career diplomat, but his innate charity and his loyal dedication to his role proved to be the best diplomacy.

Mieczyslaw de Habicht was a born diplomat. He would have been an excellent Nuncio, if that had been a lay role. From the simplest to the highest level of the ecclesiastical spectrum or of international relations, he was an accomplished 'contact' person with an authentic sense of the Church. The 'first woman in the Curia' was happy in less visible roles; but had a reputation for getting her own way, in the firm conviction that nothing would run smoothly if that way was not followed.

Glorieux was succeeded as Secretary by Mgr Marcel Uylenbroeck from Belgium, successor of Joseph Cardijn as International Chaplain of the YCW. For nearly ten years — until his death in 1979 — the Laity Council had the benefit of his dynamism, his experience (especially with young people), his understanding of the world scene, his warmth and spontaneity, his deeply pastoral spirit. However, he could not succeed in reorganising his heterogenous staff for the kind of teamwork that would be normal for an international YCW Secretariat! He soon adapted to his new environment — if not always easily to the Curia — and the diversified constituency of the Laity Council gave new depth and breadth to his ecclesial vision.

The Consilium in action

The first five-year period was experimental in every sense: in internal activities and external relationships; in theological reflection and proposals for the new Code of Canon Law that were in preparation; in the wide-ranging surveys (*tours d'horizon*) in which members and consultors brought to the Assemblies the experience of particular contexts. These surveys covered everything from difficult situations in Cuba or Poland to the Pop Festival on the Isle of Wight, as reported by Mgr Derek Worlock. After the publication of *Humanae Vitae*[12] in 1968, one Assembly was largely devoted to reflecting on the pastoral situation created in the Church by reactions to the Encyclical. A report of the discussion was sent to the Pope. Subsequently, a Commission on the Family was created within the Council.[13]

One initiative reflected the contestation and conflict of the years post–1968. This was a symposium on 'Dialogue within the Church'. In March 1971, some forty specialists in various disciplines such as theology, sociology, psychology and history analysed case studies of conflict in relation to ecclesial structures, relations between lay movements, etc. There was in-depth discussion on the nature of dialogue inspired by Paul VI's Encyclical *Ecclesiam Suam*.[14] The Pope was keenly interested and addressed the participants.[15] He also referred to the symposium in his Angelus speech[16] of Sunday, 22 March: 'Perhaps the public is unaware of the importance of such an event, but We who try to follow the life of the Church, in her intimate experiences, consider it of the utmost importance'.[17]

A new lease of life

The year 1972 opened with a new three-year experimental mandate. This was later prolonged for a further year, to allow the *Consilium* to contribute to the celebration of the Holy Year in 1975. The Vice-President was, at first, Bishop Ramon Torrella Cascante (Vice-President also of the Commission for Justice and Peace) but he was soon succeeded by Bishop (now Cardinal) Lucas Moreira Neves from Brazil. New members were appointed, giving a wider geographical distribution, but a few veterans remained, including Vittorio Bachelet and Maria Vendrik, and — among the consultors — Cardinal Wojtyla and Archbishop Jean Zoa (Cameroun).

Having survived its novitiate, although still experimental within the Curia, the *Consilium* embarked on a series of initiatives. One of the first was a meeting on 'The Christian in the University of the '70's' (13–15 October 1972).

The project emerged from an attempt during the first period to set up a Youth Service. The plan had little in common with the vast operation of the Youth Section of the present Pontifical Council for the Laity. The idea was to coordinate existing Catholic international associations for youth. But these were the post-1968 years, with the memory of the student riots. It was decided to concentrate on university youth and universities in general. Encouraged by Paul VI, the Laity Council and the Congregation for Catholic Education formed a Joint Committee. Documentation was gathered. The group which finally met included university people from different continents: professors, chaplains, students, leaders of movements, etc. The World Christian Student Federation sent an Observer.

Different types of experience emerged: campus ministry in the United States; chaplaincies for foreign students in Europe; efforts to integrate the university into Arab society in Lebanon; new political consciousness in India; the rapid increase in the number of women students; in much of the developing world, reaction against a culture identified with a colonial past, together with an excessive stress on the contribution of universities to industrial development; democratisation and radical changes within universities themselves; the impact of liberation theology.[18]

In 1976, the Joint Committee sent tentative findings to Bishops' Conferences, Catholic universities, university movements, etc. This was well received, contributing to a growing awareness of the importance of the changing university in a changing world. When, in 1982, John Paul II created the Pontifical Council for Culture, the Joint Committee became tripartite. In 1994, it published a document, 'The Presence of the Church in the University and University Culture'. Problems were no fewer than in the past but it was possible to give a fuller account of the diverse and complementary forms of the Church's presence and mission in the university world.

Many years previously, in 1951, the student Movement of Pax Romana had published a brochure entitled *University for Christ* with the purpose of presenting the reality — and diversity — of Catholic (and Christian) activity in universities with which Pax Romana had contact. It featured university federations in Austria; specialised Catholic Action for students in Belgium, Brazil, France, Peru; the missionary parish, Centre Richelieu, in Paris; Italy's FUCI; the Student Union that was attempting, pastorally, a new start in post-war — and post-Nazi — Germany; the Swiss 'Schulungsgemeinschaft' which offered intense Christian formation related to the student's future profession.

The university scene was very different from that now — or even that of the 1970s — but today there is still a need for what the philosopher, Etienne Gilson, saw in 1947 as the focus of Pax Romana: 'An association which aims to organize throughout the world the fraternity of those who place their intellect at the service of God'.[19] That was the year of the founding of the 'intellectuals' section of Pax Romana: ICMICA. But who are 'Catholic intellectuals'? And what can the definition of Pax Romana still mean by the year 2000? I quote from a talk given in 1951 by Emilio Guano for study days on 'The Intellectual Apostolate':

> The word 'intellectual' may not please us; it may sound rather arrogant. But intellectuals do exist, as well as more specifically intellectual ways of living.
>
> There is a certain intelligence in which there is no difference between the intellectual, the peasant and the worker — a capacity to know what one is, metaphysically and in relation to God,

to know God at natural level and, with the help of grace, at supernatural level. We sometimes meet people who do not know how to read but who have a marvellous sense and a penetrating knowledge of reality. In this — very basic — sense, we are all equal.

But there is a more discursive or more reflexive intelligence which gives a more systematic possession of the instruments and methods of culture and technique. Some people are more gifted or more practised in this way . . . These people are the 'intellectuals'. They have a role with regard to themselves, to enjoy God's gifts; but they also have a role, a mission in the community . . . Even beyond his own specialty, [the intellectual] should facilitate knowledge of human life, of community, of social and political life . . . He must help those who can neither read nor write, or who have no time to read, to reflect . . . to 'philosophize'; to be ever more open to the presence of God, to His Revelation . . . [20]

Post-Conciliar ecumenism

In the wake of Vatican II and after the Third World Congress, the *Consilium de Laicis* could not forget that ecumenism is 'the concern of the whole Church'.[21] But, it was perhaps inevitable that the Congress of 1967 — with its unprecedented participation of 'other Christians' — was felt by some as a *fait accompli* that must not be allowed to divert attention from differences to be overcome before Christian unity can be fully 'restored'. 'Our Churches are not ready for this', Annie Jiagge had said regretfully during the Congress. It probably did not help to overcome what resistance there might be that, in the *Consilium* ecumenism came to be dubbed 'Rosemary's baby'!

As a first experience, in February 1968, the *Consilium* was invited by the WCC Department on the Laity to take part in a joint Consultation in preparation for the Fourth WCC Assembly, to be held in Uppsala (Sweden). Two Assembly themes were discussed: 'Worship in a Secular Age' and 'Towards a New Style of Living'.[22]

In May 1968, the Joint Working Group between the WCC and the Roman Catholic Church (set up in 1965 for ongoing collaboration) made the following recommendation:

That the WCC Division of Ecumenical Action and the Roman Catholic Laity Council further explore, for presentation to their respective authorities, the possibility of the project recommended by the Consultation at Glion of a World Conference, primarily of the Christian laity, and organised on an ecumenical basis, which would be concerned with Christian witness and responsibility in the contemporary world situation.[23]

The Uppsala Assembly endorsed this recommendation. Problems arose, however, from the fact that the Catholic partner would no longer be the rather free-wheeling COPECIAL but a dicastery of the Roman Curia. When the *Consilium* received the recommendation from Uppsala, it had to reply, after consultation with the 'authorities', that 'it did not feel it was in a position to make concrete plans for an ecumenical World Conference of the Christian Laity'. The question was not raised again. But, then, neither was the possibility of another world meeting of the *Catholic* laity on the scale of the explosive post-Conciliar World Congress of 'God's People on Man's Journey'.

Joint staff meetings between the WCC and *Consilium* on matters concerning the laity did continue until the end of the experimental period, and Observers were exchanged for more important meetings. But contact became more and more sporadic, especially after laity as a theme disappeared from the WCC agenda.

One significant — if not spectacular — project was, however, realised during the second experimental period. A Consultation on 'New Trends in Laity Formation' was held at Assisi in September 1974. This turned out to be what our theological adviser, Jean de la Croix Bonadio, SS.CC. called retrospectively 'the improbable point of emergence of a renewed Christian awareness'.[24] Jointly organised with the WCC Unit III, 'Education and Renewal', the Consultation brought together fifty-three participants — Catholic, Protestant, Orthodox — from all continents: there were eleven clergy, twenty-three women and four married couples.

It will be remembered that WCC and COPECIAL had organised a joint Consultation on laity formation at Gazzada (Italy) in September 1965. Remarkable agreement on aims and principles had been reached in a Joint Statement drafted by Roberto Tucci, SJ and Mark Gibbs.[25] But the discussions stressed mainly the very different concrete approaches to formation. The WCC member Churches operated mainly through Academies and Lay Training Institutes or Retreat Centres; while, in the Catholic Church, laity formation depended largely on movements for the lay apostolate. At Assisi, the accent was not on differences, but on convergences which emerged from group discussion on theology, woman–man relationships, justice, culture, tensions between community and institutions. A final consensus stressed each person's responsibility for his or her own formation. There was consensus, above all, on 'the sign of hope that can be given to the world by a Christian community such as was formed, even momentarily, during this meeting'.[26]

On 18 September, during a general audience at Castel Gandolfo, Paul VI greeted the group:[27]

> We know that you have come from the heights of Assisi where,
> for ten days, you have been sharing your convictions, your
> experience, your questioning concerning the formation
> of the human and Christian person in today's world.
> We congratulate you and We encourage you to make fruitful,
> concretely and patiently, the light and the strength you have
> drawn from this meeting.

'Towards the Year 2000'

As I write, we are in the preparatory phase for the Great Jubilee of the Year 2000 announced by John Paul II.[28] Already in 1975, under the slogan, 'Towards the Year 2000 ... along the Way of the Gospel the *Consilium de Laicis* organised a World Consultation in Rome for the Holy Year of Renewal proclaimed by Paul VI. The aim was 'to reflect on the concrete experience of sharing, since Vatican II, in the Church's mission to modern society, and on the life of the ecclesial community'.[29] Some 250 representatives of the laity — young people and adults, men and women — took part from all over the world. As at Assisi, Bible Studies were led by Hans-Ruedi Weber; but also by Stanislas Lyonnet, SJ and Fr Jacques Loew. The prayerful and reflective atmosphere did not prevent strong reactions and debate when looking at the problems of poverty and injustice in economically underdeveloped countries.

The pilgrimage dimension of this Holy Year experience was stressed later by Katherine Strong (Episcopalian), Observer for the World YWCA:

> You may well ask what significance can a Holy Year have for one who is not a Roman Catholic! But if, as Pope Paul VI said in proclaiming it, the essential aim of the Holy Year is renewal and reconciliation, the moral rebirth of both the individual and society, then it is as relevant to me as to anyone. Do not the holy places in Rome which were the scene of the early history of the Christian Church, spiritually belong to me as a baptized Christian?[30]

Another Consultation of similar dimensions was organised at Rocca di Papa (Rome) in 1987, in preparation for the Synod of Bishops on the Laity.[31] It is arguable that this type of meeting — not a World Congress, but large enough to be representative — could be the best way of involving lay people in responsibility for the life and mission of the universal Church. It could not take the place of a Department of the Curia, staffed by competent lay people; but it could be a more flexible and more open manner of operation than the regular meetings of a small council, whose role remains necessarily consultative. This supposes, of course, that there would be authentic listening to the voices of the laity — as, indeed, there was at the Consultations of 1975 and 1987.

Towards the future . . . of the Consilium

The future in this case was more immediate than the Year 2000. Reflection began in 1975, as the end of the whole experimental period drew near. Assessments were attempted and proposals were made: personal reminiscences abounded.

At one such reflective session, Jean Zoa recalled his experience in the

Consilium as one of 'maturing', and as a prolongation of Vatican II, renewing the sense of the universal Church. From a different episcopal experience, Derek Worlock, Archbishop of Liverpool, stressed the radical changes that had taken place in Western countries in the short period since the Vatican Council. There might be fewer people occupying the pews, but 'active' laity were much *more* active. They were exercising new ministries in a Church that was more and more missionary — not only in one-time 'mission countries'. The future of the *Consilium* must be bound up with the provision of spiritual help to enable the laity to survive in modern society.

The *Consilium* had devoted much thought to the problems of lay organisations during what were difficult years for institutions as a whole. The new Council must be concerned also for the 'non-organised'. Its concern must be for the *whole* Church, not for laity as a category.

The members had not always been comfortable. They felt the confidence of the Holy Father but were they taken seriously in the Curia? People like Jeremias (Jerry) Montemayor, President of the Free Farmers Federation of the Philippines, could feel isolated from the 'masses' or the marginalised they were used to working with. Others found it difficult to keep the necessary contact with their home-base. But, on the whole, there had been adjustment to the new role. The *Consilium* was not a parliament elected to represent the laity; but it had let the voices of responsible lay people be heard in a new way.

One structural limitation was to become more evident as new Departments were set up within the Curia. Veterans from the Conference of CIO had been accustomed to assemblies dealing with all sectors of laity in a Church 'in solidarity with the world'. From the beginning, some had felt the separation from the Commission for Justice and Peace as an 'amputation'. Then the Committee for the Family became autonomous. Later, there would be the Pontifical Council for Culture. In a new generation, few would remember the problem raised during the Council: Did we want a 'laity corner' in the Holy See? Should there not be competent people — men and women — called for consultation and service in all sectors of the government of the universal Church?

Apostolatus Peragendi: *'a higher level'*

On 10 December 1976, two documents were published: the *Motu Proprio Apostolatus Peragendi*,[32] creating the Pontifical Council for the Laity (PCL), and the *Motu Proprio, Justitiam et Pacem*,[33] giving a definitive form to the Pontifical Commission (now Council) for Justice and Peace.

Apostolatus Peragendi left many questions raised during the experimental period unanswered. Its purpose — to give 'a new and permanent form at a higher level' — was expressed in the creation of a committee of three cardinals to assist the Cardinal President. Members and consultors were still mainly, but not exclusively, lay men and women. A clear distinction was established between their respective roles. (During the experimental period, the only real difference was that consultors did not vote in the Assembly.) It was stressed that the Council's mandate extended to *all* the laity in their Christian life and mission. But what that could mean concretely would have to be worked out through experience at all levels.

In one respect the Pontifical Council was clearly a step back for lay responsibility. Since the Under-Secretary had to be associated with the work of the Presidential Committee, competent for 'matters requiring the powers of order and jurisdiction'[34] (what these 'matters' were was not specified), the conclusion was that this could not be a lay person. A priest was, in fact, appointed: Mgr Peter Coughlan. This change had already been foreseen during the year 1976 — a 'limbo' year for the *Consilium* when no new initiatives could be attempted. Mieczyslaw de Habicht, after being seconded to the Central Committee of the Holy Year 1975, had been asked to retire prematurely, which he did — reluctantly. What was to be done with me? The decision was communicated to me by Archbishop Benelli on the eve of the publication of *Apostolatus peragendi*. I was to be a professor in the Pastoral Institute of the Pontifical Lateran University — the Pope's University as Bishop of Rome. The University was not new to me, nor I to the University. Since 1967, I had been giving a course on Lay Apostolate in the Pastoral Institute. But the new assignment was a much more complete immersion in ecclesiastical Academia. It was embarrassing to be parachuted into a professorship without any prior notice to any Faculty Council. But the experience, which lasted ten years, proved — at least for me — very positive. The then Rector, Mgr Franco Biffi, and the President of the Pastoral Institute, the late Silvio Riva, OFM, welcomed the appointment and I still hear from students exercising their priestly (even episcopal) ministry in the local Churches of Africa, Asia, Latin America and Europe.

I tell this story because my departure from the Laity Council was widely publicised as the 'demotion' of a woman. In February 1977, I requested and was given a brief, but memorable Audience with Paul VI. The Holy Father was most encouraging about my teaching assignment: 'You can do so much good!' But, in requesting the Audience, I had wanted also to express my own concern about the vacant place left in the Curia. There was now no woman — lay or religious — at the level of responsibility I had held 'experimentally' for ten years. Pope Paul listened, and understood my concern.

The step back for the laity has been remedied — but not for women.[35] After careful study of the new Code of Canon Law (1983), it was decided that a lay person *could* be Under-Secretary of the Pontifical Council. The post is currently held by Guzman Carriquiry from Uruguay. But there is still a long way to go, and there are perhaps some radical changes to be made, before competent lay men and women can contribute all that they could bring to the service of the Holy See.

Towards the end of the experimental period, on 26 February 1975, Maurice Roy wrote to Paul VI on behalf of the members and consultors.[36] The creation of the *Consilium de Laicis* had been 'a truly providential and prophetic gesture'. For the lay people especially:

> . . . an extraordinary ecclesial experience; and an implementation of the teachings of the Second Vatican Council . . . Called to collaborate with the Common Father in the service of the Universal Church, they have tried to communicate to others their sense of ecclesial responsibility . . . The experience shows, however, all that remains to be done. There must be a real effort, at all levels, especially in the local Churches, for a more and more effective and significant participation of the Laity in the life and the dynamism of the Ecclesial Community.

1. Austin Flannery, *Vatican Council II. The Conciliar and Post-Conciliar Documents*, op. cit.

2. The official title of this committee for Implementation was 'Coetus ad exsequendos', 26 and 90. The two paragraphs from the Council that had to be implemented are from the Decree on the Lay Apostolate, op. cit., 26 and *Gaudium et Spes*, op. cit., 90.

3. A *Motu Proprio* is a document on internal Church administration published in response to the Pope's own initiative and not in answer to a particular request.

4. *Catholicam Christi Ecclesiam*, Motu Proprio of Paul VI, 1967, *The Pontifical Council for the Laity*, Vatican City, 1997, pp. 54–9.

5. Apostolic Constitution *Regimini Ecclesiae Universae* (15.8.1967) on the Reform of the Curia.

6. Paul VI to the Commission, 21 April 1967, in *Insegnamenti di Paolo VI*, V., pp. 170–2.

7. In a statement made to the press on 3 January 1974, after thanking the Holy Father for the confidence and understanding he had been shown, Gremillion explained: '... Our Commission is now an ongoing body and movement, with the main elements of its structure, program and worldwide network rather well defined ... it no longer needs my kind of leadership and "social action" experience ... It would be easy to stay on, despite the occasional tensions and my own spirit of criticism; constructive I hope. But I believe it should become normal that clergy, religious and lay persons be invited into the Curia at a mature age. Then after making their contribution for five to eight years, be free to return to their local Church and community, or to other types of service to the Universal Church'.

8. Paul VI to the 'Consilium', 18 April 1967, in *Insegnamenti di Paolo VI*, V, pp. 160–1.

9. Paul VI to the 'Consilium', 15 March 1969, in *Insegnamenti di Paolo VI*, V, pp. 144–7.

10. Apart from the Under-Secretaries, appointed by the Pope, the staff initially included about ten people in charge of different services and with different linguistic skills, appointed by the President for an indefinite period. Papal appointments are for five years and renewable.

11. He was, above all, a delightful friend until his death in March 1971. His many interests included English literature. His Italian translation of *Murder in the Cathedral* (T. S. Eliot) and *The Screwtape Letters* (C. S. Lewis) are still in use.

12. Encyclical *Humanae Vitae* on the Regulation of Births, English text in Austin Flannery, *Vatican Council II. More Post-Conciliar Documents*, pp. 397–416.

13. The Commission later became an autonomous Committee, which, in turn, gave birth to the present Pontifical Council for the Family.

14. *Ecclesiam Suam*, 6 August 1964.

15. Paul VI, 22 March 1971, in 'Dialogue within the Church', Special Number, Laity Today 9/10, 1971, pp. 11–12.

16. An 'Angelus' speech is a brief discourse by the Pope before he recites the Angelus prayer at midday on Sunday, from his window in the Vatican or from the balcony of Castel Gandolfo.

17. Another major event took place in 1971: the *Panafrican Laity Seminar* in Accra, Ghana, which I refer to in a later chapter.

18. For the proceedings, see *The Christian in the University*, Bulletin of the Consilium de Laicis, 1973, 15–16.

19. Etienne Gilson, in *Les intellectuels dans la chrétienté*, I, Pax Romana–Movement International des Intellectuels Catholiques, Fribourg (Switzerland), published in Rome, 1948, p. 175.

20. *The Christian in the University*, op. cit., pp. 88–9.

21. The Decree on Ecumenism, *Unitatis Redintegratio*, 5, in Flannery, op. cit., states 'The concern for restoring unity involves the whole Church, faithful and clergy alike'.

22. The Consultation was held at Glion, Switzerland. In July, I had the privilege of being one of the fourteen Roman Catholic Delegated Observers at the Assembly itself.

23. Archives of the Pontifical Council for Promoting Christian Unity.

24. 'New Trends', *The Laity Today*, op. cit., 19–20, 1975, p. 86.

25. Cf. *Laity Formation*, Proceedings of the Ecumenical Consultation, Gazzada (Italy), 7–10 September 1965, Rome, 1966. *Statement Adopted by Plenary Session*, pp. 9–11. Mark Gibbs was the Anglican Director of the Audenshaw Foundation. His death, in 1986, was a great loss for the ecumenical 'cause' of the laity.

26. *The Laity Today*, op. cit., 19–20, 1975, p. 11.

27. Ibid.

28. Cf. The Apostolic Letter, *Tertio Millennio Adveniente*, 1994.

29. Introduction to the proceedings of the Consultation, in *The Laity Today*, 21–22, 1976, p. 5.

30. *The Laity Today*, 21–22, 1976, p. 16.

31. Cf. *A New Evangelization for the Building of a New Society*, World Consultation in view of the Synod of Bishops 1987. Rocca di Papa, Rome, 21–25 May 1987. Pontifical Council for the Laity, Documentation Service, 18, 1987.

32. *Apostolatus Peragendi*, Motu Proprio of Paul VI, 1976, The Pontifical Council for the Laity, Vatican City, 1997, pp. 59–65.

33. '*Justitiam et Pacem*', *L'Osservatore Romano*, 17 December 1976.

34. *Apostolatus Peragendi*, II, op. cit.

35. In 1995 it was calculated that women (religious and lay) represented about 10 per cent of Curia personnel (in Congregations, Councils, Commissions and other offices). Only about forty women had a post of recognised responsibility. The majority of these were on the staff of the Congregation for Consecrated Life or members of one of the Councils set up after Vatican II. No woman was Under-Secretary of a Dicastery. Two lay men were Under-Secretaries.

36. Archives of the *Consilium de Laicis*.

Part 4
THE LAITY, CONTINENT BY CONTINENT

God's many-coloured, multilingual people

CHAPTER 10

A voyage of discovery

The PCL, after taking over from the *Consilium de Laicis*, organised a series of continental meetings, bringing together bishops responsible for lay apostolate in their respective Episcopal Conferences, priests, religious and representative lay men and women. The meetings were held in Latin America (Bogota, 1979), Europe (Vienna, 1981), Africa (Yaoundé, 1982), Asia (Hong Kong, 1983), Central America (1984) and Oceania (Auckland, 1986). The proceedings have been published by the PCL. The most interesting point of these meetings is not so much the content of the discussions as the fact that they happened and what they signified — actually and symbolically — about the shared responsibility of pastors and laity of every race and culture. The sharing emerged in its world dimension at the Consultation held at Rocca di Papa in May 1987, during preparation for the Synod of Bishops on the Laity. These events belong — and not only chronologically — to the post-Conciliar Church. The quarter of a century between the opening of the Council (October 1962) and the Synod on the Laity (October 1987) may seem a long time in the present acceleration of history; but acceleration, we know, did not begin with Vatican II. A glance at some pre-Conciliar developments, continent by continent, will show something of the ground swell surging up into Vatican II, and overflowing into the post-Conciliar years.

My own voyage of discovery began in December 1953, when I left Rome with a round-the-world air-ticket, to explore the possibility of an

Asian meeting for the Lay Apostolate. It led to India, Ceylon (Sri Lanka), Singapore, Indonesia, Hong Kong, Taiwan, Japan, the Philippines, with a visit 'down under' to Australia and New Zealand, and a return via the United States. The first 'leg' was to Africa, where the First Leaders Meeting for the Apostolate of the Laity in Africa was about to open, organised by COPECIAL and the Uganda National Council of Catholic Action.

This was before 'jetting around' had become a fashionable pastime. Our pioneering ventures did not go uncriticised. Veronese may have won confidence across frontiers, but COPECIAL had arrived rather too suddenly on the international scene — dropped down from the Vatican, with an uncertain status. Its activity, reaching out to uncharted areas, could be seen as overlapping that of the CIO. One French cleric associated with a Catholic international organisation summed up the criticisms in a note discovered many years later in a forgotten archive. He was particularly severe on the subject of the apostolic journeys of the unimpressive female members of Veronese's staff. Their travels were suspected of being publicity stunts for COPECIAL, and could achieve nothing concrete. True, it was not usual in the 1950s for young women to be sent out from Rome to encourage lay groups in far continents and confer with their bishops. True also, there was a danger of our being taken *too* seriously. (I remember the awe of the Filipina schoolgirl who was making me a presentation: the visitor from 'Rome', straight from the Pope!) But, if there was publicity, it was also on behalf of the CIO themselves. On my Asian tour, I had a specific mandate for the preparation of Pax Romana's first Asian Student Seminar, that was to meet in Madras in December 1954.

Africans: 'missionaries to themselves'?

'Africa will be converted by Africans', said Cardinal Lavigerie, Founder of the White Fathers (1825–92). This was the conviction also of other missionary Founders, like Daniel Comboni (1831–81) and Jacob Libermann (1802–52). Paul VI, visiting Kampala (Uganda) in 1969 for the first assembly of SECAM (Symposium of Episcopal Conferences of Africa and Madagascar), told the Bishops: 'You Africans must be missionaries to yourselves'. Could this have been said to the African lay people attending the first Leaders' Meeting in 1953?

To convey something of the excitement of this pioneering event I quote an article that appeared in the Sydney *Catholic Weekly* (28 January 1954) after my arrival for the Australian stage of my tour:

> From Entebbe; political capital of the Protectorate of Uganda, where Government buildings, attractive dwellings and the White Fathers' church and mission are dotted over wide park-lands, the red clay road leads up, between Indian shops, African mud-huts and banana plantations, towards Kisubi. Just before the village, a new road has been opened up to the Minor Seminary, a fine modern building which looks over the broad expanse of Lake Victoria. It was here that some 250 delegates came from 15 territories of Africa, with experts from 14 CIO, from 8 to 13 December, for the First Leaders Meeting for the Lay Apostolate in Africa . . .

Why Africa?

It was evident at the World Congress in 1951 that regional meetings would be necessary . . . Africa was chosen for the first of such meetings, at the express desire of African Catholics and in view of the urgency of preparing lay Christians for the social transformations rapidly taking place on the continent . . . This urgency was dramatically underlined when, a few days before the Meeting, Uganda came into the limelight through events leading to banishment by the British Authorities of the Buganda King, the Kabaka Mutesa II. Despite the state of emergency in Kampala, preparations proceeded . . . Delegates from all parts of Africa, and beyond, were making their way — by bicycle, car, train, and Comet — to Kisubi.

From Mozambique came the Portuguese Cardinal de Gouveia, Archbishop of Lourenzo Marques, the first Cardinal ever seen in Uganda. The new Apostolic Delegate, Archbishop James Knox — the first Australian ever to assume such functions anywhere — made Kisubi his initial goal in his jurisdiction of East and West Africa. Archbishops, Bishops, Vicars and Prefects Apostolic responded personally to the invitation. One Bishop, who had not found any lay delegate equipped for an international meeting, came himself, to 'learn'. With them came priests and religious, but also some lay leaders, to work with the 'experts' from the international Organisations; with Prince Karl zu Lowenstein, President of the Central Committee of German Catholics, and Soeur Marie-André du Sacré-Coeur, the French White Sister known for her research and writing on marriage customs and women's status among African peoples.

> Black and white mingled happily. At the torchlight procession on December 8, over 2000 Africans sang the Latin hymns and the Lourdes 'Ave' with the same gusto as the songs in their native Luganda. At the closing session, a 'Te Deum' rocked the Seminary chapel. But, unity in diversity was expressed also by the silent presence, at every session, of one of the parish 'Monitoresses', mother of a family, who understood no word of English or French, but explained in her own tongue: 'I know what you are talking about . . . These are the things which I also believe. I want you to see that I am with you . . . '

The doctrinal element of the Meeting — presented by missionary Bishops — was essentially what had emerged from the World Congress of 1951. But an African layman, Paul Ssemakula, introduced the subject of Formation; and lay people participated actively in the forums on Education, Women and the Family, Labour and Social Betterment; Leaders' Training. It was not forgotten either that Uganda had, not only its lay Martyrs — St Charles Lwanga and Companions (Catholic and Anglican) — but also its lay apostles, active from the earliest days of the missionary Church: the catechists, men and women who numbered among them freed slaves, parents of the first generation of African clergy and religious.

Writing after the Meeting, Mgr Richard Cleire, Vicar Apostolic of the Belgian Congo, referred to Catholic Action, as it appeared from the discussions:

> Africa is feeling its way . . . In many cases, it is the Legion of Mary, the League of the Sacred Heart or other forms that adapt

best: clear formulas, with strict rules, concrete and appealing to the emotions, easily handled by the clergy, upon whom any success generally depends.[1]

Inculturation was not even dreamed of but, for the Africans, there was pride in knowing they were personally responsible for the apostolate in Africa. Archbishop Maranta of Dar-es-Salaam noted that the Meeting had dispensed with the idea that missionaries did not recognise the cooperation of the African laity in building society on a Christian basis. Already before the Meeting, the weekly paper, *Afrique Nouvelle*, published in Dakar, commented on the good that could come out of it, but also on the obstacles to be expected. This included, among others, the fears of colonial administrators, who would see any continental gathering of an African 'elite' as a threat to the artificial frontiers they had created.

In Rome also there had been fears of political repercussions. They caused the Meeting to be limited — formally, but not in fact — to East Africa. Of the fifteen territories represented, only two were independent: Egypt and South Africa. Of the Bishops present, only two were African: Bishop Kiwanuka of Masaka (Uganda) and Bishop (later Cardinal) Rugambwa of Rutabo, Tanganyika (Tanzania). But, with all its limitations, 'Kisubi' was widely hailed as a turning-point, at least for East Africa. Follow-up was intense in the six dioceses of Uganda. Enthusiastic reports came from Kenya, from Nyasaland (Malawi) . . . 'Since Kisubi', Archbishop Knox wrote, 'the Lay Apostolate has always been a subject for discussion in the meetings of the Ordinaries from the various territories of Eastern and Western Africa'.[2]

The enthusiasm was contagious. In Sudan, the Ordinaries (three Vicars Apostolic and two Prefects Apostolic) decided to sponsor a similar Meeting. For the First National Sudanese Convention of Catholic Action leaders (4–10 January 1955) help was sought from COPECIAL. Vittoria Donadeo represented the Permanent Committee. She spoke on 'Catholic Action and how to organize it' — necessarily bringing to her talk the riches and limitations of her experience. One might wonder whether an organisation modelled on the Statutes adopted for Italian Catholic Action in 1946 was exactly what was needed in the Sudan. Before the Council, it was always easy to tell whether missionaries to the 'young Churches' of Africa came from France, Belgium, Italy, Ireland . . . One had only to look at the 'map' of the lay apostolate: Specialised Catholic Action from France or Belgium; Legion of Mary which was now worldwide, combined with occasional local input such as the Guild of the Blessed Baganda Martyrs, the 'Xaveri' of the Belgian Congo, etc. At the Sudanese Convention, there were, however, also talks geared to the local situation: relations with Protestants and Moslems; family problems; trade unions; racial discrimination; defence of Catholic schools; spiritual and material help for migrants from south to north and vice versa.[3]

In October 1957, African delegates from more than twenty countries and territories came to Rome for the Second World Congress, not only to receive, but also to give. The Congress proceedings were officially opened, on behalf of the Presidency, by Joseph Amichia, President of Family Catholic Action in Ivory Coast — later to be a member of the *Consilium de Laicis*, before becoming Dean of the Diplomatic Corps accredited to the Holy See. Colourfully arrayed in national dress, he made a great impression as he politely invited Cardinal Pizzardo to address the Congress. Paul Ssemakula from Uganda presented the social, economic and political evolution at this 'most critical period in the destiny of Africa'.

When Vatican II was already in preparation, in August 1961, another East African Lay Apostolate Meeting was held at Nyegezi (Tanganyika). It was initiated and moderated by Bishop Joseph J. Blomjous of Mwanza, widely known for his strong views on the lay apostolate and his ubiquitous Dutch cigar. The Meeting was a further milestone for the local Church. After the doctrinal introduction a layman, Sebastian Chale, dealt with concrete problems of a pluralistic society that boasted the presence of 124 indigenous tribes and thirteen European nationalities, as well as Indians, Chinese and Arabs. The secretariat was reinforced by two members 'lent' for the occasion: Marie-Ange Besson of COPECIAL and Mildred Nevile, Assistant Secretary of the 'Sword of the Spirit', London.[4]

My own contribution to pre-Conciliar developments in Africa was mainly technical: as interpreter to and from English and French.

Translation was consecutive at Kisubi, but already simultaneous for two meetings organised in the Belgian Congo by George Delcuve, SJ, founder of the International Catechetical Centre, *Lumen Vitae*, in Brussels: meetings in Leopoldville (Kinshasa) and Bukavu in 1955 and 1957. This was my passport also to the first two meetings of SECAM: Kampala 1969 (with the presence of Paul VI) and Abidjan 1970. No self-respecting translator would accept the technical conditions today but it was a wonderful way of getting to know the bishops of Africa. One way also of demonstrating the usefulness of lay people — and women! — in the Church.

The Panafrican Laity Seminar

In 1967, the Third World Congress brought thirty-three African delegations to Rome. The regret was unanimous that there had not been first a continental meeting. The need was soon met. In August 1972, a Panafrican Laity Seminar was held in Accra (Ghana) on 'The Commitment of the Laity in the Growth of the Church and the Integral Development of Africa'. It was planned and prepared by a Committee of nine Africans from different parts of the continent, with technical and financial assistance from the *Consilium de Laicis*, of which John Nimo of Ghana was a member. A post-Conciliar feature was the participation of ecumenical Observers from the WCC and the All Africa Conference of Churches. This was a landmark in Africa, where divisions among Christians — mostly historical and non-theological — had been imported with Christianity.[5] The findings of the seminar were presented the following year to the Assembly of SECAM by three members of the African Committee: John Nimo, Elizabeth Namaganda of Uganda and René Huchard of Sénégal. They were substantially endorsed by the bishops. They included plans for a Panafrican Laity Secretariat which — after many vicissitudes — now exists in Accra.

At the 1987 Synod of Bishops on 'The Vocation and Mission of the Laity', out of the nineteen lay people called to address the Assembly, two were Africans: Callixta Belomo of Cameroun and Etienne Bisimwa of Zaire. Neither was to speak specifically for Africa. Callixta's subject was 'Woman and her Christian Mission', Etienne's, 'Youth and the

Mission of the Laity'. Both had international experience: Callixta in the Movement for Catholic Rural Youth, Etienne in Pax Romana–IMCS. But both were deeply committed to the Christian Mission in Africa. Callixta made full use of the twenty minutes allotted to lay speakers (as opposed to eight minutes for the 'Fathers') to deal with the Christian mission in its Christocentric, universal, socio-historical and missionary dimensions, and to sketch thirty different images of womanhood. She also defined her personal experience:

> Through baptism, I realized that I have been introduced into a great family in which relations between members are not limited by space, colour of skin or culture ...The circle of my relations no longer turns round my 50 brothers and sisters, children of one father and a dozen mothers. From now on ... the circle has the dimension of the world, which God Himself allows me to discover through my commitments and the events of my life.[6]

We had come a long way from Kisubi, but the road was the same: more and more Africans were 'missionaries to themselves'.

'Asia for Christ'

> I return to my own country more than ever a citizen of my fatherland, more than ever an Asian, more than ever a Catholic.[7]

These were the parting words of Cardinal Valerian Gracias, Archbishop of Bombay, as he left Manila after presiding over the First Asian Meeting for the Lay Apostolate: a Meeting he had described as 'Asiatic in its complexion, but Catholic in its objectives'.

From 3 to 8 December 1955, 130 delegates from fifteen countries and twenty international organisations had been meeting in the only Asian country with a large Catholic majority (more than 80 per cent) — in some ways the least 'Asian' of the continent, for its deep Asian roots mingled with a background marked by two phases of its colonial history: Spanish-style popular religiosity and American know-how. This heritage found expression in an overwhelming hospitality, the enthusiastic activities of eleven committees and a fund drive, and the triumphant language of an 'apostolic rhetoric' that was also the normal language of a popular (and solid) faith.

I had two experiences of living in this distinctively Filipino atmosphere. For a week during my exploratory visit of 1954, I had been the guest of Luisa de Lorenzo, President of the Catholic Women's League (CWL). I was a pampered guest, driven to Mass at dawn in a chauffeured Cadillac; driven later in the day to visit the institutions (mental asylum, prison, etc.) where the CWL, unable to change appalling conditions, tried to bring alleviation to the suffering. From my prison-visiting, I have two lay apostolate memories: a conversation with a member of the prison Praesidium (section for a district) of the Legion of Mary, and the group of dainty little girls in pink uniforms, shepherded by a nun to teach catechism to the youngest offenders. My second visit to Manila included six weeks helping in preparations for the Lay Apostolate Meeting. This time, I shared the life of an 'ordinary' family, as guest of Michaela Montemayor, Assistant Executive Secretary of Catholic Action of the Philippines (CAP). But most of the day was spent hard at work in the crowded secretariat of CAP.

When the Meeting opened, its wider context was at once evident. 'Unity and Diversity of Asia' was the title of the lecture by Paul K. T. Sih, Director of the Institute of Far Eastern Studies of Seton Hall University, New Jersey: diversity of races, cultures, religions, political situations; the struggle against economic underdevelopment and dire poverty; a spiritual crisis even within the great traditional religions; communist expansionism and the effects of the Cold War; a Christian presence represented — except for the Philippines and Vietnam — by a tiny minority, but also by works of education and charity that were greatly appreciated; a laity with a growing sense of responsibility for a Christian presence in social, political and cultural life.

The delegations of Asian countries — from Pakistan to Korea — as well as those from Australia and New Zealand were composed mainly of members of lay movements and different forms of Catholic Action. International experts included Mgr Luigi Ligutti — indefatigable prophet and promoter of justice for rural people on all continents; John Hofinger, SJ, and Christine de Hemptinne, as world travellers for catechetical renewal; Anthony d'Rose, Founder of the Catholic Social Guild of Malaya-Singapore; Hideo Inohara, of the YCW of Japan; Juan C. Tan, President of the Federation of Free Workers (Philippines), Vittorio Vaccari (Italy), representing UNIAPAC; Irma Amin, an Indonesian convert from Islam who addressed the Meeting on 'The Apostolate of Women'; Brian Doyle, associate editor of *The Catholic Weekly*, Sydney; Mieczyslaw de Habicht, who guided discussion on international links.

As for the African Meeting at Kisubi, the doctrinal input was essentially that of the First World Congress, at which — as Cardinal Gracias recalled — 'the subject assigned to me was the very same as that which has been allotted to me today . . . What is good for Rome is certainly good for India and the Philippines'.[8] But the Cardinal did not fail to stress difficulties and opportunities for the laity in developing 'the best of the East and the best of the West' (nor did he fail to quote Cardinal J. H. Newman, G. K. Chesterton and Jacques Maritain).

The Cardinal's doctrinal lecture had included distinctions between Catholic Action, lay apostolate and political action. These were developed in a lecture by Mgr Pietro Pavan on 'The Apostolate of the Laity in the Modern World'.[9] He was not speaking only theoretically. He had wide experience through contacts in the Americas, Africa and Europe. In Manila, he responded — without naming them — to concrete situations where religious action and political action were mixed rather too closely. Not least, in the Philippines.

On 26 February 1955, *The Sentinel*, published by CAP, had printed two declarations signed by the ecclesiastical and lay authorities of Catholic Action. One text presented an:

> unequivocal and unconditional stand behind President Ramon Magsaysay's statement that the Philippines is solidly and totally in agreement with the declaration of the United States Government that Formosa and the Pescadores will be defended as a portion of the ramparts of freedom in Asia.

This pledge of support was not intended as a political alignment, but solely 'in defence of the principle that in this epic and cruel struggle between atheistic Communism and Christian freedom there can be no compromise'. The other text was an appeal for recognition of Free Vietnam by the Philippines, addressed to President Magsaysay by the President of CAP. Commenting on these statements before the Meeting in a note for the Secretariat of State, Veronese recognised that the approach might have a salutary effect on public opinion in the Philippines, but that action of this kind, taken by an ecclesiastical Authority and by Catholic Action in an international gathering, could create problems for the Church in Asia.

The Catholic Social Movement

Pietro Pavan's distinctions between Christian-inspired lay action and Catholic Action as collaboration with the hierarchy, were addressed also to the method used in another situation. In Australia, the Catholic Social Movement had been founded in 1943 by B. A. Santamaria, who was at the time Director in Melbourne of the National Secretariat of Catholic Action. The story of the Movement has often been told. Its very effective work within the Communist-riddled trade unions claimed the authority of the hierarchy, but was carried out, more or less secretly, through the Industrial Groups of the Labor Party. It inevitably had an impact in the political field. The resulting split in the Labor Party led — not intentionally — to division within the Church in Australia, 'split' nation-wide at all levels.

I came in contact with the Movement because, in July 1953, Santamaria had suggested to Veronese that the Asian Lay Apostolate Meeting we were planning might be held in Australia. In January 1954, I was in Melbourne to discuss this suggestion. The discussion was cordial, but we agreed to differ on problems of theory and practice related to the Movement. Santamaria clearly looked for inspiration — or confirmation — to Gedda's leadership in Italian Catholic Action. Whatever the official distinction between Catholic Action and the political or union activity of Catholics, he was not convinced that effective social action was possible without direct control of the hierarchy. (This was shortly before the crisis in the Industrial Groups and the 'split' in the political world and in the Church.)

On 18 and 25 June 1955, the Bombay Catholic weekly, *Examiner*, published two articles by Santamaria.[10] They affirmed the theory of the Movement: 'It is normal and correct that a body of Catholics carrying on the work of infusing the social order with Christian principles and of opposing the enemies of Christianity in the social, industrial and political fields, should operate under the *direct control* of the Hierarchy'. When the paper reached our office in Rome, I asked that copies be sent to Jean Daly in Sydney who, I knew, was concerned about the whole situation. Jean Daly[11] gave them to Brian Doyle, associate editor of the Sydney *Catholic Weekly*.

Why was I worried about the articles? Because experience in COPECIAL, contacts with lay apostolate in most countries of Asia, and what I knew of the situation in Australia, convinced me that it was urgent to clarify the Movement's theory and to avoid the damage it could do in practice. It could be harmful, especially for the Church in India, if Catholics were considered to be carrying on underground action controlled by the hierarchy to infiltrate political life — something very different from the formation of Catholic lay people for civic and political life, which had always been a major concern of Cardinal Gracias. Fortunately, no one in India seemed to realise the possible implications of the two articles. But my concern was increased by the setting up of a Temporary International Committee to spread the ambiguity of the Australian Movement in Asia.

During preparation for the Meeting in Manila, I discussed the problem with Pietro Pavan, who was to be one of the main speakers. He, no doubt, had information also from other sources. Theologian and sociologist, he was at the time Professor (later Rector) of the Pontifical Lateran University. The distinction between Catholic Action and Christian-inspired action in social and political fields was one of his special concerns for the lay apostolate.[12]

On 6 December 1956, in an article for *The Advocate* (Melbourne), entitled 'Religious Apostolate and Political Action', Santamaria explained that the Movement was being reconstituted as a lay organisation (the National Civic Council), no longer under the direct responsibility of the Bishops. Pavan's talk at the Meeting in Manila was quoted as a factor contributing to this changed theoretical approach, defined as follows:

> Organizations of Catholic citizens (acting for the purposes of the Catholic Social Movement) are subject to the Hierarchy in all that pertains to faith or morals, but should not be under its positive direction, or its direct control, nor should they involve the authority of the Hierarchy in the policies or programmes which they put forward.

In Italy also, mobilisation of committed Catholics against the real threat of a Communist take-over in the democratic elections of 1948 had been continued after the elections, but no longer by Catholic Action as such: responsibility was taken by Civic Committees set up by Luigi Gedda, Vice-President — and later, President — of Italian Catholic Action.

'All India'

At the closing session in Manila, Veronese asked Cardinal Gracias to take back with him a 'message of fraternal solidarity' to the First All India Catholic Lay Leaders Conference, that was to be held in Nagpur, from 14 to 18 December.

For the Conference — the first of its kind — delegates came from fifty dioceses, clergy and laity, without distinction of class or caste: a cross-section of the Catholic population of India. International observers had also been invited, among them Pavan and Maria Vittoria Donadeo from COPECIAL. Predictably, at a press conference on the eve of the Conference, journalists tried to interpret the event politically; but the Conveners insisted that this was no political get-together, but a meeting of the Catholic laity to see how they could play their role in the civic, economic and cultural life of modern India, after seven years of independence.

Except for the inauguration, the Conference was held in two sessions: English and Hindi. A Central Committee for the Lay Apostolate was formed. Its President, Mariadas Ruthnaswamy, of Madras, jurist and man of letters, was to speak at the Second World Congress, in 1957, on the great need for a *social* leadership assumed by the Catholic laity, 'Of political leaders we have enough and some to spare'.[13]

Pax Romana in Asia

At Christmas 1959 and New Year 1960, Manila was the rendezvous for international conferences dealing with various aspects of the intellectual and university apostolate under the aegis of Pax Romana and in collaboration with UNESCO.

After the Christmas Midnight Mass in the Metropolitan Cathedral, on the morning of 26 December, the Interfederal Assembly of Pax Romana–IMCS and the first Pax Romana Graduate Conference in Asia opened jointly at St Thomas University to the strains of the Philippine Constabulary Band. Student delegates and graduates met separately. From 2 to 9 January, the program was further complicated by the intertwining of the two Pax Romana meetings with public sessions of a Conference of Experts on 'The Present Impact of the Great Religions of the World upon the Lives of the People in the Orient and Occident'. This was organised by Pax Romana as part of a major project of UNESCO on 'Mutual Appreciation of Eastern and Western Cultural Values'. The religions represented were: Hinduism, Buddhism, Shintoism, Judaism, Islam, Christianity (Protestantism, the Orthodox Church and the Catholic Church). The Chairman was the distinguished Orientalist Olivier Lacombe (Paris). The subjects proposed for discussion were religion and spiritual life in our technological society in relation to racial, social and economic problems, the family, culture, and the emergence of the world community.

The conference illustrated the nature — and the possibilities — of a Catholic international organisation's collaboration with the intergovernmental agencies. At the 24th World Congress of Pax Romana (Vienna, September 1958), the Director General of UNESCO, Luther Evans, had formally invited the collaboration of Pax Romana. Expressing his interest in this Catholic organisation ('in spite of my name'!), he said:

> It is not UNESCO's task to embark on the relations between religions and Churches . . . It is however possible to grant to the religious factor its due role in the development of the mutual appreciation of East and West cultural values . . . That the Western public should obtain a just idea of the richness

and depth of the spiritual traditions of the East is essential. It is equally important that the Eastern peoples should recognize that Western civilization does not amount only to the invention of machines and the improvement of material well-being, but consists as well in the maintenance and the deepening of some of the highest aspirations of humanity. The growth of understanding between East and West is one of the fields where the help of the non-governmental organizations, so valuable for UNESCO, is irreplaceable. Among all these bodies UNESCO follows with very special attention the work and projects of Pax Romana.[14]

This request to Pax Romana was made very shortly before Evans was succeeded as Director General by the founding Vice-President of Pax Romana–ICMICA, Vittorino Veronese.

Asian Laity, 1964

In November–December 1964, the 38th International Eucharistic Congress was held in Bombay, with the participation of Paul VI. This was the occasion for a meeting on lay apostolate in Asia, attended by delegates from India, Ceylon, Hong Kong, Indonesia, Japan, Malaysia, Pakistan and the Philippines, with observers from Australia and CIO. It was followed by an Indian National Convention of lay leaders, to which visiting delegates were invited.

The Asian Meeting did not show much change since Manila 1955, but a new note was sounded in the mention of 'collaboration in certain fields' with non-Catholics or non-Christians. Contact with international organisations had also developed, as witnessed by the 17th Plenary Assembly of Pax Romana–ICMICA, hosted by the Newman Association of India. The theme, 'Human Problems of Economic Development', was brought alive by the visible signs of such problems in India, reflected later in Paul VI's Encyclical *Populorum Progressio*.[15]

These various meetings were by no means devoted only to pious and apostolic rhetoric. The report presented by Fr J. B. Gauci at the Indian Convention was rigorously objective:

In India, the lay apostolate is not playing the vital role it is meant to play in the Church . . . The majority think that our lay apostolate organizations can be more aptly classified as 'pious associations' for the spiritual benefit of their individual members.

This was attributed to 'clerical domination', 'apostolic spoon-feeding', the 'ghetto complex', inadequacy of home and school training and the lack of 'status' of the laity in the Church. To help adult Christians to contribute to the political life of the country, a *non-political Association fully manned by laymen* (inclusive language was not yet on the agenda!) should be set up to (a) collect funds and help competent Catholics to stand at elections, (b) study political programs and give guidance to the general public.[16]

Before leaving the Indian scene, there is a long-standing debt to be paid. When I first thought of writing on laity history leading up to Vatican II, I promised to give due acknowledgement to the contribution of Valerian Cardinal Gracias — in India, Asia and at world level. Many publications document this contribution. As a personal comment, I quote a Profile that appeared in *The Advocate* (Melbourne) of 24 December 1964. The columnist, Florence Hagelthorn, knowing that I would be in Bombay for the International Eucharistic Congress, had asked for a few lines about the Congress host, Cardinal Gracias. I wrote:

> His Eminence is in the fullest sense a 'Prince of the Church'. It is hard to use this term today without an uneasy feeling. Between Pope John's first call to *aggiornamento* and the day when Pope Paul donated his tiara to the poor, so much has been said and written . . . about the need to return to a greater simplicity, there has been so sharp an assault on the worthy 'Monsignor' and the intricacies of 'Their Excellencies' wardrobe and procedures . . . and yet, how else describe Bombay's Cardinal Archbishop than as a 'Prince of the Church'?
>
> In saying that, I am not making him one whit the less the Pastor and servant of his people . . . If we are impressed by the majestic figure of the Cardinal, what impresses us still more is that other and truer mark of spiritual aristocracy — his serving

spirit, his personal care for every detail . . . his simply managing to be so completely himself, to be — in all the dignity of his function — an original human person.

The Laity in the Church's Life and Mission in Asia[17]

Twenty years later, this was the title of the continental meeting for Asia organised in Hong Kong by the Pontifical Council for the Laity, with the collaboration of the Committee for the Laity of the Federation of Asian Bishops' Conferences (FABC). From 2 to 6 December 1983, it was attended — under the Presidency of Cardinal Opilio Rossi — by fifteen bishops, ten priests and seventy lay people from fourteen countries.

The problems facing Christian lay people in Asian society were not new: crippling economic dependence on more developed nations; injustice and corruption in political life; demographic pressures; migrations; urbanisation; the secularisation of a technological society; discrimination against women; the caste system, etc. But there were also new accents on the mission of the laity.

After a vast *tour d'horizon* of local situations presented by delegates from the different countries, an overall view was given by Alan de Lastic, Auxiliary Bishop of Calcutta and Member of the FABC Committee for the Laity.[18] As a starting-point he took Asia as the 'cradle of the great religions of the world', asking: Why has Christianity made so little headway in confrontation with these religions? Is it only because these religions are 'closely allied to highly developed cultures', in a continent where Christianity is for the most part a 'newcomer'? But 'rapid strides' have been made in many countries of Asia to make the Gospel message more accessible through inculturation, preserving and promoting authentic values of these cultures.[19]

That is true, but how far have lay people been involved? Are not the laity in Asia still 'too heavily dependent on the clergy?' They have to be prepared to meet challenges in socio-economic and political fields — even in an international dimension; to take up, where necessary, a counter-cultural stand on questions of justice and discrimination (caste, dowry, etc.). But they have also a mission in evangelisation, and one that calls for a new maturity: an appreciation of Asian religious values, combined with a deep and informed faith in the uniqueness of Christianity and of the one Saviour and Mediator, Jesus Christ. From among such mature Christians, 'suitable lay persons', de Lastic suggested, 'should be trained to give retreats and spiritual conferences'.

Towards the Synod Assembly for Asia

Alan de Lastic's questions are reflected in the *Lineamenta*, the preparatory document for the Special Assembly for Asia of the Synod of Bishops, which is expected to take place before the Year 2000.[20] 'Greater attention is being given today to the laity and their formation' (15), also because, in the vast field for evangelisation in Asia, so many cultural and social problems are involved. 'Local Churches are becoming more aware of their missionary vocation.' Formation is helped by the development of ashram life. Especially in India, Japan and the Philippines, ashrams (under various names) become 'centres of dialogue, inculturation, spirituality, contemplation, God experience . . . and contact with followers of other religions'.

In treating the radical questions being raised about 'the uniqueness of Jesus Christ in the history of salvation' — a uniqueness and centrality that 'must be safeguarded' (23) — the *Lineamenta* does not relate this question explicitly to the formation of a mature laity. But, it is affirmed, 'Asia will increasingly welcome Jesus Christ provided that the Church's members seek to become men and women of God who have seen and touched what they proclaim' (cf. 1 Jn 1:1–2).

Seoul 1994

Following the Meeting in Hong Kong (1983), regional meetings were held for South Asia, South-East Asia and East Asia. The whole process culminated in the Asian Laity Meeting organised in September 1994 in Seoul by the Lay Apostolate Council of Korea, with the participation of the PCL and the FABC Office of Laity. The theme: 'The Commitment of the Laity in the Church's Mission with Special Reference to Implementing the Social Teachings'.

In the Foreword to the Proceedings[21] — well presented in Korean and English and profusely illustrated — Cardinal Eduardo Pironio recalls the experience as a lasting witness to the 'vitality and the enthusiasm of the laity in the young Churches that are springing up in the very ancient Oriental cultures'.

Looking back to Manila 1955, which claimed 'Asia for Christ', and to all that had gone between, one might wonder only at the Title of the Proceedings: 'The *First* Asian Laity Meeting' (my emphasis). For each new generation, history begins today!

Oceania: a far-flung 'continent'

The last of the 'continental' meetings was unquestionably a 'first'. In 1986, during preparation for the Synod of Bishops on the Laity, the PCL took the initiative for a meeting on 'The Vocation of the Laity in the Life and Mission of the Church in Oceania'.[22] This involved territories under the jurisdiction of four Episcopal Conferences: Australia, the Pacific Islands (Conferentia Episcopalis Pacifici, CEPAC), New Zealand, Papua New Guinea and the Solomon Islands.

New names appeared for the first time on the 'map' of the lay apostolate: Nauru, Papeete, Pago Pago, Samoa, Vanuatu, Tonga. The delegations from Australia and New Zealand included respectively three Aborigines and three Maoris (in each case, two women and one man). The Meeting was held in Auckland with the New Zealand Laity Commission playing a key role in its organisation.

There were vastly different contexts to be taken into account: from the modern — or post-modern — challenges of urban civilisation for the post-Conciliar Church, to young Churches, divided by wide expanses of ocean that not even modern means of communication and transport adequately span, but united in a common discovery of new possibilities for Christian life and mission. It was in French Polynesia that ecumenism was discovered in action when a new Catholic church was to be inaugurated and eager help was forthcoming from Protestant neighbours (a neighbour being anyone who lives from 100 to 300 kilometres from your home).

There were the personal situations also that were emblematic for a new generation of lay Christians — men and women — 'missionaries to themselves'. Lucy Keino, from Papua New Guinea, despite having had no formal education after leaving the mission school, was giving seminars for women and training leaders for basic communities. Rosa Lee Thaiday from Australia was a respected Church worker in Townsville; but as a child from an Aboriginal Reserve, she had known the suffering of a family disrupted by misguided 'missionary' zeal. With her husband she is deeply involved in the Australian and Islander Catholic Council. Kajetan Kado is a layman from Suva (Fiji). Fiji has been an archdiocese since 1966. It has thirty-three parishes, Catholic schools and a Teachers Training College, as well as many catechists. Old habits die hard and there are still those who think that the parish priest must do everything by himself. With others in the Parish Council, Kajetan is concerned mainly with facilitating 'a healthy Catholic relationship between the laity and priest . . . and also between the laity themselves'.[23]

The Australian delegates, meeting as a Regional Group, adopted as top priorities: forming lay people for their mission in the world and establishing a national lay voice. As a statement to the Church in Australia, they made the following submission:

> There is a need for the Church to bring a message of *Love* and *Hope* and *Special Concern* to all people, in particular those who are suffering amongst *Aboriginal Groups*, *Ethnic Groups*, *Divorced*, *Separated*, *Single Parents*, those *Re-married Outside the Church*, those going through the *Marriage Tribunal process for Annulments*, *Inactive Catholics*, who, as a group, comprise a large proportion of the Body of Christ in Australia.[24]

Latin America

I was preparing this excursus into Latin America when the television flashed on the interreligious Meeting of Prayer for Peace in Milan — the seventh in the series inaugurated by John Paul II in Assisi in 1986. On the Square in front of the great gothic cathedral, representatives of churches and world religions were seated beneath a symbolic rainbow before passing, one by one, with a lighted torch to feed a flaming brazier of Unity, and to sign an appeal to the peoples of the world. In the centre of the group I discerned a small figure in a tropical soutane and wearing a wooden pectoral cross: Helder Camara, Emeritus

Archbishop of Olinda and Recife (Brazil). As he came forward there was a round of applause from the thousands on the Square. They were greeting the apostle of the 'favelas', the shantytowns of Brazil, living symbol — with Mother Teresa of Calcutta — of the Church's option for the poor, for peace through justice and love.

Memory flashed back to the 1950s, to an insignificant little priest in a black soutane (but without the round hat, symbol of Roman clericality) who was alighting from a crowded bus in Trastevere, on his way to see Vittorino Veronese. At the time, Helder Camara, Auxiliary Bishop of Rio de Janeiro, was Director of the Brazilian National Secretariat of Catholic Action. In 1951, he had come to Rome with the Brazilian delegation to the First World Congress and with Manuel Larrain, Bishop of Talca (Chile), Ecclesiastical Assistant of the Interamerican Secretariat of Catholic Action in Santiago. Veronese had suggested forms of cooperation on international problems and in 1953, had attended the Third Interamerican Catholic Action week, held at Chimboté (Peru).

The decisive year was 1955 when about 100 Bishops met for the first General Conference of the Latin American Episcopate, held in Rio de Janeiro. The CELAM — the first federation of national hierarchies — came into being, with the approval of Pius XII. The President was Archbishop Miranda of Mexico. The first and second Vice-Presidents were Manuel Larrain and Helder Camara. In 1963, Larrain would be elected President. CELAM had a Lay Apostolate department.

We have seen that Larrain and Camara were both experienced in 'ecclesiastically assisting' Catholic Action. In Brazil, where 70 per cent of the population lived by agriculture, this would be mainly a *rural* apostolate. In 1949, Camara — not yet of shantytown fame — had been one of a group of priests attending a study session on rural problems, during which Mgr Luigi Ligutti lectured on 'Man's Relation to the Land'. But there were also other areas of lay apostolate. In Rio, the Dom Vital Centre was forming an intellectual elite. Based on the French model, there were specialised Catholic Action movements for students (YCS), Workers (YCW) etc., as well as the CFM, founded in 1949.

On the implementation — and not merely the theory — of Christian social principles, Larrain was working with Luigi Ligutti,

Pietro Pavan and others. In 1961, the bishops of Chile decided to launch agrarian reform, to combat the scandal of the vast holdings of absentee landowners and the exploitation of the 'campesinos', the rural proletariat. To give an example, they distributed lands belonging to their dioceses and they sold lands for the benefit of rural families, on a long-term loan basis at moderate rates. The venture aroused public interest. 'Land reform has begun in Chile with the soutanes!' declared the headlines. Religious congregations began to follow suit. When interviewed, Larrain insisted: 'You mustn't give a pessimistic vision of Latin America!'[25] There were reasons for hope: the growth of a social sense and of lay involvement; the pastoral sense of the clergy, their generosity and simplicity of life.

During the Council, Larrain had been one of the group of bishops who spoke out in favour of a spirit of poverty in all fields of the Church's life. In 1964, as President of CELAM, he wrote a Letter,[26] 'Failure or Success of Latin America'. Under-development was, for Latin Americans, 'a threat, as immediate, as permanent and more serious than the atom bomb' — a 'war' that could be won, a responsibility in a special way for lay Christians. This clarion call was almost a testament. On 22 June 1966, Larrain died in a car accident.

The Latin America of which Larrain wrote was briefly evoked by Pius XII in his address to the Second World Congress in 1957: demographic increase, urbanisation and industrialisation, the invasion of Protestant sects, secularisation, Marxism — the most active element in the universities and in almost all workers' organisations. The Pope's diagnosis was confirmed in the report from Latin America made to the Congress by a layman, José I. Lasaga (Cuba), President of the World Federation of Sodalities of Our Lady.[27] He spoke also of grounds for hope in a region 'whose inhabitants, in an absolute majority, consider themselves Catholics, where minority groups lead an exemplary life of faith and the great masses of the people live it partially'. The deep-rooted Catholic tradition could come to light paradoxically. A Catholic writer in Bolivia witnessed a Marxist street demonstration. The miners were shouting 'Down with the priests!' but they raised their caps as they passed the Catholic church. (A little like the good Communist matrons we saw praying the Rosary outside the Party headquarters after Stalin's death!) A few years later, the Cuban revolution was to inaugurate a period of social and ideological unrest and violence.

The response of the Latin American Church to the situation created by Vatican II came with the Second General Conference of the Bishops in Medellin in 1968. The Church sought to 'Latin-Americanise' itself. And the active laity were summoned to make their contribution. In 1970, when the tensions that had grown during the 1960s were at their height, the Secretary of the *Consilium de Laicis* Marcel Uylenbroeck, visited Brazil, Paraguay, Uruguay and Argentina. Predictably, he met complex situations and conflicting opinions. But he also met commitment that was at times authentic heroism.

In Brazil, under the military government, anyone disagreeing with government policy was liable to be branded as Communist, arrested and even tortured. Uylenbroeck reported:

> In my opinion, the most serious problem is not torture, although it is inadmissible from a human and Christian point of view. It is the climate of *non-participation*, in a society governed by an 'elite', where the mass has no role. The result is a situation of 'anti-education'. People are prevented from developing responsibly, even when they are taught to read and write, and their material situation is improved. I wonder whether, in Church circles, people are aware of this deadly aspect of the 'anti-educative' regime.

Where trade unions still existed, they were only allowed to concern themselves with the workers' free time. The groups that 'represented' students in the universities were also reduced to welfare work and leisure activities. It is no wonder that the Third General Conference of the Latin American Bishops (Puebla, 1979), meeting after the crisis years, noted a relative absence of organised lay action in society. The Conference encouraged popular piety as an authentic expression of faith and stressed the roles of family, parish and school, while encouraging lay movements. As a privileged instrument for the Church's mission, especially in rural areas, the Conference adopted the ecclesial base (grassroots) communities: cells of the Church gathered at local level around the Eucharist.

After the Puebla General Conference (1979), the Pontifical Council for the Laity sponsored a meeting of bishops and laity in Bogota.[28] During the preparation for this meeting, it was noted:

> After Medellin (1968), a growing number of militant lay groups generously threw themselves into the turmoil of Latin America's socio-political life . . . Their acute awareness of the need for greater justice, solidarity, fraternity and respect for human dignity shook vast areas of the Latin American Church. This was a qualitative leap forward . . . It resulted in a greater pluralism of political options for Christians. Whereas Catholics had traditionally supported confessional and/or conservative politics, in some countries they joined popular and nationalistic Parties, or else the newly created Christian Democratic Parties; while fringe groups within the Church adopted the political 'praxis' of the left, hegemonized by a variety of Marxist schools of thought . . . This pluralism led to a profound crisis in communion between Christians . . .

Even the Church's social teaching raised problems. Some felt that new formulations were needed to meet new situations. Some looked to Marxism for a 'scientific' outlook that could be juxtaposed to a vague sense of the Faith. The General Conference in Puebla, rising above the conflictual situation, wanted a 'preferential option for the poor' that would not be ideological, but inspired by a truly Christian vision of life.

International links

Developments among the Catholic laity in Latin America during the decades leading up to or contemporaneous with Vatican II would hardly have been possible without the stimulus and cooperation of a number of Catholic international organisations: WUCWO, World Federation of Catholic Young Women and Girls, MIAMSI, International Catholic Union for Social Service, International YCW and YCS, Christian Life Communities, International Catholic Film Organization. The fact that these and others were all based in Europe, bringing a European experience of Catholic life and apostolate, was not a cultural problem in the sense that it could be — and was — in Africa and Asia. When Pius XI issued his call to Catholic Action, it was natural for Latin American countries to look for models in Spain, Portugal, France, Italy.

Cultural links with Europe were, in particular, a natural channel for university and intellectual apostolate. Pax Romana played a special role, whether as the student organisation set up in Fribourg in 1921, or as the two Movements — IMCS and ICMICA — which together were to make up Pax Romana after its 'refounding' in Rome in 1947. Already in 1933, groups from Latin America and Spain had met in Rome and founded an Ibero-American Confederation of Catholic Students, with collaboration from Pax Romana. During the war years in Europe, the Administrative Secretary of Pax Romana, Rudi Salat (from Germany) was moving from country to country in South America, helping to found national student federations. After his return to Fribourg, most countries of Latin America could be represented at the Pax Romana World Congress of 1946. In April 1949, the Third Interamerican Congress of Pax Romana students met in Mexico. In July 1962, the 25th World Congress was celebrated by the two Movements of Pax Romana in Montevideo on the theme, 'The Social Responsibility of the University and of University People'.

For the Federations of Pax Romana, as for most organisations — at least in Europe and the Americas — the 1960s and the 'angry seventies' would mean turbulence and crisis. In November 1979, Ramon Sugranyes was in Mexico for the 23rd General Assembly of Pax Romana–ICMICA. One disconcerting aspect — but also a sign of growth — was the fact that only nine European countries were represented. The other 'disturbing' factor came from strong statements about social problems in Latin America and the Church's responsibility in relation to them. There were reactions in the Assembly and also in Rome. But misunderstandings were finally cleared up, at least as to the Movement's non-political stance.

Two main speakers at the Assembly had been Leonardo Boff and Gustavo Gutierrez. 'Liberation theology comes from the poor', Gutierrez affirmed. He continued:

I have spoken of theology because it was my theme. I hope that the idea has crept through that theology is not the most important thing. Often, friends have asked me: What is the impact of liberation theology in Latin America? I tell them sincerely that, although I am linked to this theological perspective, its impact has little interest for me. I confess that there are two things that interest me: the process of liberation of the popular classes, of the marginalized races, of the despised cultures of this continent, and the presence of the Gospel in the heart of these struggles.[29]

Europe

When I arrived for the first time in London in 1936, I discovered that I was a 'colonial' — a term that did not exist in my vocabulary. Moving to France, I 'discovered' I was Australian — a curiosity that many of my friends were meeting for the first time. My presence gave an extra worldwide dimension to international meetings. When I returned to France after the war, the world had become smaller and Australia better known. Today I have another identity. I am an 'extra-Communitarian', sharing the status with Africans, Asians and Americans. The European laity story is not my story; but it is one of which I have had glimpses from one or another vantage point over more than forty years.

Copenhagen 1960

When this story begins, the structuring of a future united Europe was already well to the fore in the thought and efforts of 'informed' Catholic circles.[30]

A significant moment was to be the first European Meeting for the Lay Apostolate, sponsored by COPECIAL in Copenhagen in September 1960.[31] It followed an Anglo-Scandinavian Meeting that brought a group of Catholics from Denmark, Norway and Sweden to London in July 1959 — an initiative that owed much to the exuberant creative energies of the Honorary Secretary of the Lay Apostolate Group for England and Wales, Jacquie Stuyt-Simpson.

It was not an easy solution to set the first European Meeting in Denmark, but it proved to be a happy one. Delegates came from sixteen countries and several CIO. The Bishop of Copenhagen, John Theodore Suhr, OSB, had granted permission — not without misgivings, for it was his 'first congress'. He entrusted local organisation to the Catholic Women's League and its President, Aase Andersen. The venue was the NIMB Restaurant, bordering on the famous Tivoli Gardens. The manager of the restaurant expressed his surprise at seeing this unaccustomed public — a joyous (and industrious) community of some 120 people, bishops, priests and laity, men and women, young and not so young.

Diversity and a common heritage

The European Lay Apostolate was approached at three levels: national, continental, and collaboration at world level.

For the national level documentation had been requested and sent to participants before the Meeting. This was the basis for a factual survey that brought out the diversity of the forms of lay apostolate and of the social, cultural and religious contexts from which they emerged. It showed also a common heritage: not only common doctrinal and spiritual bases, but an historical evolution in the idea and reality of lay apostolate that was common to almost all the countries. Bishop Jacques Ménager (later Archbishop of Reims) had distinguished four main periods:

1 The first half of the nineteenth century: growth of individual apostolate.

2 The Pontificate of Pius IX: Catholic Associations for the defence of the Church: for example, the German 'Bonifatiusverein' and the Irish Catholic Young Men's Society date from 1849; the Austrian 'Cartellverband' for university people from the same period; Italy's GIAC — Catholic Action Youth — from 1868.

3 The development of Christian Social Action: 'Action of Catholics' for Leo XIII, Catholic Action for Pius X.

4 With Pius XI, Catholic Action, defined as apostolate in the strict sense: organised action of the faithful, in collaboration with the hierarchy, for the Church's apostolic mission; the rise of specialised Catholic Action movements (YCW, etc.).

Then there were present trends including a new accent on spiritual life and evangelisation and greater collaboration across frontiers of all kinds.

Diversity in the contemporary religious situation was determined by many factors. The situation of the small Catholic minority was very different in a country marked by the Reformation (and which might still bear the scars of religious persecution), and in one where the majority were Orthodox Christians or again, as in Turkey, of Islamic tradition. Where the Protestant majority was made up for the most part of convinced Christians, the approach of the Catholic laity could not be the same as when faced with almost total religious indifference. The Catholic majority, in its turn, might be undermined by traditional anti-clericalism, or infiltrated with vague heresies, which had to be met, not with argument, but through spiritual renewal and the witness of an adult Christianity.

One point of the survey was less factual. It suggested a study of comparative psychology in relation to lay apostolate in the countries of Europe. It might show French clarity reflected in the analytical multiplication of specialised Catholic Action groups; philosophical depth and organising ability meeting in preparation of the German 'Katholikentage' (Catholic Congresses); Ireland's piety sending forth the Legion of Mary on an intrepid project of world 'conquest'; Swiss federalism expressed in three different forms of Catholic Action; the contrast between the studied informality of the English Lay Apostolate Group and the hierarchical structure of Italian Catholic Action. (In the 1960s, this might be seen as expression of 'the Italians' innate sense of hierarchy'. But what of Italy in the 1990s!)

The riches and problems of diversity were approached from a different angle by Jean-Pierre Dubois-Dumée:

> What we lack is the possibility, or the art, of looking at Europe as we look at South America or Africa . . . Being short-sighted, all we see in Europe is its extreme diversity: the overall features escape our notice. It is true that mentalities are very different in Denmark and Spain, or even in England and Scotland . . . But, from a distance, resemblances appear. I asked an American friend

what he thought of the lay apostolate in Europe. 'I admire your leaders', he wrote, 'but has not the mass been neglected in favour of the elite . . . What strikes us also is the tendency, among 'militants' and in the Church generally, to want to express ideas and construct theories while neglecting action and the setting up of institutions'. My correspondent was struck also by the *feminine* aspect of the Church — and the apostolate — in Europe. 'Look at the decorations, listen to the hymns, the sermons, the prayers. The men are like foreigners in all of that'.[32]

Achille Glorieux, in his response to the survey, saw as 'the gravest aspect of the almost general de-Christianization', the 'failure to react in the face of evil', even among 'good Catholics'.

> They go to Mass, receive the Sacraments regularly, and even belong to Catholic associations; but their faith has practically no influence on the rest of their lives: what they read, their entertainments, their reaction to other social groups, other peoples and races, their vote, their attitude on questions of conjugal and professional morality . . . But, as appearances are generally safeguarded, it would be hard to make them aware of the 'two sectors' in their life.

Later, the Scottish delegation wrote announcing plans for a national lay apostolate meeting, whose theme would be 'Mgr Glorieux's "double life" '!

Continental and Oceanic Catholicism

A particular view of European Catholics had come to light during preparation for the Second World Congress. On 26 March 1955, the review *America* published an article, 'Continental and Oceanic Catholicism'. The writer, Irish-born Desmond Fennell, after living for three years in Europe, felt he had come to know 'the life and spirit of Continental Catholicism'. He distinguished this from the 'Oceanic' brand that had emerged as a result of massive emigration, after the great famine of the 1840s, to Great Britain, Australia, the United States and scattered areas of the British Commonwealth. He wrote:

> During the last 170 years Continental Catholicism has had to contend with openly anti-Christian Liberal, Socialist and Anarchist political movements, with organized political anticlericalism and atheistic Communism as a mass phenomenon. Usually these have taken the form of breakaway movements inside the body of Catholicism. Such movements have never been important in the English-speaking countries. [Continental Catholicism was, on the whole] traditionally reactionary. [But in 'Oceanic' countries] Catholicism has not been *obliged* to accept democratic and labour movements; it has grown up with them and inside them . . . The working classes were never lost to the Church [which was] largely urban, in contrast to the largely rural Catholicism of the countries of modern Europe. [It lacked perhaps] the higher intellectual refinements (the Catholicism of the London *Tablet*).

Many things have changed since the 1950s in rural Europe and Irish-Catholic Australia but Desmond Fennell's view has at least historical interest.

The 'new Europe'

The tasks of Catholics in the 'new Europe' were introduced by Jean Kerkhofs, SJ (Louvain). He presented the findings of an international experts' Conference organised in Munich, in July 1960, on the eve of the 37th International Eucharistic Congress.

A special concern was the call to prayer, and the provision of information and concrete help (where possible) for the 'Silent Church', those deprived of religious freedom. Also discussed was the reception in Europe of Asian and African students who were coming into a society for which they were not prepared and the promotion of lay missionary groups that could help the laity in young Christian communities to take responsibility for the needs of their developing countries.

The active concern of lay Catholics for the structures of the 'new Europe' was already in evidence. The Catholic Office on European Problems (OCIPE) had been set up in Strasbourg in 1956.

Looking beyond Europe

Placing European tasks in their worldwide context, Dubois-Dumée pointed to the two main channels for international apostolate: the CIO and COPECIAL.[33]

> The CIO certainly look rather European . . . After all, was it not normal that their implantation should begin in the countries that were the most Catholic and the best equipped for international action? It is important, however, that this European — even, Latin — predominance should be attenuated. Great progress in the way of universalization has already been made. International congresses are being held in every corner of the globe. Many CIO have active national sections in from 30 to 80 countries. The role of this vast network is too little known. But, I assure you that the CIO are listened to when they speak — when they speak *well* — in meetings of the UN and its Specialized Agencies, on human rights, education, technical assistance to developing nations, etc.

Bishops and Laity in a changing Europe

Discussions at Copenhagen led naturally to proposals for future contact, and even coordination. A long process of consultation reached a solution only after Vatican II, with the creation, in 1968, of the European Forum of National Committees of the Laity.

The delegates did not feel competent to make explicit recommendations for action at hierarchical level; but the 'respectful wish' was expressed that a body be created for 'collaboration at the level of the Episcopate'. The wish met with no objection from the bishops present.[34] Subsequently, it was communicated to the Cardinal Secretary of State. In 1966, a Liaison Secretariat was set up for the Bishops' Conferences of Europe; today, there is the Council of European

Episcopal Conferences. As a direct result? — No! But the laity had the honour of providing the first occasion for expression of what was a 'felt need' of the Church in Europe.

A pilgrimage . . . and more

Sunday afternoon, 18 September, brought coaches to the door of NIMB, and a Danish interlude for the motley group of Europeans. First, there was a pilgrimage to the shrine of Our Lady of Aasebakken in the monastery of the Benedictine nuns, where Danish Catholics come each year, singing — as we did — '*Mater Christi, Mater Ecclesiae, Veneranda Patrona Daniae, O Maria . . .*'. Next, a visit to a medieval church. (I suspect that Bishop Suhr took special pleasure in introducing our Portuguese Bishop, who had surely never before met a Lutheran Rector, much less the Rector's wife!) Then, after Mass in the modern church of Knud Lavard, a Danish supper of 'smorrebrod', Compline sung in the church . . . and back to NIMB.

The Second European Meeting [35]

In May 1966, a second European Meeting was organised by COPECIAL at St Pölten, some 30 miles from Vienna, with the cooperation of Austrian Catholic Action, and the participation of the Apostolic Nuncio, Franz Zak — happy to be for a few days 'Bishop of Europe'. In an atmosphere which was still that of Vatican II, Roberto Tucci, SJ, presented 'The New Vision of the Church'. Cardinal Franz König gave a wide view of a 'changing' Europe: its responsibilities 'of service and of sacrifice'; its unity:

> which cannot be created by power and force, but only by spiritually overcoming that which separates, by believing in the future, by hoping that intelligence will achieve more than force; above all, by patience. A Europe including those countries where the Church keeps silent because she is not allowed to say what she wants to say and does not want to say what she is expected to say.[36]

As well as promoting 'fruitful collaboration in the apostolate at the European level', the Meeting was an important moment in the immediate preparation for the Third World Congress — the post-Conciliar Congress.

In July 1981, in the series of 'continental' Meetings, bishops, priests and laity from twenty-one countries of Europe responded to the invitation of the Pontifical Council for the Laity to discuss, in Vienna, 'The Pastoral Responsibilities of the Bishops vis-à-vis the Laity, Present and Committed in Society'.[37]

In 1989, the symbolic collapse of 'the Wall' would usher in a new stage in the history, not only of Europe and of the Church in Europe, but of the world.

1. Archives of COPECIAL, letter from Cleire to Veronese, 16 April 1954.

2. Archives of COPECIAL, letter from Knox to Veronese, 17 October 1954.

3. The Proceedings of the meetings at Kisubi and in the Sudan were only published in mimeographed form: 'Kisubi' in French and English, the Sudanese Convention in English.

4. The Proceedings were published in 1962 by COPECIAL for the Lay Apostolate Department of the Tanganyika Episcopal Conference.

5. 'Panafricano–Malagasy Laity Seminar', Accra, Ghana, 11–18 August 1971, Special Number, The Laity Today, op. cit., 1972.

6. Lay Voices at the Synod, op. cit., 19, 1988, pp. 72–83.

7. Acts of the First Asian Meeting for the Apostolate of the Laity, COPECIAL, Rome, 1956, pp. 9–10.

8. *Acts*, op. cit., p. 59.

9. *Acts*, op. cit., pp. 90–100.

10. The articles were excerpts from a paper Santamaria had presented at the National Conference of the Catholic Social Movement in 1953 under the title, 'Religious Apostolate and Political Action'.

11. Jean Daly, apart from being my very good friend, was an outstanding personality. She twice represented Australia in meetings of the United Nations Status of Women Commission. In 1967 she was awarded the OBE for services to the community and particularly to the welfare of women. She was an associate to her father, Justice Edmunds, before her marriage to Harry Daly, one of Sydney's leading anaesthetists. She was also the first President of the NSW section of St Joan's Social and Political Alliance.

12. Cf. Franco Biffi, *Prophet of Our Times: The Social Thought of Cardinal Pietro Pavan*, New City Press, 1992, pp. 111–16. Cf. also the Pastoral Constitution *Gaudium et Spes*, 43.

For a synthesis of the whole 'Movement' problem and its repercussions, see Dr Bruce Duncan, C.SS.R: '40 Years after the s.p.l.i.t' in *National Outlook*, Sydney, December 1994, pp. 16–19. Dr Duncan ends on a positive note: 'The Church was never quite the same after the Split . . . Yet, the Catholic community had learnt to think more carefully, to recognize more clearly the limits and ambiguities of political action, and to adapt more constructively to the dilemmas of living in a secular culture'.

13. *Laymen Face the World*, op. cit., p. 91.

14. *UNESCO Pax Romana Meeting at Manila and First Pax Romana Graduate Conference in Asia*, Introduction, Manila, (no date), pp. v–vi.

15. *Populorum Progressio*, on the Development of Peoples, 26 March 1967.

16. Cf. *Lay Apostolate*, 1, COPECIAL, Rome, 1965, pp. 21–23.

17. Cf. Documentation Service, Pontifical Council for the Laity, 14, 1984.

18. Bishop Alan de Lastic, *An Overall View of the Asian Context in which the Laity Must Fulfil Their Mission*, Documentation Service 14 of the Pontifical Council for the Laity, pp. 137–53.

19. Cf. the Declaration on Relations with Non-Christian Religion States, *Nostra Aetate*, 2, 'Let Christians, while witnessing to their own faith and way of life, acknowledge, preserve and

encourage the spiritual and moral truths found among non-Christians, also their social life and culture.

20. The full text is given in *Origins*, op. cit., January 1997.

21. *Proceedings: The First Asian Laity Meeting, 4–9 September 1994, Korea*, printed by Word of Today Publishing Company, Seoul, October 1995 for the Catholic Lay Apostolate Council of Korea.

22. Cf. Documentation Service 17 of the Pontifical Council for the Laity, 1986. The volume also documents further the 'promotion of the laity' in Asia, from the 1980s, through the activity of the Federation of Asian Bishops' Conferences (cf. pp. 160–85).

23. Documentation Service 17 of the Pontifical Council for the Laity, 1986, p. 84.

24. Ibid., p. 202.

25. *La Croix*, Paris, 1–2 January, 1963.

26. Ibid., 22 September 1965, pp. 5–6.

27. *Laymen Face the World*, op. cit., pp. 67–80.

28. Cf. *Los laicos en la vida y misión de la Iglesia*, Pontifical Council for the Laity, Vatican City, 1980.

29. *Convergence*, 1/2, Pax Romana Journal, Fribourg, Switzerland, 1981, p. 24.

30. Cf. R. Goldie, 'The Idea of Europe and the Catholic Laity', in *Pro Fide et Iustitia: festschrift für Agostino Kardinal Casaroli zum 70. Geburtstag*, Herbert Schambeck, Duncker & Humblot, Berlin, 1984, pp. 139–51.

31. Cf. *Lay Apostolate*, COPECIAL Bulletin, 1960, 3.

32. This would be the drift also of an article by Karl Rahner: 'L'homme dans l'Eglise' (The man in the Church), in the French review *Anneau d'Or*, March–April 1963.

33. Dubois-Dumée's intervention in *Lay Apostolate*, 1966, 2, p. 10.

34. The bishops present, with Bishop Suhr of Copenhagen; Archbishop Castelli, Vice-President of the Ecclesiastical Commission of COPECIAL; Mario I. Castellano, OP, Secretary of the Italian Episcopal Commission for Lay Apostolate; Léon Lommel, Bishop of Luxembourg; Bishop José Pedro da Silva, Ecclesiastical Assistant of Portuguese Catholic Action; and Mgr Jacques Ménager, General Secretary of French Catholic Action.

35. Cf. *Lay Apostolate*, COPECIAL, 1966, 2, pp. 9–15.

36. Franz König quoted in *Documentation St. Pölten, 12–15 Mai 1996*, Austrian Catholic Action, Vienna, p.32.

37. Documentation Service of the Pontifical Council for the Laity, 9–10, 1982.

Part 5

CONCERNING WOMEN

'The modern woman, anxious to participate with decision-making power in the affairs of the community, will contemplate with intimate joy Mary who, taken into the dialogue with God, gives her active and responsible consent, not to the solution of a contingent problem, but to that event of world importance...the Incarnation of the Word'.

                Paul VI, Apostolic Exhortation, *Marialis Cultus*,
                                      2 February 1974.

CHAPTER 11

'I'm not a feminist but...'

In a classification of attitudes to feminism, this is the only one with which I feel comfortable. The 'but' means, of course, that it is impossible not to recognise discrimination against women: in societies, cultures, religions throughout the ages; in families, schools and professions; in autocracies and democracies. Impossible also not to applaud the efforts of women — and of men — who have tried to create awareness of this reality; who have battled (not always by methods we would recommend) to correct injustice in relations between the sexes and its impact on society.

But (a different but), there is little in my history or my make-up that would entitle me to a place in feminist ranks. My family background would not help.[1] The grandmother who brought me up, when faced with some more than usually stupid male exploit, would exclaim: 'So like a man!' But she was a devoted wife, mother and grandmother, and my grandfather was certainly no patriarch. Scholastically, I experienced no discrimination. For reasons of finance and/or health, none of my three brothers (certainly no less intelligent than I) ever finished normal schooling; while — thanks to the kindness of the nuns — I had the best education that Our Lady of Mercy College, Parramatta, could give me, until I moved on to Sydney University and outplaced a male student for the scholarship that took me to Paris. And, if the monastic discipline of a convent boarding-school of that era frustrated some of my feminine aspirations, that was only a weak reflection of what was expected from the Religious Community by patriarchal custom and authority.² During holidays, I took my place happily among the parish Children of Mary and — when not at the beach — spent Saturday afternoon cleaning brass in the sacristy.

It might have been thought that half a century of serving this male-centred, patriarchal Church would have opened my eyes. Experience has taught me at times things I would rather not have known about the functioning of Church structures and the frustrations they can cause. But it has also allowed me to see the 'good grain' growing up to unexpected heights, and taught me to pay less attention to the 'cockle'. To share also in events that have contributed towards a more responsible participation of women in the life and mission of the Church.

As for radical feminism, I cannot even speak the language. I make every reasonable effort to use inclusive language; but I react unhappily when all the ills of humanity are summed up in the slogan word "patriarchy" which can savour of sexism in reverse, anti-male sexism. I object also to seeing women (at least half of humankind) listed simply as one more oppressed group. And, whatever concrete interpretation can be given to the term, I feel that 'Women Church' is not a happy way of indicating the effort to bring about better relationships between Christian women and men. I would like to be theologically more competent in order to respond adequately to feminists who prefer a language so inclusive that God may not even be invoked as Father (true, God is also Mother, as John Paul I pointed out!), and who see no theological significance in the incarnation of the Word of God as a male human being 'born of a woman' (Gal 4:4). I am encouraged when I see a more critical and dialogical approach developing among feminist theologians, leaving more space for an authentic expression of different experiences and different cultures.

After this confession, I take up the story of my involvement in things feminine. The Prologue recalls my early contact with the Grail Movement, founded in the Netherlands (originally, as the Women of Nazareth). It was in the Grail that I first tried to order my thoughts about women. The key word at the time was complementarity. This could imply a simplistic vision of man the maker and woman the lover, or man the head and woman the heart, etc. But, in the thought of

Jacques van Ginneken, complementarity need not be a one-to-one affair: a man and a woman, each incomplete. Rather, it could suggest the mingling — in various doses — of the masculine and the feminine, for the fullness of human personality. The women who were to 'change the world for Christ' must, indeed, be womanly, but not a stereotype of womanhood. They would also need qualities of strength, initiative, courage and steadfastness just as men needed to develop qualities of sensitivity, understanding, tenderness, etc. The model for all was the perfect humanity of Jesus.

During the 1930s, the Grail had spread, as a young women's movement, to England, Germany, Australia and the United States with all the exuberance, pageantry and triumphalism of the youth movements of the day (but with the triumph being the 'victory of the Cross'!). In Europe the war swept it all away, leaving only the essentials of a Christian commitment. Australia was isolated (it took six months to receive a Red Cross message from Europe), but we tried to keep the spirit alive. I put together a history of 'Woman's Apostolate through the Ages'.[3] They were all there, from the time of the Apostles, through the centuries: the queens and abbesses, the saints and scholars, the heroines and the missionaries; even some whom feminist writers are rediscovering today. And what of the modern world?

> Today, in our nineteen-forties, we are living in a new world (but in one which might seem to be already in the melting-pot) . . .
>
> Long before the present war, the challenge of the Lay Apostolate had brought to thousands of young Catholic women the consciousness that it was their task to use their freedom, their educational advantages and their increased self-confidence to bring about a return to Christian principles as revolutionary as the first preaching of the Gospel . . . War has brought people the world over face to face with the great realities; with life and death . . . It has shown them their great need of God. What of the post-war world? . . . One thing is certain: there will be a great task for Catholic women, not only to bind up its wounds, but also to be witnesses to the truth of Christ, ever living in his Church.

Fifty years later, a leaflet[4] distributed by the Australian Grail described the movement:

> The Grail is a vital international movement of women with indigenous members and leadership in 21 countries, in Europe, Africa, North and South America, Asia, Australia and Melanesia.
>
> It is a spiritual, cultural and social movement of women rooted in Christian faith and seeking to respond to the challenge of the Gospel in today's world and in their own lives.
>
> They are women — young and old, single and married, well known and little known, in a wide variety of life situations, with a diversity of gifts.
>
> The Grail is a movement *of* women but not exclusively *for* women.
>
> The Grail is for the world.

In North America and beyond, Grail women are exploring feminist concerns. In Oceania, from 1973 to 1987, summer schools brought together over 300 participants, from Australia and the whole Pacific area — including Aborigines, Islanders and those who had migrated to the area. In South Africa, workshops help women and girls to develop leadership skills. There is no limit to the creativity of women — young and not so young — who have a cause. But the real strength of the Grail has, however, always been its capacity to attract and foster *personal* vocations of Christian commitment in a changing world. The vocations may be spectacular, or they may move by more hidden ways. A litany of names could be a long one. I recall only a few of the Grail women for whom a world-ranging vocation has brought them into contact, at one point or another, with our laity story.

First, some Dutch pioneers: Lydwine van Kersbergen, who — before taking the Movement to the United States — led a group that brought the Grail to Australia in 1936. In the group: Judith Bouwman (1900–40), a great, warm-hearted woman, converted to Christianity by van Ginneken in 1930, and widely mourned when she died in a road accident between Melbourne and Sydney. Frances van der Schot (1912–95), leader in Australia when Judith died. Too inexperienced to deal always prudently with hierarchical diktats, Frances won the hearts of Australian youth — and not only the youth — with her radiating joy and sense of all things beautiful. Brigid Huizinga brought her spirit of tough endeavour and total dedication, together with her ready wit, not only to the Grail but also to social work for Dutch migrants, before going on to a different pioneering in Lesotho.

From the 1920s until 1949, the President of the Movement had been Margaret van Gilse (1899–1994), a great and wise Belgian woman. When she withdrew, Rachel Donders became, as International President, a world traveller — giving COPECIAL the benefit of her experience and insight at experts' meetings for the preparation of the World Congress of 1957. Later, she was to make a deep spiritual contribution in Japan, Israel and Portugal. Baroness Yvonne Bosch van Drakestein founded the English Grail in London in 1932.

After her death in August 1994, Derek Worlock, Archbishop of Liverpool, wrote of her:

> She did for professional and middle-class Catholics what Patrick Keegan and his colleagues did for the re-Christianization of the working class. They were in fact close friends . . . Their background could not have been more different: Keegan the son of a Lancashire mill-worker; the 'Baroness', as Yvonne was always known, drawn from the Dutch aristocracy, with a rich artistic culture.[5]

Led by Yvonne, the Grail helped to prepare English Catholics for what would emerge from the Council, especially in liturgy and new theological insights. In 1965, she took part in the Women's Ecumenical Meeting at Vicarello. Later, she withdrew to carry out her Grail commitment in a different way, through the semi-contemplative life of Catherine Doherty's Madonna House in Canada.

Maria Groothuizen ('Dé' for Damaris, the first Greek woman working with St Paul 1907–92) was a pioneer with the youth movement before the war, and the women's movement later. In 1961–74, her gift for helping where help was needed found an outlet as assistant to Luigi Ligutti, Permanent Observer of the Holy See to the FAO, travelling to North and South America and, in Rome, acting as pastoral counsellor for women within the Organization.

Alberta Lücker (1907–83) was the first Grail member I met, when she attended the Pax Romana Congress in Paris in 1937. Born in Bonn, she joined the Grail when it first came to Berlin. During the war she worked with van Ginneken on philological research for the University of Nijmegen. Later, while leading the Grail in Germany, she was responsible for the foreign section of the Central Committee of German Catholics, Vice-President of National and International Councils of Pax Christi and, from 1971, a pioneer member of the World Conference on Religion and Peace.

Elizabeth Reid (1915–74) was another born pioneer for Australia (which she loved dearly) and for the Grail, which she joined in 1938. In 1948, her call to join a Grail team in Hong Kong opened up a vast field for her apostolate. Starting from a press office — a one-woman enterprise at the service of the Diocese — she became journalist and photo-reporter wherever there was a danger spot (Korea, Vietnam ...) or a story that needed to be told (as at the Asia–Africa Conference in Bandung, 1955). Later, she criss-crossed the United States stirring missionary zeal in the youth, visited Grail groups in Africa, attended United Nations meetings to represent non-governmental interest in developing countries, founded the Grail in India. Her book, *I belong where I'm needed*,[6] tells it all, in a whirlwind succession of adventures and stories.

Maria de Lourdes Pintasilgo, as the President of a group of university Catholic Action in Portugal, attended a Pax Romana women's meeting in Belgium in 1952. Later, from 1956 to 1958, she was to be the first woman President of the student movement of Pax Romana. A chemical engineer by profession, she did research on nuclear energy. Her political career, begun as Minister for Social Affairs, continued as member of the European Parliament, Ambassador to UNESCO, Prime Minister of Portugal for a brief period in 1979 and, in 1986, candidate for the Presidential election. As member of an Inter-Action Council of former heads of government, she has scope for her insight into concrete problems of human development at all levels. At one time, Maria de Lourdes was also Vice-President of the Grail. The Movement is still her support as a community. Interviewed for the French magazine *Panorama* in February 1992 she said: 'I cannot imagine committed Christians whose life would not include sharing, not only possessions, but their talents, themselves and what is dear to them'.

1. For my family, I refer the reader to the forthcoming autobiography of my mother Dulcie Deamer, which is to be published by the Queensland University Press.

2. Cf. Madeleine Sophie McGrath, *These Women: Women Religious in the History of Australia. The Sisters of Mercy of Parramatta*, NSW University Press, Kensington, NSW, 1989.

3. An article in the small volume, *Youth Lives with the Church*, published by The Grail, Melbourne, 1944.

For The Grail in Australia, see Sally Kennedy, *Faith and Feminism, Catholic Women's Struggle for Self-Expression*, Studies in the Christian Movement, Manly, NSW, Australia, 1985.

4. Grail leaflet, The Grail, 22 McHattan St, North Sydney, NSW, Australia.

5. *The Tablet*, London, 13 August 1994, pp. 1030–31.

6. The Newman Press, Westminster, Maryland, 1962.

CHAPTER 12

The Women's Ecumenical Liaison Group

Maria de Lourdes Pintasilgo was one of the five Catholic women appointed through the Laity Council to the Women's Ecumenical Liaison Group (WELG). WELG was set up to implement, in 1968, a Recommendation adopted in November 1966 by the Joint Working Group (JWG) between the WCC and the Roman Catholic Church.[1] It was intended as a follow-up to the ecumenical consultation held at Vicarello during the Council.

The other Catholic members were Pilar Bellosillo, President of WUCWO; Marianna Dirks, President of the Federation of Catholic Women's and Mother's Groups in Germany; Sister St Charles Henaff, Vice-Provincial in Greece of the Ursuline Sisters, representing the International Union of Superiors General of Women Religious; Maria Meersman (Belgium) from the World Movement of Christian Workers.

The five members appointed by the WCC were: Athena Athanassiou, of the Greek Orthodox Church, President of the World YWCA; Marga Buhrig of the Swiss Protestant Church Federation; Liselotte Nold, of the Evangelical Church in Germany (Lutheran); Margaret Shannon, of the United Presbyterian Church in the United States, Executive Director of Church Women United; Ruth Walker, Secretary of the Council for Women's Ministry in the Church of England.

Co-Chairpersons were Marga Buhrig and Maria (Rie) Vendrik, member of the Laity Council. Co-Secretaries were Brigalia Bam, of the Anglican Church in South Africa (later, Secretary General of the South African Council of Churches) and myself.

WELG held its first meeting in Rome in December 1968. Thomas Stransky, CSP, of the Secretariat for Promoting Christian Unity, provided the context for the group's exploration in a talk on 'Current trends of the Ecumenical Movement'. He pointed to a generation gap:

> Between 1961 and 1964 a different type of person became interested for the first time in the Ecumenical Movement. This type of person thinks differently from the pioneers . . . The 'younger' ecumenical generation (but this has little to do with age) may be freer for what can actually be done at this time. But young revolutionaries themselves age. The 'aggiornamento' cries of one generation sound hollow in t
> he next.

A press release, issued at the close of the meeting, summed up the results:

> The women voted to give priority to projects that would further the renewal of the Church, education for ecumenical action, and Christian unity. They set as their first topic for discussion, 'Christian Women Together for Social Change'.

Four full meetings were held during the four years of the Group's existence, two in Rome and two in Geneva. There were three major projects. The first was intended to test the ecumenical situation through case studies which looked at Protestant–Catholic collaboration at parish level in Switzerland; 'living-room dialogues' in the Philippines; the Women's World Day of Prayer in Tanzania; work with migrant women in Scotland; the Australian ecumenical group: 'Christian Women Concerned' from the Sydney area.

The other two projects were more ambitious. In June 1970, a conference on 'The Image of Women in the Mass Media' brought 120 women together in Vienna, mainly from denominational women's organisations in fourteen European countries where the 'Women's Lib' element, brought by the North Americans, was a new experience for most of the Europeans. Five or six men from the media were present. (One of them felt that the experience helped him to understand 'the normal position of women at international meetings'!).

The Conference had been prepared by a scientific survey conducted in France, based on a questionnaire that required respondents to monitor a medium of their choice — mainly television — and a particular female character. The overall result, from the 350 replies, indicated that the mass media largely reflect (rather than create) the images the public has of women. Geneviève Poujol, who prepared the survey, remarked: 'It would be pointless to smash this mirror or to draw a curtain over it . . . A society gets the media it deserves . . . Christian men and women should ponder this truth, whether they be image consumers or producers'. If the image is that of a 'helpful, cheerful idiot' or a 'sex object' or a woman interested exclusively in her own career, the responsibility is not only that of the media.

The third project emerged from a Consultation on Christian Concern for Peace organised by SODEPAX in April 1970. SODEPAX and WELG decided to co-sponsor a meeting on 'Women's Role in Peace Education', to be held at Nicosia, Cyprus, in May 1972. The meeting was to be 'informal and open-ended', fostering a 'fresh outlook' that could contribute to 'the so far men-dominated approach to the problem of peace'. It was to develop 'concrete strategies to promote peace and justice on the community level . . . investigating the social and cultural hang-ups in reconciling people, organizing explore-units centring on special "sorespots" ', etc. Follow-up would be the respon-sibility of the participants, who would be chosen both for their personal qualities and for their ability to act as catalysts and 'multipliers'. The criteria for selection were faithfully observed. The list of participants — about fifty from twenty-nine countries of all continents, included only two men: the husband of one participant and Kinhide Mushakoji, of Sophia University, Tokyo, member of the Pontifical Commission for Justice and Peace.

No overall report was foreseen. But groups of participants produced notes and comments — serious and less so — theatrical interpretation, dramatic real-life experiences, social analysis. It was not all work either. When the whole group was received on 18 May by His Beatitude Makarios, they assured the Archbishop that they had enjoyed, not only the hospitality of the island, but something of its life, its culture and its beauty. They had much to take away, but no illusions about the task ahead. It was not really going to be:

> As Easy as That
> By coffee time
> we had decided a fair and equal
> distribution of power.
> We had granted every person
> mankind's basic rights . . .
> We decided that participation in decision-making
> is as necessary as the daily bread
> the poor world is craving for . . .
> We made love and human concern
> the guiding principles of all our actions
> and advocated a new ethics
> for the fast-changing relationships
> in mass society . . .
> To change the international monetary system
> took us to tea . . .
> We had come to terms with the most pressing problems
> the have-nots are facing
> and we started to change the patterns
> of aid giving and receiving of governments and churches.
> We even convinced the affluent ones to consume less
> in order to preserve the finite resources for all of us
> poor and rich alike.
> It is as easy as that
> to create conditions for peace.
> We agreed completely
> on what we wanted to see happen.
> There were some arguments however
> on how to make it happen.

> We broke for dinner
> to avoid major dispute
> and outbreak of hostilities
> among our peaceful group.

Why WELG?

The fourth and last meeting of WELG was held at Cartigny (Geneva) in October 1971. There was input from invited Observers but unfortunately only five of the actual members of WELG could be present for this meeting of evaluation. It was agreed unanimously that some kind of WELG should continue. This should be a think-tank, rather than an operational group. There should be official links with the JWG, the WCC and the Roman Catholic Church, but freedom enough to act as a liaison with both official and non-official bodies.

The final (unpublished) Report recalled the steps leading to the creation of WELG, the context in which it had emerged and the subsequent evolution in 'the thinking, feeling and style of action of the more vocal sectors of mankind — not least of womankind'. The evolution only confirmed the need for WELG:

> The *raison d'etre* for such a group may be summed up by saying that the wholesome development of women's participation in the life of the Church and society is an ecumenical concern; further, that it is a matter, not only for women's organizations, but for the Churches as such . . .
> *Women in the Churches* is an ecumenical concern:
> – because it involves an essential element in the life of any Church and in the 'self-consciousness' of any Church or ecclesial community;
> – because it touches a field where there is a rapid evolution . . . a field where the Spirit would seem to be speaking in a special way to Churches at the present time;
> – because the full participation of both men and women is an element of renewal for the Church; it concerns the Church's mission, 'in order that the world may believe'.

The members of WELG had been grateful to have their ecumenical task spelled out in the words that Pope Paul VI addressed to them on the occasion of their meeting in Rome in October 1970:

> How many situations require your joint study, situations in which you are committed as women and where you must bring your specific witness as Christian women! How many fields to be explored, in domestic and social life, in which personal relations must be transformed by love! How many experiences of your various Christian movements to be pooled, how many considerations to be pursued in the light of faith, and perhaps new activities to be undertaken in the charity of Christ, so that men and women of our time, our brothers and sisters, may respond more perfectly to their vocation as children of God![2]

In spite of these encouragements and of general agreement that 'something of WELG' should continue, nothing more was done after the presentation of the report to the JWG in June 1972. From the side of the Holy See, there was 'an increasing reluctance to be identified with efforts which led to the creation of joint bodies with an identity of their own'.[3] The example most in view was SODEPAX which was to continue for some years but with a limited form of collaboration between the WCC and the Pontifical Commission for Justice and Peace. There were also reasons internal to WELG. Almost from the beginning, there had been tensions on both sides, largely due to a lack of clarity. To whom was the Group really responsible: to the JWG, the WCC, the RCC through the Laity Council or the Secretariat for Promoting Christian Unity? To whom personally? How were projects to be financed? Only by temporary expedients? Through normal channels of the sponsoring bodies? How were members to be appointed? Observers to be invited?

On the WCC side, there was restructuring to be taken into account. On the Catholic side, the *Consilium de Laicis*, renewed in 1972, had its own internal working-group of women and men, that treated concerns raised within WELG. Some of these concerns were listed in the WELG Report:

Women's potentiality for service within the Church at all levels.
- Women's contribution to Christian unity and to education for ecumenism at the level of daily life (including the life of couples in 'mixed marriages').
- The contribution of both religious and lay women to the Church's action for justice and peace at all levels.
- The role of the single woman and a deeper understanding of celibacy.
- Women's liberation movements: a critical evaluation, including meaning of liberation, of freedom, for both men and women.
- The need to review women's groups and organizations, at all levels and in different cultural contexts.[4]

On the Catholic side there was, above all, the Recommendation adopted by the Synod of Bishops of 1971:

> We urge that women should have their own share of participation and responsibility in the community life of society and likewise of the Church. We propose that the matter be subjected to a serious study employing adequate means: for instance, a mixed commission of men and women, religious and lay people, of different situations and competence.[5]

The Secretariat for Promoting Christian Unity hoped that the Commission would have an ecumenical dimension. This was not to be possible, in view of the nature of the Commission and the limited time at its disposal; but also because of the radical feminist approach that was to mark much ecumenism in the 1970s. Women's ecumenical collaboration was taken off the official agenda of the Catholic Church. It continued, however, at international level, especially through WUCWO and other Catholic organisations that stimulated the ecumenical involvement of Catholic women at national and grassroots levels.

1. 'The JWG recommends to the authorities of the RCC and the WCC the appointment of a joint group of ten, representing the women of the Churches, five from either side, to be responsible for keeping in touch with and coordinating plans which are now developing for common study and action by Christian women on social questions.' Archives of Pontifical Council for Promoting Christian Unity and WCC.

2. Pope Paul VI to WELG, 28 October 1970, original French text in *Insegnamenti di Paolo VI*, VIII, 1970, p. 1075.

3. Cf. S. Herzel, *A Voice for Women*, Women in Church and Society, WCC, Geneva 1981, pp. 58–9.

4. WELG Report, eight pages with various annexes, signed by the co-chairpersons, Marga Bührig and Maria Vendrik, and dated 15 March 1972. Available in English, French and German editions.

5. Synod of Bishops, *Justice in the World*, Vatican Polyglot Press, Rome, 1971, p. 17.

CHAPTER 13

Commission on women in Church and society[1]

Approving the Report from the Synod of Bishops of 1971, Paul VI also approved the Synod's recommendation on the 'mixed commission',[2] proposed, on behalf of the Canadian bishops, by Cardinal George Flahiff.

Implementation could not be immediate. There were problems to solve, conflicting expectations to take into account. The delicate task was entrusted by Paul VI to Bishop Ramon Torrella Cascante, Vice-President of the Pontifical Commission for Justice and Peace (and, from 1983, Archbishop of Tarragona, Spain).

It is rarely possible to know exactly by what mysterious processes Vatican appointments are made. The Study Commission was no exception. When, at last, on 3 May 1973, the press conference was held to present the Commission, it was found to be composed of twenty-five members: twelve lay women, two women religious, one member of a Secular Institute, seven ecclesiastics and three lay men. Of the lay women, seven were married and leaders of Catholic organisations: Eugenie Bahintchie (Ivory Coast), President of the International Committee of Catholic Nurses; Pia Colini Lombardi, President of the Italian Committee for the Moral and Social Defence of women; Claire Delva (Belgium), President of the International Association of Charities of St Vincent de Paul; Marie-Thérèse Graber-Duvernay (France), Consultant of WUCWO; Marina Lessa (MIAMSI, Brazil); Mary Pyne, President of the National Board of Catholic Women of England and Wales; Dulcinea Rodrigues, President of the National Council of Catholic Women of India. The single women were Pilar Bellosillo, President of WUCWO, Maria Vittoria Pinheiro (Portugal), of the World Movement of Christian Workers; Maria Vendrik and myself from the *Consilium de Laicis*; Deborah Schellman — who became Mrs Seymour in the course of the Commission's work. Debbie was a delightful and competent young American, fresh from college, who played her part well, but — at that critical time — could hardly represent the thousands of women in the United States who were looking to the Commission for an answer to their questions and demands.[3]

The women religious were Claire Herrmann (France) of the Daughters of Charity and Teresa Avila MacLeod, OP (Scotland), President of the Pontifical (University) Institute Regina Mundi in Rome. Emma Seger (Germany), Professor of psychology, was a member of the Schönstatt Secular Institute. The lay men were Guzman Carriquiry of the *Consilium de Laicis*, and Mario Petroncelli (Italy), canonist. A well-known Catholic journalist, Angelo Narducci, had been appointed but, after the first meeting, was unable to give time to the Commission. The ecclesiastics were prelates from Vatican Departments, theologians (biblical, dogmatic and moral theology) and the Rector of the Pontifical Lateran University, the Swiss sociologist, Franco Biffi. The President of the Commission was a great friend of Paul VI: Enrico Bartoletti, formerly Archbishop of Lucca, General Secretary of the Italian Bishops' Conference.

L'Osservatore Romano of 3 May 1973 explained that

> the new Commission is of a temporary character and will
> present its conclusions to the Holy Father . . . It will be up
> to the Commission to ascertain what elements, in attitudes of
> mind, structures of different cultures and social milieux, need to
> be altered in order to guarantee the authentic advancement of
> [and] recognition for the position and role of women in the
> Church.

Pilar Bellosillo had been an expert at the Synod Assembly of 1971. After the press conference, she commented:

> The Synod created a new climate in the Church, a climate of hope. The Christian Churches have been very slow to respond . . . to the evolution of women's situation, which now finds expression at universal level through a new personal awareness on the part of women themselves.

She recalled also that:

> When Barbara Ward spoke in the Synod hall on Justice in the world, the Fathers were deeply impressed by the quality and the personality of the famous economist. One Bishop asked: 'Can we deprive the Church of this important contribution that women are able to make?'.[4]

Clouds on the horizon

Careful calculations had been made in order to allow the Commission to embark serenely on its task but an important element had not been taken into account. The two years separating the Synod's proposal from its implementation had seen a rapid rise in feminist temperature, both outside and inside the Church. WELG had started from a relatively calm approach to what was already felt as the need for radical change in the role of women in Church and society. At the time, Catholic women had been collaborating, in WELG, with the WCC Department on Cooperation of Men and Women in Church, Family and Society, as Madeleine Barot had envisaged and developed it. Madeleine was succeeded by Brigalia Bam, who knew all too well what it was to be a victim of oppression from her experience under South African apartheid. The new 'women's desk' was sensitive to a new radicalism. In 1974, the WCC Consultation, 'Sexism in the 1970s', brought together in West Berlin 170 women (no men) from fifty countries. Its goal was 'liberation' from the 'heresy of sexism'. This was a turning-point in the feminist struggle.[5]

In the ecclesial context, WELG had made only general approaches to the question of ministry for women and cursory references to priestly ordination. When the Study Commission was set up in 1973, ordination, for much of the WCC 'constituency', was not so much a problem as a reality for women, or at least an immediate project. In the Catholic Church, the question had begun to be raised at the time of the Third World Congress for the Lay Apostolate. By the 1970s it was an objective for many Catholic women's groups in North America and some countries of Europe. In 1972, the flame was fanned by the publication of *Ministeria Quaedam*.[6] According to the terms of this Motu Proprio, Minor Orders for the clergy were replaced by the 'Instituted Ministries' of acolyte and lector. These, based sacramentally on Baptism and Confirmation, were to be open to the laity, but '*they are reserved to men, in keeping with the venerable tradition of the Church*' (7) (my emphasis). Many Catholic women might scarcely have noticed this 'traditional' clause (which, clearly, lacked any theological basis); but for those committed to the cause of women's ministerial responsibility in the Church, and especially to some who were already convinced of the rightness — if not the right — of priestly ordination for women, this was a setback, even a scandal.

It was unfortunate, therefore, that before the Study Commission could even begin its work, a confidential *Pro-Memoria* had (inevitably) been leaked to the press. It stated that the Commission should, indeed, study the question of ministries, but that women's ordination to the priesthood was not part of its agenda. The *Pro-Memoria* was probably intended to calm certain apprehensions. To say the least, it was unnecessary. Composed as it was, the Commission could not, in any case, have treated the complex question of priesthood for women. It did not improve the atmosphere around the Commission that members first learned of the existence of this document through the press.

Real problems soon came to the surface. Whatever the care taken in its composition, it became clear that the group was only apparently well balanced. Of the fifteen women, only one — Teresa Avila MacLeod — was a theologian. Others who felt they should voice questions that were emerging in feminist and ecumenical circles were not equipped to dialogue with theologians who spoke the language of biblical symbolism or of a theology that for some was too traditional. Others again regretted that there was not more opportunity to discuss concrete problems related to women's life in modern society. The main difficulty was that the Commission had been asked to face a huge and complex task in a very limited time. Its mandate had been originally only for one year. This was extended, in March 1974, until January 1976 — but only to make it possible for the Commission to contribute to preparation for the participation of the Catholic Church in International Women's Year in 1975.

After the first two plenary sessions, five members — all from international organisations[7] — wrote to Paul VI saying they would regretfully have to resign if the Commission did not improve its method of work and widen its approach. They pinpointed real — but inescapable — difficulties. The Commission had no independent secretariat. (The *Consilium de Laicis* provided meeting-rooms and helped with secretarial and administrative problems.) I had become the de facto secretary — a situation which had its limitations also for me during this final experimental year of the *Consilium*. The reply to the letter came only after some months. The five members were asked to continue as before — which they did, but not too happily. For the final session, in January 1976, they prepared a 'Note of the Minority'. The Assembly decided that this would not be included in the dossier of texts the Commission would submit to the Holy Father. Substantial issues (as distinct from criticism of methods, etc.) would, however, be included in a text identifying 'problems that remain open'. Regrettably, more that ten years later, in 1987, the 'Minority' felt it necessary to publish their Note in *Bulletin* 108 of the research centre *Pro Mundi Vita*. Taken out of context, the text presents an unrelievedly negative image of a group which had done useful work under difficult circumstances. This, unfortunately, was the image that had been given, almost exclusively, in the press — even in serious reviews — during and after the life of the Commission.[8]

An interim report

On 23 October 1974, Archbishop Bartoletti presented an interim report to the Synod of Bishops.[9] Three plenary sessions had been held. A study on 'The Human Being, Male and Female, in God's Plan' was being completed by elements of philosophical anthropology and dogmatic theology. A group of studies dealt with the participation of women, religious and lay, in pastoral responsibilities, and with the admission of women to non-ordained ministries. The Commission was in contact with the International Theological Commission and the Pontifical Biblical Commission. A sociological study was in preparation.

A series of Recommendations distributed to the Synod Fathers dealt with: (1) *recognised and effective responsibility* for women in evangelisation; (2) women's participation in ecclesial bodies for reflection and *decision-making*; (3) participation of women religious in accordance with their *specific vocation* and the charism of their Institute; (4) opening *non-ordained ministries* as much to women as to men; (5) education for a *change of mentality* to promote better collaboration between women and men; (6) *education of the clergy* for collaboration with women; (7) *faith education* for women; (8) clarification of *terminology*: 'ministry', 'apostolate', 'service', etc.; (9) a deep study of the question of *ordained ministry for women*, in order to provide a satisfactory answer — not only disciplinary, but ecclesiological — which would give 'intelligibility' to the practice of the Church.

Time was short, but the bishops were allowed several interventions before the Assembly broke for coffee. These stressed the diversity of situations; the necessity, while seeking 'equality', of respecting women's 'specific nature' (a question, Bartoletti replied, that was causing much debate within the Commission); the importance of women's tasks and feminine 'genius' in the contemporary process of socialisation — with special attention to Mary as 'perfect realization of femininity' (Cardinal Wojtyla). In answer to another intervention on Mary as 'model', Bartoletti pointed to the difficulty caused by certain excesses in Marian devotion but he stressed the enthusiastic assent of the members of the Commission to the image of Mary given in the Apostolic Exhortation of Paul VI, *Marialis Cultus* (1974). Cardinal Suenens would have liked a recommendation denouncing as 'discriminatory' the 'excessive dependence' of women's congregations on the masculine branches of their Order. Mention was made of the Diaconate, which was being studied by the Biblical and Theological Commissions. Finally, Joseph Lécuyer, CSSp wondered why there was no Commission for *men*, and would have liked a woman to have been called to speak to the

Assembly. (With Sr Claire Herrmann, I had accompanied Archbishop Bartoletti, but we were silent witnesses.)

Paul VI was not present in the Synod on this occasion but he followed closely the work of the Commission. During the first plenary session, he had defined its task as 'gathering, verifying, interpreting, reviewing society'. (This was the vast undertaking that the 'Minority' — not without reason — thought had not been fully carried out.) At the last session, on 31 January 1976, he expressed his satisfaction at the work that had been done through reflection, documentation and proposals. The Study Commission had also accepted since April 1975, as an extra task, to act as the central group of the enlarged committee of the Holy See for the preparation of International Women's Year (IWY).[10]

International Women's Year 1975[11]

The International Women's Year must be 'a new point of departure', Paul VI said on 31 January 1976. It was 'urgently necessary to make the climate of public life ... more wholesome and more respectful of woman's dignity'. Whatever the progress in claiming women's rights, 'discrimination still exists', and even 'in the most highly developed countries the accession of women to posts of reflection and decision-making which condition all spheres of life in society needs to progress with wisdom and realism'.

The Pope had already expressed the support of the Church for the aims of IWY — equality, development, peace — when receiving the Secretary General of IWY, Helvi Sipila, in November 1974. It was expressed more fully in a Message addressed to the World Conference (Mexico, June 1975), and read in plenary session by Bishop Ramon Torrella Cascante, as Head of the Delegation of the Holy See.[12]

Paul VI even canonised a Saint for International Women's Year. IWY coincided with the Holy Year for Renewal and Reconciliation, proclaimed for 1975. Women's Day in the Holy Year program was marked by the canonisation, on Sunday, 14 September, of Elizabeth A. Bayley Seton. During the ceremony on St Peter's Square, the figure of the new Saint was illustrated, not — as usual — by the Postulator of the

Cause, but by four women, representing the stages in the life of 'Mother Seton': a young girl, a wife, a widow, a religious of the Sisters of Charity of St Elizabeth Seton.

To make something of the Study Commission's work available and to involve local Churches in preparation for IWY, a study kit was sent, early in 1975, to Bishops' Conferences, Catholic international organisations, religious congregations and to others interested. It contained information and proposals, the Addresses of Paul VI for IWY, biblical studies from the Commission,[13] a document from the Congregation for the Evangelization of Peoples on 'Women in Evangelization', the Recommendations made to the Synod of Bishops, and a Questionnaire — an instrument for reflection — on the actual participation of women in the life of the ecclesial community. Recipients were not obliged to respond, but there was considerable feedback from more than fifty countries.[14]

Meanwhile, in the context of the IWY and using available documentation from the United Nations and its agencies, a sociological text was prepared by Franco Biffi and Guzman Carriquiry. It summed up the situations of women throughout the world especially, (but not exclusively,) the evidences of discrimination. It was structured on the model of Part II of *Gaudium et Spes*,[15] according to the five 'great spheres': marriage and family; socio-economic life; culture; political life; international life. Unfortunately, the text could only be ready towards the end of the Commission's work. It must have found favour even with the more feminist members. To quote from the Introduction:

> The will to promote and the efforts to liberate women are among the outstanding phenomena of our time . . .
>
> Moving away from a type of society that laid all its stress on masculine roles, and forgot, or discriminated against, and not infrequently oppressed women, there has been a gradual change towards a new type of society in which women are evolving from a state of dependence to one of autonomy, from constraint to freedom, from passivity to initiative, from resignation to a desire for action, and from subordination to responsible participation.[16]

In spe fortitudo

Concluding the final session on 31 January 1976, Bartoletti recalled the life of the Commission as he had experienced it:

> We can look at the work we have done with great humility, but not with scepticism or destructive self-criticism. Humility needs always to be founded on truth. We can point to the positive elements: above all, the sincere commitment on the part of each one, bringing a communion, not only of effort, but also of prayer, faith, charity . . . even if at times there were difficulties, slight misunderstandings, shared suffering, such as can never fail to accompany a work for the Church, and in the Church.
>
> Another positive element to be underlined: the pluralistic contribution of competence in specific fields . . . and mutual listening. Between the first texts we examined and the conclusions we reached, we note changes that are solely the result of this mutual listening.
>
> I think it is right also to stress that, in spite of the limited time available and the composition of our Commission, as well as other circumstances — such as full-time work outside (for myself, to begin with) — we have been able to identify the essential points that, from a Christian standpoint, throw light on the sociological situation of women today in society and in the Church. Indications have also been given for a conversion of mentalities in an ongoing education at all levels, so that the Church can be effectively present in the situations of the human family today.
>
> But we cannot overlook negative aspects, due to a great extent to the objective difficulty of our subject matter . . .
>
> The seed we have sown may be poor, but the Word of God and of the Spirit of the Lord, still speaking in the Church, is rich. Our hope must be serene and generous. When I had to choose a motto that could support me in my life as a Bishop, there came to my mind, from the Old Testament, the words inserted in my crest: '*In spe fortitudo*' (In hope: strength).

For the Commission this was Archbishop Bartoletti's testament. Scarcely more than a month later he had a heart attack and died on 5 March 1976. The news was a sad shock, even for the most critical members of the Commission. This holy Pastor, this aristocratic Florentine, with his fine intellect, with the courtesy and the patience of dialogue that come from true humility and charity, had won the esteem and affection of all at a time when he carried a heavy burden in the Bishop's Conference: a difficult moment in Church–State relations and the preparatory period for the first National Meeting of the Church in Italy.[17] The death of Bartoletti was a grave blow also for Paul VI. He came to the chapel of the Bishops' Conference, to pray near his friend, before the funeral Mass in the Basilica of St John Lateran.

Afterwards, it fell to me to prepare for Paul VI the Dossier of the Study Commission's work.

1. As announced, the Study Commission was to be on 'The Role of Women in Church and Society'. From the start, we quietly dropped the 'role'. There was no official comment.

2. 'A mixed commission of men and women, religious and lay people, of different situations and competence'.

3. At the request of the Conference of Bishops of Northern Europe, Inger Saxild (Denmark) attended some of the sessions.

4. After the Synod, in a bookshop near St Peter's (a centre of Vatican gossip), I overheard the remark, from one prelate to another, '*That woman* [Barbara] is the one who should preach the retreat in the Vatican!'.

5. Cf. 'Sexism in the Seventies', meeting held in Berlin, 1974, discussed in Susannah Herzel, *A Voice for Women*, WCC, Geneva, 1981, pp. 71–9.

6. Austin Flannery, *Vatican Council II, The Conciliar and Post-Conciliar Documents*, op. cit., pp. 429–32.

7. Pilar Bellosillo, Maria Vendrik, Claire Delva, Vittoria Pinheiro, and Marina Lessa.

8. I was able to complete this image to some extent when Peter Hebblethwaite interviewed me in Rome while writing his biography of Paul VI, *The First Modern Pope*, HarperCollins, London, 1993, pp. 640–4.

9. Cf. Giovanni Caprile, *Il Sinodo dei Vescovi 1974: Terza Assemblea Generale*, Edizioni La Civiltà Cattolica, 1975, pp. 697–705.

10. Ibid.

11. Cf. *The Church and the International Women's Year 1975*, Documentation Service of the Pontifical Council for Laity, Vatican City, 1976, p. 167, available in English, French and Spanish.

12. The other members of the Delegation were: Mother Teresa of Calcutta; Bernadette Kunambi (Tanzania); Sr Teresa Botello (Mexico); Guzman Carriquiry, Marina Lessa, Mgr James T. McHugh (United States), Sr Rae Ann O'Neill (United States); Fr Paul Toinet (France); Maria Teresa Vaccari (Italy); and Rosemary Goldie (Secretary).

13. Cf. *The Church and International Women's Year 1975*, 'Women in Holy Scripture', Ignace de la Potterie, SJ, pp. 76–89; 'The Novelty of the Evangelical Outlook on Women', MJ, Le Guillou, OP pp. 90–4.

14. Ibid, pp. 112–14.

15. Austin Flannery, *Vatican Council II: The Conciliar and Post-Conciliar Documents*, op. cit.

16. Cf. *The Church and International Women's Year 1975*, p. 119. One theologian at least — Edouard Hamel, SJ, Canadian and Professor of Moral Theology — won general approval with three texts prepared for the first Plenary Assembly: on 'Christ and Women', sexuality in the human person and the *exercise* of authority, as distinct from 'jurisdiction', which is reserved to ordained ministers.

17. The Meeting was held in October/November 1976, on the theme 'Evangelization and Human Development'.

CHAPTER 14

Ordinatio Sacerdotalis:
The ordination debate

When Archbishop Bartoletti presented to the Synod of Bishops the Recommendations from the Study Commission on Women, he stressed the necessity to give intelligibility to the norm that excludes women from the ministerial priesthood. The question:

> should receive a reply that would be motivated not only from a disciplinary standpoint but also with an ecclesiological motivation, based on biblical, theological, historical studies, etc., and on the living tradition, not only of the Latin, but also of the Oriental Church.

The question, we know, was not new. It was raised at the time of Vatican II. But it was still a very recent question in the Catholic Church. The majority of the faithful would have been more or less unaware of it — except, perhaps, from some reference in the context of 'women's promotion' or of developments in other denominations, where ministry has varied connotations. Some would have become aware of it in 1958, when for the first time an Episcopal Church, the Lutheran Church of Sweden, decided (under political pressure) to ordain women, thereby creating grievous divisions within the Church itself.

To verify how recent the question really was, I once searched through Catholic literature on women's issues from before 1958. I found no mention of ordination as a prospect, or even a problem. But in 1952, at a Pax Romana meeting of university women, for the first time I heard a woman say she felt 'called' to ministerial priesthood. This, if not unique, was so rare that the impression remained.

In the Church of England[1]

In the Church of England, there had been a campaign for women's ordination in the first decades of this century. It did not make much headway. In 1930, the Lambeth Conference even reversed an earlier ruling that deaconesses were part of Holy Orders. In 1962, the question was reopened. A Committee, headed by the Archdeacon of Westminster, produced a report, *Gender and Ministry*.[2] It stated: 'The various reasons for this withholding of the ordained and representative priesthood from women, reasons theological, traditional, instinctive, anthropological, social, emotional, should be more thoroughly examined'. In the same year, a Commission was set up under the chairmanship of the Bishop of Chester. Its report, *Women and Holy Orders*,[3] issued in 1966, made no specific recommendations, but set out arguments for and against ordination. In 1973, the question was referred to every diocese for discussion. In 1975, two motions were discussed in the Synod. The first was carried: 'This Synod considers that there are no fundamental objections to the ordination of women to the priesthood'. The second, calling for implementation, was rejected 'in view of the significant division of opinion'. The campaign continued. The final vote in favour of women's ordination was taken in the Synod on 11 November 1992. On 12 March 1994, the Church of England ordained its first women priests. In the meantime, ordinations — to priesthood and episcopate — had taken place in other provinces of the Anglican Communion.

Less than fifty years had passed since, in 1948, a *Revised Interim Report* for the First Assembly of the WCC had reported the position of the Anglican Churches on the question of ordination:

> Any major alteration such as the admission of women to the priesthood is not within the competence of any Province, or

indeed any part of the Catholic Church less than the whole body of Easterns, Romans and Anglicans acting in concert under the guidance of the Holy Spirit.[4]

In the Catholic Church

Campaigning in favour of women's ordination escalated after Vatican II. In 1967, a group, 'Cooperation between Men and Women' had been set up in the Netherlands within the ecumenical St Willibrord Association. In June 1970, it reported that a strong majority of the Dutch Pastoral Council had voted in favour of the rapid access of women to all ecclesial functions where their presence creates 'no problem or few problems', and in the future to *all* functions, 'including the presidency of the Eucharist'. (The Bishops taking part in the Pastoral Council did not vote on this occasion.) Here, as in other forums, the aim was to promote women's effective participation in the life of the Church; but, in a clearly superficial approach, the refusal of priestly ordination was considered 'the tip of the iceberg' of discrimination against women.[5] In 1970, the group 'Femmes et Hommes dans l'Eglise' (Women and Men in the Church) was created in Belgium.[6] In the N.O. of its Bulletin, the group called for 'openness' on the question of women's ordination.

In Canada, in April 1971, sixty-five of the seventy-five members of the Canadian Bishops' Conference met with about sixty women from all parts of the country. They accepted to study recommendations on equal rights and responsibilities for women and men in the Church, on the revision of Canon Law, etc. In the Synod, on behalf of the Canadian Bishops, Cardinal Flahiff made the intervention on diversification of ministries and ministries for women which led to the creation — on the Synod's recommendation — of the Study Commission on Women in Church and Society.

In the United States, women religious were becoming ever more aware of their immense potential for the mission of the Church. The National Assembly of Women Religious, meeting in Minneapolis on the eve of the 1971 Synod, called not only for the diaconate but also for the priestly ordination of women.

An unlooked-for result of the Synod's discussions was the creation in Belgium of an Association of Women Aspiring to Priestly Ministry (AFAMP).[7] By 1975, AFAMP had seventy members (from twenty to eighty years of age). Documentation on the nature and aims of the group was sent to Bartoletti by Valentine Buisseret, OP. Bartoletti expressed great respect for the spirit of the group, but obviously could not promote its cause. He received much less seriously, but with wry humour, a series of buttons offered by the representative of St Joan's International Alliance in the United States. Among the slogans they flaunted were: 'Equal rites for women'; 'No mini-ministries'; 'Don't make coffee, make policy'; and, more aggressively, 'Ordain women or stop baptizing them'.

In the meantime, the publication of *Ministeria Quaedam*, excluding women from the instituted ministries of lector and acolyte, had produced reactions even in more moderate circles. In October 1972, WUCWO adopted a motion protesting against this discrimination affecting women as lay people. Predictably, some protests went further, claiming women's right to priestly ordination. The bishops of the United States responded with the publication of a document, *Theological Reflections on the Ordination of Women*.[8] The stated purpose was 'to encourage further study and discussion'. The bishops were 'conscious of the deep love for the Church which underlies the growing interest of many women in the possibility of ordination'. Among arguments against ordination, they stressed 'the constant practice and tradition of the Catholic Church'. They explicitly rejected any right to ordination and the understanding of priesthood as 'power' rather than 'service'.

In Europe, a Colloquium of PRO MUNDI VITA, in September 1973, reached a consensus that was generally favourable to women's ordination. The material presented included a report by Agnes Cunningham, SSCM,[9] in which the perspective did not go beyond the diaconate for women.[10]

It was on the diaconate that attention was mainly focused during the year leading up to the Synod of Bishops on Evangelization (1974). Already before the Council, especially in Germany, there had been much discussion of what was to become the permanent diaconate. In March 1974, a meeting organised in Paris, with the collaboration of major specialists,[11] issued an appeal to the coming Synod:

> How could this ministry have its full meaning and efficacy if its restoration concerned only men? ... Exegetical and theological studies show that the call of women to the Diaconate does not raise any objection and can find support in tradition, even if the present legislation is opposed to it.

The diaconate was considered, not as a concession to those excluded from priesthood, but as a ministry at the service of a renewed pastoral community; not as an archaeological restoration, but an 'invention' in the line of the tradition.

In spite of expectations, the question of ministries for women remained marginal during the Synod. The Post-Synodal Exhortation of Paul VI, *Evangeli Nuntiandi*[12] (1975) makes no specific reference to women's ministry, but contains an important number (73) on diversified ministries. During IWY, Paul VI repeatedly encouraged women's involvement in the Church's pastoral mission. The only passages quoted from his Addresses were generally those that reiterated the impossibility of priestly ordination.

More insistent voices

In August 1975, PRO MUNDI VITA organised a Colloquium in Louvain, in collaboration with the WCC, WUCWO and the Lutheran World Federation. The theme: 'Women and Men as Partners in Christian Communities'.

The ecumenical input must have been considerable. During the same year, the 5th Assembly of the WCC, meeting in Nairobi, charged the Churches that practised women's ordination not to let themselves be 'hampered by ecumenical objections'. An English-speaking workshop of the Colloquium adopted the following Recommendations:

> Women who want to be ordained should be ordained. We recommend that some of these women seek ordination in the Church from a Catholic Bishop willing to take the risk. If this is not possible, a majority of our group recommends that they seek ordination outside the institutional Catholic Church.

> The institutional laws defining ministers of the Eucharist as men, selected by men, trained by men and ordained by ordained men, are obstacles to the formation of *real* Eucharistic communities. We recommend that those communities who are ready appoint their own ministers of the Eucharist — men or women, married or single.[13]

The meeting that had the greatest repercussion was, however, the Conference: 'Women in Future Priesthood Now. A Call for Action', held in Detroit in November 1975. It was organised by a group of some thirty women, including members of associations of women religious and of AFAMP. The forecast was for 600 participants. The site had to be changed to deal with 1300 registrations (1100 sisters, 100 lay women, 100 men, clergy and laity). Five hundred persons remained outside the hotel. Of 313 invited bishops, only three attended, in a personal capacity. Others expressed interest and support. Commenting in the review *America*,[14] one of those present, Carroll T. Dozier, Bishop of Memphis, expressed regret at the absence of the Bishops' Conference: 'These Sisters are too important to be treated as though they did not exist; and the talks were well prepared, and deserve to be studied'. In spite of some rhetorical excesses the general impression was of serious research, of solidarity and love for the Church. During one celebration, 300 women (some of them married and studying theology) declared that they felt called to the priesthood.[15] After the meeting, the Women's Ordination Conference was set up. Among its supporters were members of 'Priests for Equality'.

A later event that had a wide impact was the publication in June 1976 of the Conclusions from a subcommission of the Pontifical Biblical Commission. A majority (twelve members against five) supported the statement that, if the Church, in certain circumstances, should ordain women to the priesthood, it cannot be proved from Scripture that such action would be contrary to the will of Christ.[16]

Inter Insigniores

In this climate, the Congregation for the Doctrine of the Faith published, on 28 January 1977, its Declaration *Inter Insigniores*[17] on 'the

Question of the Admission of Women to the Ministerial Priesthood'. The Declaration clearly affirms the traditional norm excluding women:

> In execution of a mandate received from the Holy Father . . . the Congregation for the Doctrine of the Faith judges it necessary to recall that *the Church, in fidelity to the example of the Lord, does not consider herself authorized to admit women to priestly ordination.*

At the same time, an attempt is made to point towards the 'intelligibility' of which Bartoletti expressed the need in 1974. Arguments are proposed: the Church's constant tradition; the attitude of Christ; the practice of the Apostles; the Mystery of Christ, expressed in the 'sacramental sign' of the priest who acts 'in persona Christi capitis' (representing Christ the Head); the Mystery of the Church. It is recognised that 'some women feel they have a vocation to the priesthood'; but 'such an attraction, however noble and understandable', cannot of itself suffice for a 'genuine vocation' without the Church's 'authentication'.

The Commentary accompanying the Declaration recalls developments within other Christian denominations since the action of the Lutheran Church in 1958, and especially since similar action taken within the Anglican Communion by Churches which 'considered that they preserved the apostolic succession of Order'. The resulting ecumenical problem had been pointed out to the Archbishop of Canterbury, Donald Coggan, by the Orthodox Church in Britain, as well as in two letters from Pope Paul VI. The Commentary goes on to develop the arguments proposed in the Declaration. It distinguished between those that concern the Church's teaching with regard to Tradition, the attitude of Christ and the practice of the Apostles, and reflections which clarify this teaching through the 'analogy of faith', but do not involve the Magisterium: 'In solemn teaching, infallibility affects the doctrinal affirmation, not the arguments intended to explain it'. (Infallibility is not mentioned anywhere else in the Declaration or its Commentary.) Clearly, reflection, not only could, but must continue.

Negative, and even polemical reactions were not lacking. There were also positive comments, even where the normative content was difficult to accept. It was appreciated that the Declaration distanced itself explicitly from the anti-feminism — the misogyny even — of some theologians and Doctors of the past. If women were excluded from the priesthood, it was not because they were 'inferior' or 'impure' or necessarily 'subordinate' to the male, nor on account of any psychological handicaps (unable to keep a secret, inapt for public speaking ...). The criticisms and overall rejection regarded fundamental arguments put forward in the Declaration and Commentary and developed in a series of articles appearing in *L'Osservatore Romano* and signed by specialists in various theological areas.[18] This marshalling of the 'big guns' of theology was a positive action. The campaign for ordination had, in fact, obliged theologians to delve into questions that had seemed either unimportant or unanswerable. It revealed the complexity of a question that could not be dismissed either by claiming rights or distributing anathemas.[19]

Another positive aspect of the early stage of the ordination debate was the impulse it gave to the theological commitment of women, once the Faculties of Theology were at last opened to them after the Council. It was unfortunate, however, that women studying theology was too often equated with women seeking ordination, which did not help their integration into the mainstream of academic achievement. What was needed was the equipping of women theologically in view — among other motives — of the ecumenical contacts and collaboration that many were seeking enthusiastically. Instead of being ready to dialogue from a Catholic standpoint with women (and men) from other denominations, where ordained ministry could have a different connotation from that of priesthood in the Catholic tradition, Catholic women too often took over uncritically positions of their 'other Christian sisters'.

As Avery Dulles has pointed out,[20] 'during the decade of confusion that followed Vatican II, the question [of women's ordination] was allowed to be treated as dogmatically open, so that many Catholics in good faith became convinced that the Church was free to overturn its earlier practice'. They were encouraged by the fact that well-known theologians were speaking and writing in favour of ordination. It is not surprising therefore that, even after the traditional teaching was definitively reaffirmed by John Paul II in the Apostolic Letter *Ordinatio Sacerdotalis*[21] in terms that the Congregation for the Doctrine of the Faith later interpreted as a use of 'infallibility':[22]

> Catholics in good faith will in some cases find it difficult to proffer the kind of interior assent for which the Pope is asking. Time and education may be required for them to resolve the tension they feel between loyalty to the tradition and desirable modernization.[23]

Too often, even today, theological arguments against ordination are countered with pastoral considerations (lack of priests, women's 'success' in pastoral work, etc.), if not with sociological or cultural arguments (damage to the image of the Church from the absence of women priests in a society where almost all other professions are open to women).

The definitive statements issued by the Holy Father and the Congregation for the Doctrine of the Faith must not be seen as putting an end to discussion of the questions involved. They should rather be a stimulus to the search for intelligibility.[24] Indeed, their definitive character underlines the necessity for an overall review of the Church's ministerial activity in order to make women — religious and lay — more effectively present at all levels, up to the ordained diaconate. The arguments against priestly ordination do not apply to this ministerial service. And, after the restoration of the permanent diaconate by Vatican II, it would seem necessary, in any case, to take a deeper look at the three degrees of the Sacrament of Orders: deacon, priest and bishop.

But, without waiting for a ruling on the diaconate, it is imperative that every possibility open to lay people — including women — in the 1983 Code of Canon law should be put to good use. That alone could give the Church a 'new look'. The ministerial priesthood could then develop in its right context, as an irreplaceable service, instituted by Christ to be appropriately exercised by men. The Post-Synodal Exhortation *Christifideles Laici*[25] points to 'new roles' for women and others not so new. Its most important statement is, no doubt, that 'the *acknowledgement in theory* of the active and responsible presence of women in the Church must be *realized in practice*' (51).

Implications of this had been spelt out already before the Synod — as a contribution to its work — at a meeting held in Brussels in June 1987, sponsored by the Conference of CIO. Some forty women came from all over the world. They defined themselves as[26]

> Women involved at the grassroots, working for development, in situations of poverty or conflict; in social, political, economic sectors and others. Some are teachers, theologians, writers, psychologists. Others hold positions in the Church or ecumenical bodies at various levels. We love the Church and we want to be truly a Church of all women and men. We feel we share fully the responsibility of its mission, with a view to reflecting God's love for the world.

I see hope for the future in the 'Pastoral Reflection on Women in the Church and in Society', published in November 1994 by the bishops of the United States under the title, *Strengthening the Bonds of Peace*.[27] This authoritative pastoral statement continues the dialogue the bishops pursued from the 1980s with many thousands of women in all parts of the country in their attempt to produce a 'Pastoral Letter on Women's Concerns'. The Pastoral Letter did not materialise (fortunately, I think), but the bishops earned the right to speak as having listened and learned.

The Reflection of 1994 points to all the possibilities for women's leadership in the Church — a leadership which, as for the ordained, must be one of servanthood. It sees the Pope's definitive statement as providing 'a graced moment in the life of the Church, which enables us to take a fresh and deeper look at the relationship between jurisdiction and ordained ministry'.[28] It rejects, on the one hand, sexism and, on the other, extreme feminist positions which impede dialogue and divide the Church. It encourages the many ways in which women today carry out pastoral activity with their personal gifts and trained competence. In conclusion, the bishops quote from the Pope's Letter:[29]

> The role of women is of capital importance for the rediscovery by believers of the true face of the Church . . . The true face of the Church appears only when and if we recognize the equal

dignity of men and women and consistently act on that recognition.

Towards intelligibility?

The norm of women's exclusion from ministerial priesthood, definitively reaffirmed by John Paul II, is not likely to be changed. But, even supposing that it could be changed, this would not be an enrichment for the Church.[30] Rather, it would deprive the Church, not only of a rich diversity but, more deeply, of a full expression of the symbolic meaning of the Christian priesthood, as preserved in the Catholic tradition. The problem remains: how to make the norm, if not fully intelligible (we are, in fact, in the realm of mystery), at least more acceptable to those who rightly want to avoid anything savouring of unjust discrimination.

We must, in the first place, avoid irrelevant arguments. It is true, for instance, that Mary has the highest dignity of any purely human being, but she was not a priest. It is true that holiness is more important than ministry. But these irrefutable facts remain beside the point. Can the example of Jesus and the constant Tradition alone give intelligibility?

It may never be possible to reach an explanation that will satisfy all who are now unconvinced. But we can, at least, try to satisfy ourselves! We need to see *together* the elements of a complex — but not necessarily incomprehensible — whole:

(a) The interpersonal pattern of the man/woman relationship in creation, seen in a biblical anthropology and interpreted in the Church's Conciliar and post-Conciliar Magisterium, while taking into account the findings of modern science;

(b) the consequent 'appropriateness' of the incarnation of the Word as a male human being: a man, 'born of woman' — a woman who, as his Mother, gave him his physical body and nourished his human and spiritual growth; the 'Woman' whom Jesus addressed at the beginning of his public life (at Cana), and again from the cross on Calvary;

(c) the relation of Christ to the Church, his Body, as expressed in Paul's spousal symbolism (cf. Eph 4,5);
(d) in Catholic tradition, the sacramental sign of the priest, acting 'in persona Christi Capitis'.

Finally, it has often been pointed out that, if Jesus chose only men to be his Apostles, it was not because of any compulsion from contemporary Jewish culture. He showed Himself, on the contrary, to be supremely free as regards the customs and taboos of his day. The disciples were amazed even to find Him speaking to the Samaritan woman (cf. Jn 4:27). It is true that an argument from his attitude to culture has also been used in the opposite sense: Jesus went along with contemporary custom in calling his Apostles, but his general attitude to women suggests that He would expect their successors to take advantage of future contexts favourable to women's leadership, even in ministerial priesthood. Neither of these arguments seems to have convinced anyone not already convinced, whether for or against women's ordination.

We need to look more carefully at what the Gospels tell us of Jesus' dealings with his disciples, both men and women. The 'Twelve' were called to a role of authority that could reflect a masculine image; but a role that was to be exercised in a way quite uncongenial to any masculine propensities for domination — as the service of one humble enough to wash the feet of his brothers. The women do not seem even to have waited to be called. They were there following Jesus and serving Him, regardless of public opinion. He accepted their service, almost as a matter of course. He welcomed their discipleship: Mary listening raptly while Martha toiled; the veneration expressed in precious oil poured out; Bethany's warm friendship; the keen wit and the tenacity of the Canaanite woman in her dire need; the love of Mary Magdalen, who would not let Him go so easily until He sent her off with her Easter message . . .[31] All those women's ways of being, thinking, doing, praying, loving, that would be so necessary, and that the successors of the Apostles must learn to appreciate for the good of the Church in all her God-given diversity.

1. Cf. Brenda Conlon, 'The ordination of women: the broken silence, *The Month*, London, March 1995, pp. 111–16.

2. The *Gender and Ministry* report is quoted textually in Part 2 of the Introduction to the *Report of the Archbishops' Commission on Women and Holy Orders*, Church Information Office, London, 1966, p. 7.

3. Ibid.

4. *Revised Interim Report of a Study on the Life and Work of Women in the Church*, Ed. W. A. Visser't Hooft, Archives WCC, Geneva, 1948, p. 7.

5. The report is from a mimeographed circular of the St Willibrord Association, Driebergen, Netherlands.

6. rue de la Prévoyance 58, Brussels..

7. *'Amicale des Femmes aspirant au Ministère Presbytéral'*. Arguments against women's ordination were refuted in a printed Address to the Fathers of the Synod.

8. *Theological Reflections on the Ordination of Women*, Committee on Pastoral Research and Practices of the National Conference of Catholic Bishops, Washington, 1972.

9. Sr Agnes Cunningham, Lecturer at Saint Mary of the Lake Seminary, Mundelein (United States), later (1976) prepared for the Bishops' Conference a synthetic study: *The Role of Women in Ecclesial Ministry: Biblical and Patristic Foundation*.

10. The International Research Centre PRO MUNDI VITA (rue de la Limite, 6, Brussels), from 1964 published a bulletin several times a year, edited by Jean Kerkhofs, SJ. It later ceased publication for financial reasons.

11. Among others: Yves Congar, M. D. Chenu, Hervé Legrand, J. M. Aubert, Yvonne Pellé-Douel.

12. *Evangelii Nuntiandi*, in Austin Flannery, *Vatican Council II: More Post-Conciliar Documents*, Dominican Publications, Dublin, 1992, pp. 711–61.

13. PRO MUNDI VITA Bulletin, 59, March 1976, p. 22.

14. 'Impressions from Detroit', *America*, America Press, New York, 17 January 1976, pp. 26–35.

15. Cf. *Impressions from an Ordination Conference*, in Bulletin of the International Grail Movement, 17, April 1976, pp. 16–22.

16. Cf. *Origins*, op. cit., 24 June 1976.

17. *Inter Insigniores* in Austin Flannery, *Vatican Council II. More Post-Conciliar Documents*, op. cit., pp. 331–45.

18. Between 29 January 1977 and 26 March 1977, articles appeared over the signatures of R. Spiazzi, A. L. Descamps, H. Urs von Balthasar, A. G. Martimort, G. Martelet, J. L. Bernardin, J. Ratzinger. Archbishop (Cardinal) Bernardin's article of 19 November 1977 was a positive approach to 'women's promotion' in the Church, but in roles other than the ministerial priesthood.

19. It is significant that the Orthodox Churches are also seeking to deepen their approach to a question which has been for them unquestioned. In November 1988, the Ecumenical Patriarchate convened an Inter-Orthodox Theological Consultation in Rhodes on 'The Place of Women in the Orthodox Church and the Question of the Ordination of Women'.

Cf. *Women and the Priesthood*, (ed.) Thomas Hopko, St Vladimir's Seminary Press, Athens Printing Company, NY, 1983.

20. In an address to United States Bishops on 22 June 1996; cf. *Origins*, op. cit., 29 August 1996, pp. 177–80: 'Pastoral Response to the Teaching on Women's Ordination'. Cf. also A. Dulles, 'Gender and Priesthood: Examining the Teaching', in *Origins*, 2 May 1996.

21. Pentecost, 22 May 1994: 'I declare that the Church has no authority whatsoever to confer priestly ordination on women and that this judgment is to be definitively held by all the Church's faithful' (4).

22. Reply to a *dubium* (doubt) about the Church's teaching as contained in *Ordinatio Sacerdotalis*: This teaching belongs to the 'deposit of faith'. It requires 'definitive assent'. It has been 'set forth infallibly by the ordinary and universal magisterium' (28 October 1995).

23. A. Dulles, in *Origins*, op. cit., 29 August 1996, p. 180.

24. A starting-point can be a volume edited by the Congregation for the Faith and presented in italian in the Vatican in January 1997: *From Inter Insigniores to Ordinatio Sacerdotalis*. It contains, with the text of these two documents and of the Reply to the *Dubium*, concerning *Ordinatio Sacerdotalis*, two series of comments published in *L'Osservatore Romano*: three unsigned articles and two groups of articles signed by theologians, respectively in 1977 and 1993.

25. *Christifideles Laici*, op. cit., pp. 1967–2082.

26. *Women in the Church and in Society*, Proceedings of the Colloquium, Brussels, 9–14 June 1987, published by Chairwoman of the Colloquium, Evi Meyer, Am Janshof, 3; D–5040 Brühl, West Germany, p. 3.

27. Cf. *Origins*, op. cit., 1 December 1994.

28. The 1983 Code of Canon Law (Can.129) provides for the cooperation of lay people in the *exercise* of authority, of governance in the Church, without exercising 'jurisdiction' in the strict sense.

29. *Ordinatio Sacerdotalis*, Apostolic Letter of John Paul II on Ordination and Women, 22 May 1994. Text and comments in *Origins*, op. cit., 9 June 1994.

30. This is well expressed in two articles by John McDale, SJ, Editor of *The Month*, London: Editorial, December 1992 and 'Gender Matters: Women and priesthood', July 1994, pp. 254–9.

31. For the Gospel references, cf. Luke 8:1–3; 10:38–42; Mark 14:6–8; Matthew 15:21–26; John 20:16–18.

CHAPTER 15

John Paul II and women

John Paul II has himself given us the key to his approach to women, an approach that reflects his personal background, but has matured in response to the questionings and the ever-widening horizons of our day. In his book, *Crossing the Threshold of Hope*,[1] we read:

> If our century has been characterized in liberal societies by a growing *feminism*, it might be said that this trend is *a reaction to the lack of respect accorded each woman*. Everything that I have written on this theme in *Mulieris Dignitatem*[2] I have felt since I was very young and, in a certain sense, from infancy. Perhaps I was also influenced by the climate of the time in which I was brought up — it was a time of great respect and consideration for women, especially for women who were mothers.
>
> I think that a certain *contemporary feminism* finds its roots in the absence of true respect for woman . . .

It is in this context of contemporary feminism that the Pope sees the rebirth of 'the authentic theology of woman', and the rediscovery of woman's 'particular genius'. This rediscovery is inextricably linked, for John Paul II, with the inspiration of Mary — the Virgin Mother of the Incarnate Word of God — as she is depicted in Vatican II. Chapter VIII of the Constitution *Lumen Gentium* recalls, for him, the 'earlier youthful experiences' which would lead him to place his Pontificate in the hands of Mary. His papal motto, '*Totus Tuus*' (I am wholly yours), expresses the devotion which the young Karol Wojtyla, while employed as a factory worker, discovered in the writings of St Louis de Montfort (1673–1716) and made his own.³

In *Mulieris Dignitatem* we see Mary as the highest expression of feminine dignity and 'genius', of woman's vocation within the 'order of love'. This vocation can be lived both by the married and by the unmarried, and in all the concrete situations of a woman's life. It is seen as a 'spousal' love — woman's part in the 'unity of the two', in the vocation of motherhood and in consecrated virginity. In *Crossing the Threshold of Hope*, we are told how, as a young priest, Karol Wojtyla had 'learned to love human love' and how, as a professor writing his book *Love and Responsibility*,⁴ he had learned from his young friends an approach that anticipated Paul VI's *Humanae Vitae* (1968); anticipated too, no doubt, the systematic reflection on theology of the body and of sexuality that would be given during Wednesday Papal Audiences in the 1980s.

Mulieris Dignitatem was received by many with enthusiasm — once it had been ascertained that pre-publication information about the Pope's reaffirmed 'no' to women's ordination ignored or deformed his real message. 'This is a Pope who believes in women!' was the title of an article by an Italian journalist, Maria A. Macciocchi,⁵ who records spontaneous reactions to the Pope's Apostolic Letter she had met with in Madrid, Paris, Brussels . . .

There were, of course, criticisms. In particular, this 'unhistorical' meditation was seen as out of touch with reality. This was the time when, in the United States, the bishops were struggling to produce the first draft for a Pastoral Letter that was to be a response to dialogues in process across the country. But the Pope's meditation was not a dialogue. Nor was its aim to make concrete proposals for women's participation in the life of the Church and of society.⁶ Its roots were deeply embedded in the mysteries of Creation, Incarnation, Redemption and the Love of the Triune God.

Towards a dialogue?

The International Women's Year in 1975 had been the occasion for Paul VI to encourage all that was positive in a feminism that pointed to needed changes — of mentality especially — in society and within the Church. Another IWY — 1995 — would give John Paul II the occasion for a more direct approach to the concrete problems of women than had been possible in *Mulieris Dignitatem*. The occasion was the preparation of the 4th United Nations World Conference on Women, held in Beijing in September 1995, proposing — as in previous Conferences — the theme: Equality, Development and Peace.

The Pope's annual Message on 1 January 1995 was devoted to a reflection on 'Women — Teachers of Peace'.[7] In his Letter for Holy Thursday, he invited Priests to read *Mulieris Dignitatem* and to 'reflect on the important role which women have played in their lives as mothers, sisters and co-workers in the apostolate'.

Receiving the Secretary General of the Conference, Gertrude Mongella, on 26 May, the Pope entrusted her with his Message for Beijing. This was afterwards sent to all Bishops' Conferences, so that local Churches could associate themselves with the IWY. As Head of the Delegation of the Holy See for the Conference, the Pope appointed — for the first time — a woman: Mary Ann Glendon from Harvard and a member of the Pontifical Academy of Social Sciences. In the Message, he pointed out 'man's enormous debt' to women in every realm of social and cultural progress. Unjust discrimination must be eliminated in education, health care and employment, and the 'terrible' sexual exploitation of women and girls.

But this was not enough. John Paul II wanted to make a direct approach to all women and to every woman. As a 'sign of solidarity and gratitude', he wrote his *Letter to Women* (29 June, 1995).[8] In it, he thanks God for the 'mystery of woman' and women themselves for all they represent in the life of humanity. There follows a courageous apology: women's dignity has often not been recognised. They 'have been prevented from being truly themselves . . . If objective blame, especially in particular historical contexts, has belonged to not a few members of the Church, for this I am truly sorry'. The regret must be transformed into 'a renewed commitment of fidelity to the Gospel vision'.

Reactions to the Letter were naturally diverse.[9] There was general appreciation of its 'warmth and honesty' mingled with more than a little surprise at the Pope's personal apology. It was even described as 'undoubtedly a love letter to a frustrating, bewitching creature, modern woman'; yet, one that many women would dismiss, saying the Pope 'knows nothing of his subject' (but 'even a thank-you might be in order'). For others it was an example of what they saw as contradictory in the Church's practice: 'Many of us are professionally trained theologians, speakers, teachers, counsellors, spiritual directors. We ask that our gifts be integrated more fully into the local and national life of the Church'. Pat Jones, Assistant General Secretary to the Bishops' Conference of England and Wales, was glad to see the Pope's Letter contradicting 'the stereotypes about the Church's view of women':

> Increasingly there are Catholic women who express another voice: that it is possible to be faithful to the Church, and to be active within it in ministry and leadership, while also asking hard questions and seeking change. They believe it is right to develop new roles and greater participation for women; indeed, the Pope himself asks us to so.

Introducing his Letter, the Pope speaks of a dialogue. There are, indeed, essential elements of dialogue: listening and a direct approach. But dialogue, in the full sense, supposes partners who can meet, more or less, on an equal footing. The nature of the Pope's unique 'listening-post' hardly allows for anything more than an 'ideal' dialogue with all women and every woman. The Letter remains, however, an essential reference for the effective dialogues that need to develop at all levels: dialogues between women themselves, between women and men, women and clergy ... in all the diversity of persons, age-groups, situations and cultures, from East and West, North and South of our planet.[10] With the patience to listen, with honesty and good will, with openness to the Spirit, something more may be revealed of the 'truth about women' about women and men, created in the image of God.

Epilogue

The journey has been long. It has brought us glimpses — often only fugitive glimpses — of important moments, events and people seen from the limited perspective of one onlooker. Rather than a calm glance from a quiet window, the impression may have been at times more like that of the passing scene from a jolting Roman bus, or some jetlag memories of intercontinental travel.

We set out on the eve of the Holy Year in 1950 into a 'world becoming one'. We are preparing to pass into the third millennium through the Holy Door of the great Jubilee. What does the 21st century reserve for the world? What will it bring for the generations who will be the Christian laity of a universal Church of truly planetary dimensions? What will they bring to the growth of the People of God, to which — Vatican II tells us in *Lumen Genium* — all humankind are called?

I am no prophet. And, insofar as my personal story has emerged in these pages, it will have shown how I learned from experience that God's ways are unpredictable. I was the shy schoolgirl cleaning brass in the sacristy of the parish church. Later, the slightly less shy student from Paris who thrilled to the universality of the Church, on Easter Sunday 1938, as Pius XI performed a triple canonisation in St Peter's Basilica, with all the pomp and colour of a pre-conciliar Papal liturgy. Perched up at the back of the tribune of St Andrew (left-hand side as you look at the main altar), I could hardly guess that, about a quarter of a century later, I would be sitting demurely (but excitedly) at the front of the same tribune, while a far more representative gathering of the universal Church debated the tasks of God's People in solidarity with the modern world. Nor that, soon after, I would be hailed, jokingly, journalistically — but not altogether erroneously — as the 'First Lady of the Vatican' (although one journalist — to the delight of a cardinal friend of mine — decided on the 'bambina vaticana'!). Perhaps that only goes to show that God who 'writes straight with crooked lines' (according to the Portuguese proverb) has also a sense of humour.

Without trying to prophesy I can only ask: To what extent will the third millennium, and already the 21st century, see lay men and women — in all the vast diversity of their Christian vocations — deeply involved in the new evangelisation proclaimed by John Paul II? Will new approaches have been found, new ways of bringing Christian witness to — and within — a more and more secularised, globalised and computerised world? Will inculturation no longer be an abstract term but the true blending into Christian life of the riches of all cultures, old and new? Will the great dream of the full restoration of Christian unity have become reality or be, at least, much closer to its realisation? Will the 'spirit of Assisi 1986' be bringing a great upsurge of energies from the Holy Spirit in all religions, making an end to the tragedies of war and heralding the dawn of lasting peace?

We cannot know. But a backward glance at the changes seen from our 'window' suggest, rather than apocalyptic or utopian developments (the 20th century has not lacked its apocalyptic moments) a process of growth. It may not always seem a steady growth (two steps forward and one backwards!), nor even at once a visible growth, but surely a growth that, in God's good time, will not fail to come to visible fruition. The good seed may not all bring forth fruit a hundredfold, but neither is it all destined to fall by the wayside.

When Pius XI called all the laity to Catholic Action, not all, but many responded; and fruits of those early days are still visible, under many names and through many unwritten personal stories. We have seen, after the Second World War, how the seed was sown more widely in a multiform lay apostolate, encouraged by Pius XII. It became easy to say that all Christians must be apostles although not so easy to demonstrate what that meant. But concrete responses were not lacking among committed laity in the crisis of the modern world: the response of a spiritual quest, and of action and reflection at the service of the Church's mission, leading up to Vatican II. Then, when the 'windows' —

not really closed — were thrown wide open by John XXIII, horizons also widened. *All* baptised Christians were seen to be co-responsible in the People of God. The way was clearly pointed for Catholic lay people to join with other Christians in prayer, in witness to the Gospel, and in world-changing endeavour for what has lately been summed up as justice, peace and the integrity of creation.

True, since Vatican II, there has sometimes been more vague invocation of the spirit of the Council than concrete implementation (or even exact knowledge) of what the Council actually taught. True, it is easier to speak of solidarity, even of a preferential love for the poor, than to adopt new life-styles that would make it possible to share out the world's riches: food, clothing, housing, work, and joy for all. True, it is necessary to affirm strongly the dignity of the human person, but does this always correspond to a delicate respect for the just claims of the individual man or woman? True, we need to stress, with the Council, the importance of dialogue, but is this often more of a slogan word than a concrete approach to diversity, conflict and Christian leadership? True, we acknowledge the universal call to holiness, but it can be tempting to delegate the response to the 'saints' — canonised or not!

We must be realistic. But our shortcomings must not prevent us from accepting the invitation of John Paul II to 'cross the threshold of hope'. During the last decades, he has been stirring the youth — and not only the youth — of all continents with his challenge to the new evangelisation. Enthusiasm can be short-lived when difficulties abound. But very many of those who have acclaimed the Pilgrim Pope during a pastoral visit or a World Youth Day, will surely look back to that moment as a high-point of spiritual experience, and a challenge that is meant to last.

Each time again, the good seed is sown more widely. Only God can know when, and to what extent, it will come to full maturity. But growth there will surely be. The Sower has said: 'I am with you always to the close of the age'(Mt 28:20).

1. Published by Jonathan Cape, London, 1994, pp. 216 and 217

2. *Mulieris Dignitatem*, Apostolic Letter of John Paul II on Dignity and Vocation of Women on occasion of Marian Year, 15 August 1988.

3. Cf. *Crossing the Threshold of Hope*, p. 213.

4. *Love and Responsibility*, first published in Polish by the Catholic University of Lublin, 1960. French translation, *Amour et Responsabilité*, published in 1965 by Société d'Editions Internationales, Paris. English translation (by H. T. Willette) published by Collins, 1981.

5. *Amica* (a popular Italian women's magazine), 21 November 1988.

6. That would be left to the Post-Synodal Exhortation, *Christifideles Laici*, 49–52, op. cit.

7. The message for 1 January 1995 and the *Letter to Women* are published, with other texts, in the booklet *Dear Sisters . . . John Paul II Speaks to Women*, published by the Pontifical Council for the Laity, Vatican City, 1995.

8. Ibid.

9. The quotations are from a selection of reactions published in *The Tablet*, London, 15 July 1995, pp. 920–1.

10. Much may be learned from the four-year process of study and dialogue on the 'Community of Women and Men in the Church' that was initiated by the WCC, culminating in a Consultation held in 1981; cf. Constance F. Parvey (ed.), *The Community of Women and Men in the Church: The Sheffied Report*, WCC, Geneva 1983. Many Catholics were involved in the groups for study and sharing that were set up in different parts of the world. Catholics are also involved in the activities of the 'Ecumenical Decade: Churches in Solidarity with Women' that the WCC launched in 1988 and that will be concluded in 1998. (Cf. *Decade Link*, published three to four times a year by Unit III, WCC, Geneva.)

The complex theological questions involved, not only in the Ordination debate, but in contemporary feminism as a whole, have been treated comprehensively and in depth in a recent book by Francis Martin: *The Feminist Question. Feminist Theology in the Light of Christian Tradition*, William B. Eerdmans Publishing Company, Grand Rapids, Michigan, 1994.

Sources

Documents of the Second Vatican Council

The official source is the Latin Text in the *Acta Synodalia Concilii Vaticani Secundi*.

The first English translation of the collected documents was edited by Walter M. Abbott, SJ, The America Press, New York, 1966.

I have quoted mainly from the volume of Austin Flannery, OP, *Vatican Council II. The Conciliar and Post Conciliar Documents*, The Liturgical Press, Collegeville, Minnesota, 1975.

For the Pastoral Constitution *Gaudium et Spes* on the Church in the World of Today, the translation is that of Rev. William Purdy, published by the Incorporated Catholic Truth Society, London, 1966.

For the Decree *Apostolicam Actuositatem* on the Apostolate of the Laity the translation is generally that prepared by the Permanent Committee for International Congresses of the Lay Apostolate (COPECIAL) in liaison with the Council Commission on the Lay Apostolate, on the basis of a text endorsed by the American Bishops.

Papal Documents

Pius XII is quoted from the volume *Discorsi e Radiomessaggi di Sua Santità Pio XII, VII*. The public addresses of Paul VI, greetings to various groups, etc., are quoted, unless otherwise indicated, from the volumes *Insegnamenti di Paolo VI* (Vols I–XVI).
Documents addressed to the whole Church — Encyclicals, Apostolic Exhortations, Apostolic Constitutions, Apostolic Letters, 'Motu Proprio's' — are published in the original Latin in the *Acta Apostolicae Sedis*. Translations in English and other languages are published by the Vatican Polyglot Press and in the Vatican daily paper *L'Osservatore Romano*.

Papal Encyclicals are published in English by Australian Catholic Truth Society (ACTS) Publications, 143 A'Beckett St., Melbourne.

Important documents following Vatican II were published in the volume of A. Flannery quoted above, *The Conciliar and Post Conciliar Documents*, and in *Vatican Council II. More Post Conciliar Documents*, Costello Publishing Company, Inc., Northport, New York, 1982.

Publications of the Pontifical Council for the Laity (Vatican City)

The departments ('dicasteries') of the Holy See publish their own documents. Much material used here is taken from publications of the *Consilium de Laicis* (the first form of the Council, 1967–76) and of the Pontifical Council for the Laity (PCL) (1976–). The PCL publishes in English (and in other languages):

An annual Review, *Laity Today* (formerly *The Laity Today*), which is monographic.

A Documentation Service, which reports on meetings, events and studies relating to the lay apostolate.

An Information Service on the Council's activities.

Another very useful source is the CNS Documentary Service, *Origins*, published weekly by Catholic News Service, 3211 4th Street NE, Washington, DC 20017–1100.

Publications of COPECIAL

For the earlier part of our history I quote largely from the publications of the Permanent Committee for International Congresses of the Lay Apostolate (1952–68).

COPECIAL published the proceedings of the three World Congresses of the Lay Apostolate:

> *Actes du Premier Congrès Mondial pour l'Apostolat des Laïques*, Rome, 1952. Two volumes, mainly in French, but with summaries in English and other languages of the main texts in the first volume.
>
> *Texts of the Second World Congress for the Lay Apostolate*, Rome, 1958. Three volumes: *I Laymen in the Church, II Laymen face the World, III Forming apostles*.
>
> *Proceedings of the Third World Congress for the Lay Apostolate*, Rome, 1968. Three volumes: 1. *God's People on Man's Journey*, 2. *Man Today*, 3. *The laity in renewal of the Church*.

Other publications include: *Acts of the First Asian Meeting for the Apostolate of the Laity*, Rome, 1956.

From 1960 to 1967, COPECIAL published a Bulletin, *Lay Apostolate* three times a year and in three editions: English, French, Spanish. The Bulletin gave news of international and national activities of 'lay apostolate', as well as of COPECIAL's activities. During the Second Vatican Council, it gave news of the Preparatory and Conciliar Commissions on the Lay Apostolate, on involvement of lay people, etc.

The archives of COPECIAL, including much unpublished material, are preserved in the historical archives of the Pontifical Council for the Laity.

Publications of Rosemary Goldie

The following articles are particularly relevant:

Lay Participation in the Work of Vatican II, in *Miscellanea Lateranense*, 'Lateranum', Rome, 1974–75, pp. 503–25.

Lay, Laity, Laicity. A bibliographical Survey of Three Decades, in: Pontifical Council for the Laity, *The Laity Today* 26, 1979, pp. 107–44.

The Laity in the Ecumenical Movement, in *Lay People in the Church Today*, 'Gregorianum', Pontifical Gregorian University, Rome, 1987, pp. 307–36.

L'avant-Concile des 'Christifideles Laici' (1945–59), in *Revue d'Histoire Ecclésiastique*, Vol. LXXXVIII, Louvain, 1993, pp. 131–7.

Index

Adenauer, Konrad 38
Adjakpley, Eusèbe 73
Africa 157–63, 165
Alivisator, Hamilcar 103
Alonso, Sara 24
Amichia, Joseph 161
Amin, Irma 165
Andersen, Aase 182
Asia 163–74
Association of the Fraternity of CL 124
Association of Women Aspiring to Priestly Ministry (AFAMP) 221–2, 224
Athanassiou, Athena 199
Australian Association of University Women 9

Bachelet, Vittorio 93, 123, 143
Bahintchie, Eugenie 207
Bam, Brigalia 200, 209
Barot, Madeleine 81, 83, 101, 103, 209
Barry, Michael 98
Bartoletti, Enrico 208, 211, 212, 213, 215, 218, 221, 224
Baur, Hermann 39
Bea, Agostino 34, 83, 105
Bellosillo, Pilar 73, 83, 199, 208, 209
Belomo, Callixta 162–3
Benelli, Archbishop 150
Besson, Marie-Ange 24, 90, 161
Betz, Regina 25
Biffi, Franco 151, 208, 214
Bisimwa, Etienne 162–3

Blomjous, Joseph J. 161
Bliss, Kathleen 96
Blyth, Ann 39
Boff, Leonardo 180
Bonadio, Jean de la Croix 146
Borovoi, Vitaly 83
Bouwman, Judith 195
Bringmann, Karl 38
Brown, Ann Porter 82
Buckley, Vincent 54
Buhrig, Marga 81, 82, 199, 200
Buisseret, Valantine 221

Caggiano, Antonio 19, 26
Callahan, Daniel 57, 59, 60
Camara, Helder 176
Canossian Laity 125
Cardijn, Joseph 6, 17, 18, 25, 26, 34, 35, 48, 56, 95, 141
Caritas Internationalis 47
Carmelite Family 125
Carosi, Maria 24
Carriquiry, Guzman 125, 151, 208, 214
Carter, Alexander 69
Cascante, Ramon Torrella 143, 213
Casey, James V. 58
Castelli, Alberto 138, 141
Catholic Action 6, 8, 15, 16, 17, 18, 19, 23, 33, 34, 48, 55, 56, 89, 120, 122, 126, 157, 164, 166, 176, 180, 237
Catholic Action Girl's Movement 24
Catholic Charismatic Conference 124

Catholic Charismatic Renewal 123
Catholic International Organizations (CIO) 46–50, 52, 70, 74, 126, 157, 227
Catholic Office on European Problems (OCIPE) 186
Catholic Social Movement 166–8
Catholic Worker 54
Centro, Fernando 69, 74, 94
Cercle St Jean Battiste 25
Chale, Sebastian 161
Chang, John Myung 39
Chesterton, G. K. 19, 165
Ching-Hsiung Wu, John 40
Christian Family Movement (CFM) 55, 56, 57
Citrini, Tullio 117
Cleire, Richard 159
Coderre Gérard 68, 77
Coggan, Dennis 224
Cogley, John 57–8, 60
Comboni, Daniel 157
Commission on the Lay Apostolate 74, 137
Conference of Catholic International Organisations (CIO) 26, 33, 89, 92, 141
Congar, Yves 51–2, 55, 56, 97, 101, 114, 116, 118
Cooperators of the Salesians of Don Bosco 125
COPECIAL 22–8, 33, 41, 45, 50, 52, 58, 68, 74, 83, 84, 88, 89, 92, 93, 94, 99, 138, 141, 157, 160, 167, 196
Copenhagen 181–2

INDEX 243

Corçao, Gustave 39
Cordes, Paul 127, 129–30
Coughlan, Peter 150
Crookall, Adelaide 8
Cunningham, Agnes 221

Daly, Jean 167
Daniélou, Jean 25, 43
Davis, H. F. 45
Dawson, Christopher 40
Day, Dorothy 55
de Franch, Ramon
  Sugranyes 50, 83, 93, 94
de Gasperi, Alcide 44
de Gouveia, Cardinal 158
de Habicht, Mieczyslaw 48, 91, 139, 141, 150, 165
de Hemptinne, Christine 165
de la Bedoyere, Michael 53
de Las Casas, Bartolomeo 38
de Lastic, Alan 172, 173
de Lorenzo, Luisa 164
de Lubac, Henri 55, 56
Delcuve, George 162
Delva, Claire 207
Dezza, Paolo 28, 32
Dirks, Marianna 199
Dohen, Dorothy 55
Doherty, Catherine 196
Donadeo, Vittoria 160, 168
Donders, Rachel 196
d'Ormesson, Count
  Wladimir 40
Doyle, Brian 165, 167
Dozier, Caroll T. 223
d'Rose, Anthony 165
du Rostu, Marie 26
Dubois, Marc 7
Dubois-Dumée, Jean-Pierre 32, 68, 183, 186
Duff, Frank 34
Dulles, Avery 117–18, 225
Dumas, André 83
Dupuy, Claude 76

Ecumenical Council 66–86
Episcopal Council for Latin
  America (CELAM) 45

Eppstein, John 45
European Forum of National
  Committees of the Laity 186

Federation of Asian Bishops'
  Conferences (FABC) 172
feminism 192–198, 206, 210, 233, 232
Fennell, Desmond 185
Flahiff, George 207, 220
Flory, Charles 20
Folliet, Joseph 22, 36, 40
Forte, Bruno 117
Fraser, Ian 103
French Federation of
  Catholic Women Students 7
French Revolution 21
Frotz, Augustin 77

Gauci, J. B. 170
Gedda, Luigi 23
George, Chakko 102
Gibbs, Mark 147
Giese, Vincent J. 54, 55
Gilson, Etienne 144
Giussani, Luigi 124, 125, 129
Glendon, Mary Ann 234
Glorieux, Achille 24, 69, 78, 137, 141, 184
'God's People on Man's
  Journey' 88, 92–3, 146
Graber-Duvernay, Marie-
  Thérèse 208
Gracias, Cardinal 19, 163, 165, 167, 168, 171–2
Grail Movement 8, 10, 193, 194, 195, 196, 197
Greene, Michael J. 58
Gremaud, Abbé Joseph 10
Gremillion, Joseph 139
Grootaers, Jan 52
Groothuizen, Maria 196
Guano, Emilio 26, 32, 75, 83, 144
Guitton, Jean 73

Gutierrez, Gustavo 180

Hagelthorn, Florence 171
Hallinan, Paul 78
Hamer, Jerome 83
Häring, Bernard 75, 81, 82
Hebbelthwaite, Peter 107
Helmsing, Charles H. 60
Herger, Alma 94
Herrmann, Claire 209, 213
Hofinger, John 164
Huchard, René 162
Huizinga, Brigid 196
India 164, 168, 169–70, 170–1

Inohara, Hideo 165
International Association of
  Charities 125
International Catholic Child
  Bureau 47
International Catholic
  Movement for Intellectual
  and Cultural Affairs
  (ICMICA) 10, 180
International Federation of
  Catholic Universities 28, 128
International Federation of
  University Women 9
International Movement for
  Apostolate in
  Independent Social
  Milieux (MIAMSI) 71
International Movement of
  Catholic Students
  (IMCS) 10, 54, 180
International Union for
  Social Studies 47
International Women's Year 211, 213–14, 233
Italian Catholic Action 16, 17, 18, 23, 31, 122, 123, 132, 160, 166
Italian Federation of
  Catholic University
  Students (FUCI) 18, 37, 123, 132

Jackson, Barbara Ward 73, 96, 137, 209
Jeunesse Ouvrière Chrétienne (JOC) 6, 48
Jiagge, Annie 102, 145
John XXIII 1, 23, 41, 49, 60, 65, 68, 73, 75, 89, 238
John Paul I 78, 80
John Paul II 4, 121, 127, 131–3, 137, 144, 147, 226, 228, 233–6, 237, 238
Jones, Patricia 35, 235

Kado, Kajetan 175
Keegan, Patrick 25, 72, 93, 196
Keino, Lucy 174
Kennedy, John F. 57
Kerkhofs, Jean 185
Kerstiens, Thom 94, 95
Kirchner, Ed 8, 11
Kiwanuka, Bishop 160
Klompé, Marga 39
Knox, James 158, 160
Kominek, Bolislao 121
König, Franz 187
Kopling, Adolph 125
Korea 173–4
Kuriakose, P.T. 96

La Pira, Giorgio 40, 44
Lacombe, Olivier 169
Larrain, Manuel 36, 176
Lasaga, José I. 177
Lateran Treaty 2
Latin America 175–9
Lavigerie, Cardinal 157
Lazzati, Giuseppe 117
Lebret, Louis-Joseph 37
Leckey, Dolores R. 118
Lécuyer, Joseph 212
Lee, Hainam 90
Legion of Mary 48, 126, 159
Leo XIII 19
Lessa, Marina 208
Libermann, Jacob 157
Ligutti, Luigi 164, 176, 177, 196

Littleton, John 102
Loew, Jacques 148
Lombardie, Pia Colini 207
Lopez, Alfredo 36
Lorscheider, Aloisio 129
Lowenstein, Karl zu 159
Lubich, Chiara 124
Luciani, Albino 78–80
Lücker, Albert 197
Lyonnet, Stanislas 147
Lyons, Dame Enid 9

MacLeod, Teresa Avila 208, 211
McDivitt, James A. 96
McDonnell, Kevin 45
McEnroy, Carmel E. 72
McFadden, Agnes 7
McGuire, Paul 56
Macciocchi, Maria A. 233
Maione, Romeo 25
Maranta, Archbishop 160
Maritain, Jacques 11, 165
Marshall, Bruce 40
Martelet, Gustave 67
Martini, Carlo Maria 130
Matracia, Anna 24
Maurin, Peter 55
Meany, George 39
Ménager, Jacques 182
Meersman, Maria 199
Moeller, Charles 83, 97
Mongella, Gertrude 234
Monnet, Jean 71
Monnet, Marie-Louise 71
Montemayor, Jeremias (Jerry) 149
Montemayor, Michaela 164
Montini, Giovanni Battista 12, 15, 18, 36, 37, 44, 47, 132
Moro, Aldo 37, 95
Movimento Laureati 18
Murphy, Dick 7
Mushakoji, Kinhide 201

Namaganda, Elizabeth 162
Narducci, Angelo 208

National Assembly of Women Religious 220
National Council of Catholic Men (NCCM) 55, 91
National Council of Catholic Women (NCCW) 55, 91
National Lay Apostolate Committees 33
Neves, Lucas Moreira 143
Neville, Mildred 161
Newman, Cardinal 19, 165
Nicholson, G. G. 5, 6, 9
Nimo, John 162
Nissiotis, Nikos 83
Nold, Liselotte 199
Norris, James 73, 137

Oceania 174–5
O'Gara, James 97
Ozanam, Frederick 125

Palace of St Calixtus 1–2
Panafrican Laity Seminar 162–3
Paronetto, Sergio 44
Paul VI 1, 12, 18, 37, 49, 67, 69, 70, 71, 73, 75, 88, 92, 97, 99, 109, 116–17, 121, 123, 138, 140, 142, 143, 147, 151, 157, 170–1, 204, 222, 224
Pavan, Pietro 20, 24, 26, 165, 166, 167, 169, 177
Pax Romana 7, 8, 10, 11, 12, 48, 49, 144, 169–70, 180, 197
Permanent Committee for International Congresses of the Lady Apostolate 23, 24
Petrarca, Maria 17
Petroncelli, Mario 208
Philippines 164–5, 167, 169
Philips, Gérard 20, 26, 32, 36, 41, 52, 56, 89, 114
Pinheiro, Maria Vittoria 208

Pintasilgo, Maria de Lourdes 197, 199
Pironio, Eduardo 174
Pius XI 1, 6, 16, 120, 180, 237
Pius XII 11, 12, 15, 16, 20, 22, 32–5, 41, 44, 49, 53, 54, 57, 65, 99
Pizzardo, Cardinal 23, 161
Pocock, Philip 68
Pontifical Council for the Laity (PCL) 50, 126, 129, 143, 150, 156, 179
Pontifical Council for Justice and Peace 150, 204, 205
Poujol, Geneviève 201
Putz, Louis J. 56
Pyne, Mary 208

The Quest 8

Rahner, Karl 53, 114
Ramsay, Michael 101
Riccardi, Andrea 127
Reid, Elizabeth 197
Riegner, Gerhart M. 100
Righetti, Igino 18
Riva, Silvio 151
Rodhe, Birgit 83
Rodrigues, Dulcinea 208
Rommerskirchen, Joseph 20
Rossi, Opilio 172
Roy, Maurice 76, 107, 137, 138, 141, 151
Rudahigwa, Charles Léon Pierre 39
Rugambwa, Cardinal 160
Ruiz-Gimenez, Joaquin 98
Rupasinghe, Rienzie 97
Ruthnaswamy, Mariadas 168

Sacred Congregations 1
Salat, Rudi 8, 180
Santamaria, B. A. 166–7
Schaeffer, Catherine 20
Schauff, Johannes 137
Schellman, Deborah 208

Schema 13 69, 73, 74–6, 77, 78
Scheyven, Raymond 39
Schillebeeckx, Edward 52, 114
Second Vatican Council 17, 66, 67, 68
Serger, Emma 208
Serrarens, Pierre 20, 26
Seton, Elizabeth A. Bayley 213–14
Severi, Francesco 39
Shak, Therese 99
Shannon, Margaret 97, 199
Sheed, Frank 19, 36
Shields, Mrs John 108
Sih, Paul K. T. 164
Sipila, Helvi 213
Siri, Giuseppe 20
Slade, Ruth Reardon 100
Soeur Marie-André du Sacré-Coeur 159
Souttar, Elizabeth 82
Spiazzi, Raimondo 26
Ssemakula, Paul 159, 161
St John Bosco 125
St Vincent de Paul Society 47, 125
St Vincent Pallotti 125
Stern, Karl 39
Stransky, Thomas 101, 102, 200
Strong, Katherine 148
Stuyt-Simpson, Jacquie 181
Suenens, Léon-Josef 32, 72, 115, 124, 212
Suhard, Cardinal 16, 19, 55, 56
Suhr, John Theodore 181
Swanstrom, Edward E. 137

Taggart, Nancy (Anne) 6
Tan, Juan C. 165
Tanaka, Kotara 39
Thaiday, Rosa Lee 175
Third World Congress for the Lay Apostolate 88–110, 145, 161, 188, 212

Thomson, Ian 105
Thorman, Donald J. 57, 59
Thurian, Max 67
Tobin, Mary Luke 72, 81, 84
Todd, John M. 53–4
Trastevere 1, 2
Tromp, Sabastian 41
Tucci, Roberto 32, 78, 147, 188

United Nations, Scientific and Cultural Organisation (UNESCO) 11, 41, 44
University Catholic Federation of Australia (UCAF) 8, 9, 10
University Grail Group 9
Uylenbroeck, Marcel 141, 178

Vaillancourt, Jean-Guy 107
Valier, Maria Luisa (Marisetta) Paronetto 44
van Berckel, Charlotte 48
van Bismarck, Klaus 83, 96
van der Schot, Frances 195–6
van Drakestein, Baroness Yvonne Bosch 196
van Gilse, Margaret 196
van Ginneken, Jacques 8, 10, 194, 195
van Kersbergen, Lydwine 195
Vanistendael, Auguste 26, 45, 137
Vatican II 1, 2, 4, 6, 18, 19, 20, 21, 23, 24, 26, 27, 32, 34, 38, 48, 49, 52, 58, 64, 65, 78, 89, 92, 99, 114, 115, 122, 132, 137, 145, 178, 218, 225, 226, 238
Vazquez, Juan 72
Vendrik, Maria (Rie) 83, 91, 93, 140, 143, 200, 208
Verghese, Paul 81, 82, 84

Veronese, Vittorino 15, 17–18, 19, 22, 23, 24, 25, 37, 38, 41, 43, 50, 73, 94, 137, 166, 168, 170
Villot, Cardinal 80
Vischer, Lukas 83
von Balthasar, Hans Urs 67
von Le Fort, Gertrud 41

Walker, Ruth 199
Ward, Barbara see Jackson, Barbara Ward
Ward, Mary 20
Weber, Hans-Ruedi 34–5, 104, 148
Wedel, Cynthia 81
Willebrands, Johannes 81, 83
Wojtyla, Cardinal Karol 48, 121, 140, 143, 212, 233
women
  and the Council 76–8
  and John Paul II 232–5
  ordination 210, 212, 218–29

Women's Ecumenical Liasion Group (WELG) 199–206
Women's Ordination Conference 223
Work, Martin H. 58, 59, 60, 109
World Congress of the Lady Apostolate 12, 15, 18, 31
World Council of Churches (WCC) 80, 81, 82, 83, 100, 114, 139, 146–7, 199, 204, 209
World Federation of Sodalities of Our Lady 126
World Student Christian Federation 100
World Union of Catholic Women's Organizations (WUCWO) 46, 47, 70, 179, 205, 222
Worlock, Derek 142, 149, 196

Wright, Lance 26
Wu, John 36

Young Catholic Students (YCS) 35–6, 55, 57, 179
Young Christian Workers (YCW) 6, 16, 17, 25, 34, 35, 36, 48, 56, 57, 141–2, 179
Young Men's Christian Association (YMCA) 100
Young Women's Christian Federation (YWCF) 100

Zoa, Jean 143, 148
Zotti, Mary Irene 56